Challenging Welf____
in the Global Countryside

Challenging Welfare Issues in the Global Countryside

Edited by

George Giacinto Giarchi

Blackwell Publishing

CONTENTS

Notes on Contributors   vii

Preface   ix
George Giacinto Giarchi

1   Redefining the 'Rural Question': The New 'Politics of the Rural'
and Social Policy   1
Michael Woods

2   Rural Movements in Europe: Scandinavia and the Accession States   18
Vanessa Halhead

3   Market-based Governance and the Challenge for
Rural Governments: US Trends   34
Mildred E. Warner

4   Between Decentralized Planning and Neo-liberalism: Challenges
for the Survival of the Indigenous People of Kerala, India   53
Darley Jose Kjosavik and Nadarajah Shanmugaratnam

5   Child Health in Rural Mexico: Has Progresa Reduced
Children's Morbidity Risks?   72
Maria C. Huerta

6   Rurality and Social Inclusion: A Case of Preschool Education   97
Mark Shucksmith, Janet Shucksmith and Joyce Watt

7   Jobs in the Bush: Global Industries and Inclusive
Rural Development   111
Robyn Eversole and John Martin

8   Older People 'on the Edge' in the Countrysides of Europe   123
George Giacinto Giarchi

9   Spinning the Rural Agenda: The Countryside Alliance,
Fox Hunting and Social Policy   140
Alison Anderson

Index   157

NOTES ON CONTRIBUTORS

Alison Anderson is Reader in Sociology in the Department of Law and Social Science, University of Plymouth.

Robyn Eversole is Programme Director, Regional Development in Global Context, at RMIT University, Victoria, Australia.

George Giacinto Giarchi is Professor of Social Care Studies in the School of Applied Psycho-Social Studies, in the Faculty of Health and Social Work at the University of Plymouth.

Vanessa Halhead is a researcher on Rural Policy at Scottish National Heritage.

Maria C. Huerta is Research Fellow at the Centre for Analysis of Exclusion, London School of Economics.

Darley Jose Kjosavik is Associate Professor (Development Studies) in the Department of International Environment and Development Studies (Noragric), at the Norwegian University of Life Sciences, Aas, Norway.

John Martin is Director of the Centre for Sustainable Rural Communities, La Trobe University, Victoria, Australia.

Nadarajah Shanmugaratnam is Professor (Development Studies) and Head of the Research Department of International Environment and Development Studies (Noragric), at the Norwegian University of Life Sciences, Aas, Norway.

Janet Shucksmith is Professor of Public Health in the School of Health and Social Care at the University of Teesside.

Mark Shucksmith is Professor of Planning in the School of Architecture, Planning and Landscape at Newcastle University.

Mildred E. Warner is Associate Professor in the Department of City and Regional Planning at Cornell University, USA.

Joyce Watt was formerly Senior Lecturer in the Department of Education, University of Aberdeen.

Michael Woods is Reader in Rural and Political Geography in the Institute of Geography and Earth Sciences, University of Wales at Aberystwyth.

Preface

The rural domain occupies much of the earth's surface and is populated by billions of its people. However, until recently a greater concentration on urban social policy issues and urban deprivation has tended to engender an urban sociological and urban welfare bias that has sometimes resulted in shunting rural social policy and countryside welfare studies into the sidelines. Currently, there has been a reversal of this trend and an increased interest in countryside issues and rural social welfare. This has led to a quest for British and transnational rural studies. Here, in this edited collection the focus is upon rural welfare and social countryside issues in areas ranging from rural localities in the more industrialized regions of Britain, Continental Europe, the USA and Australia, to rural localities in the less industrialized contexts of India and Mexico.

At the outset, conceptual difficulties need to be addressed. The contents of this special collection have to be set against a background of polemics and contested notions of what constitutes the rural in industrialized societies. Concepts and definitions of what a rural area actually consists of are complex and elusive (Cloke 2006), in much the same way as are concepts of community. Woods (2005: 6) has observed that government agencies have produced more than 30 definitions of rural areas. Population-based descriptors of rural settlements vary enormously – ranging from settlements of 300 (Iceland) to 30,000 persons (Japan). They are based upon descriptive definitions of rurality determined by what governments and statisticians regard as the 'maximum population of a rural settlement' (see Woods 2005: 5–6). The question is: when do a given number of people in a rural area make it into an urban area? Distinctions between urban and rural made on the basis of population alone are arbitrary and unworkable.

Socio-cultural and socio-political indicators of rurality need to be taken into account, as the chapters in this volume will demonstrate. They show that there are degrees of rurality in widely different types of countryside, spanning multiple rural welfare and political issues. These have to be set against a community studies backdrop responsible for first introducing some of the major socio-political concerns and contested notions of what rurality is.

Debate first emerged over what is rural in the late nineteenth and first decades of the twentieth centuries. Ferdinand Tönnies (1887) inspired a plethora of sociological and anthropological studies in the 1920s and 1930s, focused upon the urban threat to the rural idyll and rural sense of community. Later, the protracted postwar period up to the late 1970s witnessed the publication of conceptual, largely systemic analyses of what constituted the rural. Rural community was examined in contradistinction to the urban, triggering a protracted debate over the rural–urban continuum and rural way of life: for instance in studies and critiques by Stacey (1969), Ronald Frankenberg (1966), Howard Newby (1971), and Paul Cloke (1977). Interests widened between the 1970s and late 1980s because of global changes affecting rurality; these resulted in many sociological, anthropological, political, economic and social geographical studies by mainline British rural researchers, such as Anthony Cohen (1982), Clare Wenger (1984), Joseph Alun and David Phillips (1984), Anthony Russell (1986), Brian McLaughlin (1987) and Anthony Champion (1989). Something of a lull then occurred – and in 1989 Ruth Glass cynically referred to urban and rural studies as 'the poor sociologist's substitute for the novel'.

However, a year later Marc Mormont (1990) ushered in a revival when he focused on the different meanings attached to rurality – that provided a handle for the exercise of power by the global over the local, indicative of struggles for legitimation between urban and rural domains. A whole new genre of geopolitical and socio-economic rural studies has been published, mostly by social geographers and rural sociologists, such as Graham Crow and Graham Allan (1994), Paul Cloke and Jo Little (1997), Keith Halfacree (1997), Terry Marsden (1998), Anthony Barnett and Roger Scruton (1999), Mark Shuck-smith (2000), Michael Woods (2005), and Philip Lowe and Lynda Speakman (2006). These researchers among others have striven to focus the attention of governments, as well as service providers and academics, upon the struggle for rural citizens' political representation, for fairer rural governance and for better countryside welfare provision in the global arena. Chapters in this volume show how urban and rural localities can at times be drawn together – and how at others they can collide or be thrown apart or left to drift in disparate directions.

Certain global factors bear particularly upon welfare and health care services. There is the global, outward flow of younger populations in rural localities, who seek jobs in cities, often leaving older, unsupported family members behind. Inversely, people flow into other rural areas because of global counter-urbanization – the commodification of the rural by retailing, tourism and recreation. Welfare and health care agencies in regional centres can find it difficult to cope with unforeseen rural demands. The relocation of financial and service sector employers and corporate service employers in the countryside – dictated mainly by lower land tax – leaves them still firmly integrated into urban-centred networks and specialist labour markets. Consequently, in some areas an urban imported service class culture infiltrates the rural social landscape. Contrasts can be drawn between those residents who are excluded and deprived, lacking the power to alter their lives in rural areas, and those who are privileged and enjoying a comfortable lifestyle. These incomers (sometimes described as urban villagers) are often able to outbid disadvantaged locals in village halls and countryside forums and may alter local politics. More affluent migrants seeking the rural idyll move into rural housing, often as second homes, disadvantaging established local residents. Again, countryside studies focus on the contrasting values associated with rurality: how it is socially constructed and expressed by idyllic symbols, associated conservative traditional values, pastoral signs, media images and notions about rural bliss and the proverbial rose-wreathed cottage. More importantly, these include values of planning significance: not merely about what rural in-migrants may seek to enjoy in the countryside ('aspirational migration'), but also those values and rural concerns influencing 'people-led' social movements that protest about and seek to block urban intrusion into rural ways of life. All these factors, taken together, can help formulate an eclectic, holistic approach (Jones 1995) that incorporates the key concepts of space, power and values in countryside peripheries beyond urban centres.

Rural health and welfare issues have recently been put on the public policy agendum, at least in the UK. In November 2000, the government published two papers, one for urban policy and two others for rural policy (Defra 2000; Cabinet Office 2000). This was a departure from previous health and social care issues and policies, which did not expressly take the rural into account. (The 1990 NHS and Community Care Act, for instance, did not refer at all to rural community care provision, even in passing.) Since the start of the new millennium there have also been significant published contributions to rural welfare issues by major bodies such as the Countryside Agency (2000, 2003, 2004) and the BMA Board of Science (2005).

Whatever the import of these UK factors, there is a need to look beyond the confines of Britain's rural case material, which may indeed be 'untypical'. This collection sets out to broaden perspectives with regard to rural welfare issues and policies within a global world. The impact of social and health care policies on certain vulnerable groups is explored within rural settings in India, Mexico, Australia, New Zealand, the USA, Scotland, England and Wales, as is the counter-reaction of rural movements to rural social exclusion in sixteen European countries – in contested rural areas where space, power and values are central elements.

However dominant the urban is, generally, over the rural, the socio-political tensions and conflicts between urban and rural domains can at times shift in favour of the rural. In some localities and regions, entrenched endemic internal forces may shape the destinies of their peripheral communities, while in others the 'life-world' of people residing in rural areas may be subjected more to external urban market forces (Bradshaw and Wallace 1996). Globalization is not a single, unidirectional force (Pieterse 1996). There are several competing globalizations, which can be open-ended. For example, centralization and decentralization may rotate in accordance with socio-political forces and competing ideologies. There is yet a further situation where global forces can be diverted away from rural localities isolated in a rural limbo or regional backwater, deprived of resources and marginalized. All of these factors, related to space, power and values in rural areas, are discernible in the chapters that follow.

Michael Woods's opening chapter brings us up to date on the ramifications of the new 'politics of the rural', as this has affected rural communities from the 1980s and 1990s through to the first years of the new millennium. The rural question is no longer confined to issues of agriculture. Socio-economic restructuring has brought about a widespread shift away from old-style 'rural politics'. Woods's exemplars in Britain, North America, Australia and New Zealand show how political debate and campaigning are assertive over conflicts, not only regarding the development of rural space, but also over the development of rural social policy issues as variegated as the rights of rural citizens, the provision of services, access to housing, the intrusion of wind farms, the closure of rural schools and the treatment of different social groups. He argues that a new social rural movement is gathering momentum transnationally, and in some areas gaining considerable political influence.

Vanessa Halhead next focuses upon rural/village movements that have spontaneously responded to rural decline by striving to influence regional, national and EU policies from the bottom up. Her focus is on the 'accession' countries of Eastern Europe together with Scandinavia – which is an interesting combination in itself. The picture that emerges challenges the view that the rural is necessarily subject to the vagaries of central national and international political and market forces. She provides evidence of motivational forces that have empowered village movements to voice their local concerns about deteriorating rural infrastructures and the destabilization caused by migration. Her studies suggest how peripheral communities have opened up effective channels of communication and alternative rural developments to national policy-makers in their distant urban centres. On this evidence, distinct rural global political agenda are emerging, as centres and peripheries are brought closer together within an urban–rural dialogue.

Mildred E. Warner, by contrast, draws our attention to the rural situation in the USA. In a meticulous study she shows how market-based approaches to governance and the implementation of privatization and decentralization systems can have an uneven effect upon rural areas. Decentralization can increase spatial inequality. The reduction in subnational governance in rural US areas does not explain the shortfall in market-based service deliveries. Warner concludes that increased regional spatial inequalities in the USA result from a trend towards more and more competitiveness based upon investment in centres of growth. Socio-economic outcomes are decided by the struggle for governance between town and country and the relative political standing of each.

Darley Jose Kjosavik and Nadarajah Shanmugaratnam offer a contrasting, instance of rural people being disadvantaged, in spite of decentralization and neo-liberal privatization. These authors focus upon the effects of planning decentralization on a community of rural people (*adivasis*) in Kerala in Southern India. The objective was to set in motion 'destatization' and liberalization, i.e. to relocate tasks formerly carried out by the state to NGOs, private agencies and elected village bodies (*grama panchayat*). The decentralization process (described as the 'state in society') was to replace a previous 'oppressive' state regime. However, the shift from government to local governance and privatization has not been successful for the *adivasis*, who remain the most disadvantaged group in rural Kerala. In the process of the changeover, they have suffered from increased social exclusion, exacerbated by a market-led programme of what was regarded as progressive privatization. So the second state of affairs has proved worse than the first for the poorest rural people.

The next four chapters further extend discussion with regard to the centre–periphery pressures being exerted by the contrasting socio-political impacts of centralization and decentralization, together with the outcome of interrelationships and conflicts between urban planners and rural consumers/users of services.

In the first of these studies, Maria Huerta examines the effectiveness of the children's health programme, Progresa, in rural Mexico. Children aged less than 5 in countryside areas are more than twice as likely as other children to be malnourished. However, major infant health care programmes are usually centralized, in many developing countries, and hence are of immediate benefit only to those living in urban areas. In this case, although the rural scheme was initiated by government from the centre, it was momentum from the rural areas that drove forward the localized rural anti-poverty programme. This bottom–up programme empowered local groups to reduce the morbidity of disadvantaged under-5-year-olds in poor homes in Mexico's vast peripheries. In fact this rural programme was later adopted in urban areas. Huerta's chapter shows how rural public health priorities (in this case for infants) – sanctioned from the centre, but devolved and driven from the 'local bottom up' – can be highly effective in deprived rural areas.

Next, Mark Shucksmith, Janet Shucksmith and Joyce Watt turn our attention to the issue of exclusion and inclusion in rural settings, in the context of the provision of preschool education in more remote rural areas in Scotland. Central administration and providers have failed to respond to rural need, which has resulted in the exclusion of rural children from preschool education. Shucksmith and colleagues identify the universal geo-economic constraints associated with distance, high transport costs and the overheads in providing for small, dispersed populations. These have affected preschool attendance, but have also created difficulties for children's mothers travelling to work. Yet rural remoteness was not the salient problem. The authors' work demonstrates how, in Scotland, the lack of preschooling in some areas – together with the poor quality of preschool provision in others – is also a result of local authorities' restrictive interpretation of government guidelines. They argue that there is a need to politicize the preschool issue from the bottom up and initiate a rural agendum to redress the uneven provision of preschool provision. Account has also to be taken of the entitlement of parents and children to treatment as fair as that enjoyed by their urban counterparts. Here equity is a central issue. The authors have urged the need not only for a rural–urban dialogue with local authorities, but for the politicization of these concerns by rural action involving the whole local community in partnership with voluntary agencies.

Robyn Eversole and John Martin then shift our attention to the weakness of local governance in the rural Western District of Australia. Local institutions, government schools and health services – and distribution of intergovernmental revenues to meet local rural needs – tend to be dictated 'from afar' by the arbitrary decisions of metropolitan policy-makers. Outside industries move into the rural environs under the specious claim that their industrial developments will be good for the region but, as the authors point out, they are not necessarily good for job-seekers and small businesses not protected from global exposure. The interests of outside agents are dictated by the world stage and by neo-liberal 'runaway' privatization. The Australian Federal Government does not actually have a rural development policy – so a politics of the rural does not exist and the rural community 'will remain the poor cousin of urban Australia'. The authors conclude by urging the need for better structures for community governance and local agency controls, to ensure that economic and human development go hand-in-hand.

The editor's own chapter offers an overview of the *Lebenswelt* (life-world) of Europe's seniors in their countrysides. Rural areas in the continent have a higher proportion of older people than do urban areas, yet there have scarcely been any major European comparative studies of senior citizens in rural areas. The chapter tackles the need for a contextual framework within which the study of Europeans aged over 50 can be carried out, beginning with the uneven impact of globalization upon diverse countrysides. The argument rotates around the socio-cultural and socio-political interconnectivity between urban centres and their rural peripheries. It identifies the rural benefits some enjoy and the rural deprivation others endure. These outcomes are dependent upon the socio-cultural and socio-political relationship between the urban and rural domains regionally, as well as upon the availability and accessibility of health and social care provision for residents in four identifiable types of countryside. Four parameters are regarded as significant. The first focuses upon the two-way urban–rural socio-economic flows which are more likely to benefit older residents in urban 'fringe' or 'shadow' countrysides, than their counterparts in less accessible and remote areas. The second takes account of the impasse – or socio-economic and socio-political blockage – that can exist between some urban centres and rural areas in their hinterland. The third identifies a situation when regional and local urban centres actually prevent or cut socio-economic flows to the countryside. The fourth takes account of the effects when rural communities take it on themselves to resist socio-economic urban flows. Exemplars within each of the four parameters help to show the applicability and workability of this four-way exploratory approach.

Finally, Alison Anderson echoes Woods's opening views regarding the 'politics of the rural' by discussing the controversial countryside issue of 'fox hunting by dogs' in rural Britain. Her chapter provides a pertinent example of the 'politics of the rural' in full swing – and of the urban–rural biases cutting across society. These are 'spun' by right- and left-leaning newspapers, consorting with social movements for and against such hunting. Anderson shows just how powerful the partisan press can be over rural issues and how the spin in the public arena has triggered biases for and against the issue in question. She notes that social science researchers have tended to overlook how the media has framed the countryside agenda to suit its own political ends – and how each side in the public debate has waged a symbolic war based upon deep-seated constructs about rurality. An urban–rural debacle has emerged from the altercations at protest rallies which have succeeded in diverting attention from major rural problems, such as rural poverty.

The chapters in this edited collection have directed attention to multi-dimensional factors affecting rural space, socio-political urban–rural power relations, conflicting urban–rural tensions and conflicting values. The authors have offered case material to inform contemporary urban–rural dialogue, in respect of social policy and rural welfare in the changing global countryside.

Professor George Giacinto Giarchi
School of Applied Psycho-Social Studies
Faculty of Health and Social Work
University of Plymouth, UK

References

Alun, J. and Phillips, D. (1984), *Accessibility and Utilization*, New York: Harper and Row.

Barnett, A. and Scruton, R. (eds) (1999), *Town and Country*, London: Vintage.

BMA Board of Science (2005), *Health Care in a Rural Setting*, London: British Medical Association.

Bradshaw, Y. W. and Wallace, M. (1996), *Global Inequalities*, California: Pine Forge Press.

Brody, H. (1973), *Inishkillane*, London: Norman and Hobhouse.

Cabinet Office (2000), *Sharing the Nation's Prosperity: Economic, Social and Environmental Conditions in the Countryside. A Report to the Prime Minister by the Cabinet Office*, London: Cabinet Office.

Champion, A. (1989), *Counterurbanization*, London: Edward Arnold.

Cloke, P. (1977), An index of rurality for England and Wales, *Regional Studies*, 11: 31–46.

Cloke, P. (2006), Conceptualising rurality. In P. Cloke, T. Marsden and H. Mooney (eds), *Handbook of Rural Studies*, London: Sage, pp. 18–28.

Cloke, P. and Little, J. (eds) (1997), *Contested Countryside Cultures*, London and New York: Routledge.

Cohen, A. (ed.) (1982), *Belonging, Identity and Social Organization in British Rural Cultures*, Manchester: Manchester University Press.

Countryside Agency (2000), *The State of the Countryside*, Cheltenham: Countryside Agency.

Countryside Agency (2003), *The State of the Countryside*, Cheltenham: Countryside Agency.

Countryside Agency (2004), *The State of the Countryside*, Cheltenham: Countryside Agency.

Crow, G. and Allan, G. (1994), *Community Life: An Introduction to Local Social Relations*, Hemel Hempstead: Harvester Wheatsheaf.

Defra (2000), *Our Countryside: the Future, a Fair Deal for Rural England*, CM 4909, London: Stationery Office.

Frankenberg, R. (1966), *Communities in Britain*, Harmondsworth: Penguin.

Glass, R. (1989), *Cliches of Urban Doom and Other Essays*, Oxford: Basil Blackwell.

Halfacree, K. (1995), Talking about rurality: social representations of the rural as expressed by residents in six English parishes, *Journal of Rural Studies*, 11: 1–20.

Halfacree, K. (1997), Contrasting roles for the post-productivist countryside: a post-modernist perspective on counterurbanisation. In P. Cloke and J. Little (eds), *Contested Countryside Cultures*, London: Routledge, pp. 70–93.

Jones, O. (1995), Lay discourses of the rural: development and implications for rural studies, *Journal of Rural Studies*, 11: 35–49.

Lowe, P. and Speakman, L. (eds) (2006), *The Ageing Countryside*, London: Age Concern.

McLaughlin, B. (1987), Rural policies into the 1990s: self-help or self-deception? *Journal of Rural Studies*, 3: 361–4.

Marsden, T. (1998), Economic perspectives. In B. Ilbery (ed.), *The Geography of Rural Change*, Harlow: Longman, pp. 13–30.

Mormont, M. (1990), What is rural? Or how to be rural: towards a sociology of the rural. In T. Marsden, P. Lowe, and S. Whatmore (eds), *Rural Restructuring: Global Processes and Their Responses*, London: David Fulton, pp. 21–44.

Newby, H. (1971), *A Green and Pleasant Land? Social Change in Rural England*, Harmondsworth: Penguin.

Pieterse, J. (1996), Globalization as hybridization. In M. Featherstone, S. Lash and R. Robertson (eds), *Global Modernities*, London: Sage, pp. 45–68.

Russell, A. (1986), *The Country Parish*, London: SPCK.

Shucksmith, M. (2000), *Exclusive Countryside? Socal Exclusion and Regeneration in Rural Areas*, York: Joseph Rowntree Foundation.

Stacey, M. (1960), *Tradition and Change: A Study of Banbury*, London: Oxford University Press.

Stacey, M. (1969), The myth of community studies, *British Journal of Sociology*, 20, 2: 134–47.

Tönnies, F. (1887), *Community and Association*, London: Routledge and Kegan Paul.

Wenger, C. (1984), *The Support Network: Coping with Old Age*, London: George Allen and Unwin.

Woods, M. (2005), *Rural Geography*, London: Sage.

1

Redefining the 'Rural Question': The New 'Politics of the Rural' and Social Policy

Michael Woods

Introduction

> From now on, if what could be termed a rural question exists it no
> longer concerns issues of agriculture or of a particular aspect of living
> conditions in a rural environment, but questions concerning the specific
> function of rural space and the type of development to encourage
> within it. (Mormont 1987: 562)

Twenty years on, the above words – written in the 1980s against the background of social and economic restructuring that was unsettling conventional
understandings of rural space and that introduced new actors into rural
politics – have a prophetic ring. Over the course of the intervening decades,
local politics in many rural regions have seemingly become dominated by
debates over the development or protection of the countryside, revolving
around proposals for new housing, roads, windfarms, quarries, extraction
pits, waste dumps and other similar land uses that are the antithesis of some
conceptions of rurality, but which can be accommodated within others
(see, for example, Murdoch and Marsden 1994; Walker 1995; Woods 1998,
2003a, 2005a). In other contexts the function of rural space has become
contested through conflicts over the exploitation or conservation of resources
such as water and forests (Doremus and Tarlock 2003; Magnusson and
Shaw 2003), and between the interests of wildlife conservation and those of
traditional rural activities such as hunting (Woods 2005a).

Less certain, however, is the implication in Mormont's statement that the
rise of such conflicts around the development and regulation of rural land
has involved the marginalization of rural social issues on the political agenda.
Rather, issues such as access to services, affordable housing, the standard and
extent of health care and education provision, poverty, crime and the integration or otherwise of various social groups in rural society all remain
central to the everyday conduct of political debate and campaigning in rural
areas. Moreover, these issues do not constitute a rural social agenda that is

counterpoised to an environmental and land use agenda as an example of 'old rural politics' against 'new rural politics'. Instead, it is notable that many rural advocacy groups are concerned with both social issues and development issues, and that debates over rural social issues are increasingly framed around questions of rural identity, the meaning of rural community and the rights of rural citizens (Woods 2006). As such, contemporary debates around rural social issues, like those over the function and development of rural space, form part of a new 'politics of the rural' in which the meaning and regulation of rurality itself is the primary focus of conflict and debate (Woods 2003b).

This chapter explores how the transition from a traditional 'rural politics' to a new 'politics of the rural' has been manifested in the arena of rural social policy. It first introduces the argument for a transition from 'rural politics' to a 'politics of the rural' and describes the transformations in the institutions and practices of rural governance and rural political representation that have accompanied this shift. The chapter then proceeds to focus on three arenas in which social policy issues have been contested through the lens of the meaning and regulation of rurality: the provision of rural services; rural schools and community life; and the presence of minority groups in rural areas.

From Rural Politics to a Politics of the Rural

Rural politics and agricultural policy as social policy

Rural politics has traditionally been identified with policies and political debates concerning agriculture or forestry, or the management of rural land more broadly (Winter 1996). To the extent that social issues were also included within some definitions of rural politics, these were largely restricted to contexts framed by agriculture or other land-exploiting industries. Thus, the political relations between farm workers and their employers could be seen as falling within the realm of 'rural politics', as might policy issues concerning problems of poverty and social adjustment arising from declining agricultural employment; but the mainstream politics of education, health, social welfare, public service provision and social justice issues were generally regarded as lying outside its scope.

This was in marked contrast to urban politics, which was widely accepted as having a social dimension as well as physical and economic dimensions. Indeed, Castells (1977, 1978) sought to redefine urban politics as struggles over 'collective consumption', or the intervention of the state in organizing the reproduction of labour power through, for example, providing health care, education, social security and so on. In doing so, Castells denuded 'urban politics' of its geographical referent, such that the logical extension of his work is to categorize struggles over housing, education or public services in rural areas as part of *urban* politics (Pickvance 1995). Consequently, the narrow identification of rural politics with agriculture and conservation was reinforced by default.

The narrow conception of rural politics was reflected in the structures of rural governance and rural representation, which from the 1920s onwards had in most developed nations involved an internal/external division of labour (Woods 2003b). Internally, rural leadership and government were provided by elites composed of farmers, landowners and business owners, whose position was intricately entwined with the interests of the rural resource economy (Newby *et al.* 1978; Woods 2005a). Externally, the representation of rural interests was performed by formally constituted unions and pressure groups, of which the most important were farm unions. During the first part of the twentieth century, farm unions had established themselves as 'insider' groups with a central role in the governance of rural regions, working closely with powerful agriculture ministries in tight-knit and exclusive policy communities (M. Smith 1993; Winter 1996).

Together, the combined influence of the local agrarian elites, farm unions, rural-leaning parties and agriculture ministry officials not only controlled the direction of agricultural policy but also ensured the primacy of agricultural interests within the rural political sphere. This was further assisted by the institutional structure of the state, with little integration or coordination of rural policy across government departments, meaning that the assumptions of agricultural policy could not be challenged by other interest groups.

As the interests of resource capital, and particularly agrarian capital, were prioritized, social policy issues were rendered subservient to these interests. At a local level, agrarian-dominated elites protected their power base by restricting social provision. Rural councils in Britain, for example, provided significantly less public housing than their urban counterparts, thus requiring agricultural workers to continue to depend on tied accommodation (Milbourne 2004; Newby *et al.* 1978). More broadly, local elites sought to retain control over local institutions of welfare provision and public services and were resistant to policies of nationalization, amalgamation and rationalization.

At the national level, agricultural exceptionalism in effect turned rural politics into a form of industrial politics, concerned with the workings of one industry, and social policy could only therefore be approached in relation to its implications for agriculture. Consequently, the farm lobby came to adopt a paradoxical position on social issues, on the one hand opposing 'big state' tax-and-spend solutions and emphasizing the tradition of 'self-help' in rural communities, yet on the other hand creating an agricultural system that depended on state intervention and subsidization. Sheingate labels this creation the 'agricultural welfare state', resembling 'a sector-specific form of social insurance' (2001: 3), in which economic and social goals became blurred in policies such as the commodity programmes, production controls and price supports that underpinned American agriculture from 1933 onwards, and the Common Agricultural Policy in Europe.

As long as the perceived social problems of rural areas could appear to be addressed by raising farm incomes, securing the family farm as the primary social unit of rural life and maintaining agricultural employment, then rural 'social policy' could be absorbed within agricultural policy. At the same time, rural social problems that could not be addressed in this way were strategically kept off the policy agenda. Thus, rural poverty was generally only acknowledged as an issue at times of plummeting farm incomes when price support and subsidy payments could be presented as the solution (Browne 2001;

3

Milbourne 2004). The persistent poverty of those rural residents 'left behind' by agricultural modernization remained a non-issue for agricultural policy, and certainly the role of capitalist agriculture in reproducing rural poverty through the payment of low wages, the rationalization of farm workforces, and the increasing reliance on seasonal and migrant labour, was strictly off-limits. Browne (2001) notes that concessions towards coalition-building did lead to the incorporation of some wider social programmes into US agricultural policy, including the rural mail service, electrification and some extension education initiatives. Yet, as he comments:

> These efforts had to be small because any extensive policy initiatives would have acknowledged farm policy failure and brought resulting policymaker skepticism about this assistance. Thus, the limited size, funding, and means of evolution of rural programs always made clear that this sort of farm policy accommodation did not bring forward a decisive national policy for those left behind by farming. (Browne 2001: 43)

Towards a politics of the rural

The failures of farm policy could not, however, be disguised for ever. By the 1970s the power of the agricultural policy communities and the unchallenged supremacy of productivist agricultural policies were beginning to look vulnerable to charges of economic inconsistency and shifting public opinion. Several factors contributed to this change in fortune. Firstly, the economic significance of agriculture has decreased. The average contribution of agriculture to gross domestic product in developed countries at the start of the twenty-first century was just 2.6 per cent (FAO 2004) and as other industries became increasingly significant in the rural economy and labour market, so the rationale for continuing to prioritize agricultural interests in policy-making has been questioned, particularly as many of the growth industries, including tourism, rely on a different representation of rural space to that of productivist agriculture.

Secondly, public attitudes towards agriculture have changed as concerns have grown about the environmental impact of productivist farming, about animal welfare, and about the quality of the food produced. While agricultural policy communities battled to exclude environmental and consumer interests, these critical voices have gained increasing influence elsewhere in government, such that the grip of agricultural policy communities over 'rural policy' has eventually been loosened in many countries in a move towards more integrated approaches to rural policy.

Thirdly, the population of most rural regions in the developed world has changed dramatically as a consequence of counter-urbanization. Rural societies have been reconstituted by the influx of a diverse cohort of migrants attracted by the amenity-value of the countryside and the lure of the 'rural idyll', most with no connection or familiarity with agriculture. The new in-migrants have challenged the authority of agrarian elites and increased pressure for social and economic policies that address the needs of the non-agricultural countryside (Woods 2005a).

Fourthly, the swing towards neo-liberalism has provided an ideological challenge to established rural politics. Neo-liberal reforms in Australia and New Zealand have deregulated agriculture and dismantled systems of price support and producer subsidies, and there are pressures for Europe, the United States, Japan and other states to follow (Cloke 1989; Cloke and Le Heron 1994; Pritchard 2000). While larger producers and exporters have benefited, deregulation and exposure to global competition have been disastrous for many smaller farmers, who have felt abandoned by their one-time representatives (Cocklin and Dibden 2002; Halpin 2004; Halpin and Guilfoyle 2004). At the same time, the privatization of public services and the application of commercial principles to utilities that remain under state control have led to the controversial closure or downsizing of 'uneconomic' services and facilities in rural communities (Warner and Hefetz 2003), and neo-liberal principles have informed the retreat of state intervention in rural development and the promotion of community self-help strategies, creating new arenas for rural political mobilization (Edwards and Woods 2004; Herbert-Cheshire 2000, 2003; Murdoch 1997).

Collectively, these factors have changed the rural political landscape. Established rural interest groups that had enjoyed considerable insider influence as part of small policy communities suddenly found their authority questioned as they struggled to deliver results to their constituents. Disillusioned members drifted to more militant groups, threatening to pursue their objectives through direct action (Woods 2003b, 2005a). New groups also emerged from the action networks set up by rural in-migrants to protect their financial and emotional investment, from local conflicts over planning or development issues, and from the advocacy groups representing previously marginalized rural interests, such as the poor or ethnic minorities. These new rural interest groups tended to differ from their more established counterparts in their organizational structures, tactics and strategies and political objectives, such that they might be argued to constitute an emergent rural social movement (see Woods 2003b).

Moreover, the terms and focus of rural political discourse have changed. It is in this respect that we can identify a transition from 'rural politics' to a 'politics of the rural'. The old-style 'rural politics' took the 'rural' as the uncontested context for political debates, conflicts, negotiations and campaigns that were essentially concerned with the regulation and management of agriculture and other resource-exploitation industries, the supply of labour for these industries, and the conservation of environmental resources. However, in the new 'politics of the rural' it is the meaning and regulation of rurality itself that is the primary focus of conflict and debate.

As Mormont (1987) observed, this new politics is most visibly articulated in struggles over the development of rural space. From small-scale disputes over barn conversions, blocked footpaths, streetlighting or tree-felling, to large-scale conflicts over new roads, windfarms, waste dumps and major housing developments, the appropriateness of the development to the rural setting and the impact on the rural character of the locality are commonly evoked alongside issues of environmental impact, pollution, noise disturbance, traffic, property devaluation and so on (Woods 1998, 2003a, 2005a).

Increasingly, agricultural politics is also framed in the language of rural distinctiveness, with family farm campaigners emphasizing the importance of farming to the rural landscape and the rural way of life in opposing policy reform and trade liberalization.

Finally, issues of the meaning and regulation of rurality are beginning to feature in debates over social policy. Far from refocusing the 'rural question' away from the condition of rural society, the new 'politics of the rural' has liberated rural social policy from the shadow of agricultural policy, providing a new language and context through which rural social issues can be placed on the political agenda. The remainder of this chapter discusses three examples of this, starting with the provision of public services in rural areas.

Rural Services and Rural Rights

The provision of public services to rural areas has been returned to the political agenda by the combined effects of neo-liberal state restructuring and an increasingly vocal rural population, including both in-migrants who expect urban levels of service and established residents concerned at the gradual dismantling of rural infrastructure. Historically, the development of public service provision in rural regions during the twentieth century was undertaken and underwritten by the state, informed by two distinct imperatives. Firstly, the rolling out of services such as electrification and communications systems was driven by the need to support resource capitalism and, in North America, Australia and New Zealand, to encourage the economic colonization and settlement of frontier regions. The provision of public services to rural households was hence largely a side-benefit of the primary economic purpose (Browne 2001), although the social concerns of groups such as the American Country Life Association did play a role in lobbying for improvements (Wunderlich 2003). Secondly, the principle of universal access to vital public services informed the development of education, health care, public transport and other key services, particularly under social democratic governments in Europe, Australia and New Zealand (Cloke and Little 1990).

Recently, however, the involvement of the state in providing and underwriting public services in rural areas has been challenged by neo-liberal reforms. The privatization of nationalized industries and utilities such as banks, electricity suppliers and telecommunications companies drastically reduced the role of the state in rural service provision and exposed these services to the demands of market forces. In some cases a degree of regulation has remained, offering some protection to rural services, but more broadly neo-liberal reforms have also included the deregulation of sectors such as public transport, ostensibly to increase competition but in effect encouraging providers to focus on the most profitable services. Even those services that have remained within the state have usually been required to find efficiency savings and adopt more commercial practices, including the rationalization of branches into larger units.

Collectively, these reforms transferred the risk involved in public service provision from the state to the private sector and to consumers, with two main consequences. Firstly, branches and services that were considered to be inefficient, uneconomic or insufficiently profitable have been closed or curtailed. Secondly, the principle of standard pricing for public services has been eroded, with differential pricing introduced for some services to reflect geographical variations in the actual cost of delivery. These impacts are not restricted to rural areas but they are more prevalent in rural regions because diseconomies of scale mean that services in remote areas with sparser population densities are generally more expensive to deliver and produce a lower rate of return.

The privatization of the state-owned Commonwealth Bank in Australia, for example, was followed by a programme of rural branch closures (Tonts 2000), matching the strategy of rationalization pursued by other commercial banks both in Australia and elsewhere, which has contributed to growing problems of financial exclusion in rural communities (Argent and Rolley 2000; Leyshon and Thrift 1994; Midgley 2005). Reforms to postal services have similarly provoked both branch closures and differential charging. In preparation for the end of its letter monopoly, New Zealand Post – a government-owned corporation – closed a third of its branch network and increased the delivery charge to rural areas in 1988 (Geddes 2003), while the restructuring of Australia Post as a government-owned enterprise in 1989 led to the closure of unprofitable rural post offices, although a standard postal charge was maintained and concerns over the impact on rural communities have continued to militate against full privatization (Geddes 2003; Tonts 2000). Concern about the impact on rural areas has also featured in recent debates over the privatization or deregulation of postal services in Japan and Britain.

Cuts and closures of this kind have provoked local campaigns and protests. One resident of an Irish town facing the closure of its last bank branch mounted a hunger strike until the bank agreed to install an ATM as a replacement (Skillern 2002), while demonstrators staged a sit-in at a bank earmarked for closure in the village of Terrington St Clement, Norfolk, England (Randall and Gregoriadis 2000). Protests against rural post office closures have been reported in New Zealand, Germany, France, Ireland, Austria and Britain, with varying degrees of success (Postcomm 2003). In Canada, proposals to close around 5,000 rural post offices in the early 1990s were dropped after 1,500 closures, following a national campaign that included demonstrations at the Canada Post headquarters and the Governor General's residence (NUPGE 2003). In many cases, however, the 'rural' has simply provided the context for these protests, with debates revolving around issues of social justice, the quality of service provision or job losses.

It is therefore interesting to note that over the last decade the question of rural service provision has increasingly been picked up by mainstream rural lobby groups, and that the language in which public service provision in rural areas is debated increasingly reflects the concerns of the 'politics of the rural' with rural identity and the meaning of rurality. In particular, threats to public services in rural areas are presented both as threats to a rural way of life, and as discrimination against rural people. The Countryside Alliance in Britain, for example, includes opposition to the closure of rural post offices, banks, shops and public houses, and to the differentiation of postal charges, and support for rural bus services and health care, among its campaign priorities, describing rural services as the 'glue' of rural life and threats to them as 'discrimination' against rural communities (Countryside Alliance 2004). Conversely, the advocacy group Rural Dignity in Canada established itself in campaigns against post office closures in the 1980s and 1990s and has since expanded its focus to embrace transportation and other rural services as well as wider social justice and trade issues.

The connection between rural service provision and the struggle for the rural way of life has been explicitly drawn by several campaign groups in Australia. While rural politics there has generally revolved around issues of agricultural restructuring, indigenous rights and environmental regulation (Halpin 2004; Pritchard and McManus 2000), groups such as the Regional Women's Alliance (RWA) and the Foundation for the Bush, which emerged from the rural women's movement in the late 1990s (but were frequently short-lived), put the rural community at the heart of their campaigning (Halpin 2003). The primary objective of these groups was to protect and promote the 'country way of life' through education of the urban population, support for rural enterprises and initiatives to sustain rural crafts and traditions, and, crucially, the defence of rural services and exertion of the right of rural residents to public services. Campaigning against proposals to rationalize rural service provision is hence identified as a key battleground, as one activist told the *Weekend Australian* newspaper:

> Over the past nine years we've had an education standards issue, a hospital downgrade issue, a railway closure issue. I do feel embattled. I've been fighting for so long. (RWA activist, quoted by Rothwell 1997: 29)

As such, groups such as the RWA became some of the foremost critics of neo-liberal economic rationalism in Australia and its impact on rural communities, but combined their political-economic critique with an identity politics in which they called for discrimination on grounds of geographical isolation to be covered by human rights legislation. As another RWA activist explained, 'all we can do is be in everyone's faces, and then people will recognize that we are human beings and have rights' (quoted by Rothwell 1997: 29), while one of the movement's leaders, Betsy Fysh, told a radio discussion programme: 'We need to start seeing ourselves as a minority group, and we need to start playing politics by the rules that minority groups play by' (Radio National 1996).

The Heart of the Community

In some cases, debates over the provision of rural services revolve not only around their functional properties but also around their symbolic properties, as core components of an idealized notion of the rural community. According to popular discourses of rurality, the ideal rural community is defined by the presence of certain facilities and services, and the disappearance of these can be perceived as undermining a traditional rural way of life. Thus, the closure of village shops, post offices, public houses and bars can all be contested by local campaigners concerned at the impact on community life, but some of the most hard-fought campaigns involve the closure of rural schools.

The village school plays a multidimensional role in a rural community. It is not only an educational establishment, but also a focal point for community life. It can be used as a venue for community meetings and events, and fundraising activities, and informal school-gate conversations between parents contribute to the structuring of community engagement. Local schooling reinforces identification with a community and friendships formed in the classroom may shape the social networks of a community for decades. Moreover, the closure of a school not only removes these functions, but can also make a village less attractive to in-migrants, with families with school-aged children being less likely to move to a village without a school, thus contributing to an imbalance in the age profile of the population (Woods 2005b).

Yet, the consolidation of rural education provision was a prominent trend in most developed countries for much of the twentieth century. Rural depopulation, which reduced enrolment; the growing mobility of rural residents, meaning that children could travel further to school on a daily basis; together with efficiency and pedagogic arguments, all contributed to the closure of small rural schools. This trend was generally supported by rural modernization campaigners, for whom 'the one-room schoolhouse was the very symbol of rural inefficiency and institutional poverty' (Lapping et al. 1989: 28). More recently, the higher value placed on the aesthetic quality of rural life and the allure of the rural idyll within a consumption-based countryside has challenged the logic of this approach and led to a greater contestation of school closure proposals.

Nonetheless, the rationalization of rural schools has continued to be a feature of education policy in a number of countries including the United States, Britain, Canada, New Zealand, Ireland, Germany, Sweden, Finland and Hungary (Ribchester and Edwards 1999; Robinson 1990). In France over 1,400 rural communes lost their school between 1988 and 1994 (INSEE 1998), while 415 small rural schools closed in the United States between 1986–7 and 1993–4 (NCES 1997). The arguments in favour of school rationalization focus on the perceived pedagogic benefits of larger schools and cost-effectiveness analyses, particularly the costs of staffing and maintaining buildings for schools with few pupils (Ribchester and Edwards 1999; Woods 2005b). Supporters of small schools, in contrast, tend to emphasize the impact of closure on the rural community, both functionally and symbolically. Thus, a campaigner against the proposed closure of 57 rural schools in British Columbia in 2002 warned that 'when you close a school in a small community, you attack and undercut and potentially destroy the centre of community life. We have precious few institutions that build community life left in our province any more, and 57 of those are about to close' (quoted by Knickerbocker 2002). In New Zealand, the *Manawatu Evening Standard*, in an editorial on plans to rationalize nine rural schools into three in the Dannevirke district of North Island, also invoked a sense of rural discrimination:

Such schools are an integral part of the fabric of many country com- munities, and their loss feels like another nail in the coffin of rural life, somewhat similar to the closure of the post office, hotel or petrol station. For parents, of course, there remain the sheer practicalities of the new situation: new timetables due to the longer trips to the new school, greater stress, higher costs, and so on. Not a happy thought, but seemingly the price New Zealand families are increasingly being forced to pay for the privilege of living in the countryside. (*Manawatu Evening Standard*, 17 June 2003)

Similarly, a rural commentator testifying to the Nebraska Legislature on a proposed Bill establishing a 'School Structure Task Force', declared that:

If the intent of the Legislature is to kill Nebraska's rural communities, [this Bill] is the perfect prescription. [It] would eventually close schools in certain communities in rural Nebraska ... Forcing the closure of schools in rural Nebraska will also have a consistent result – towns and villages will become poorer, smaller, and less viable communities. Taking away the heart and soul of the community will eventually kill its body. Is 'efficiency' in the context of school structure actually synonymous with the slow but certain death of rural Nebraska and its communities? (Bailey 2003)

In each of these cases, as in others, opposition to school closures was also mounted by vigorous local campaigns initiated by grassroots activists. Often, campaigns against school closures are the first or most substantial expressions of collective political action in a rural community, uniting long-term residents and in-migrants in a common cause. In this way, Mormont saw campaigns against village school closures as prime examples of his embryonic rural social movements, representing 'a multiclass movement [that] managed to raise the question of the right of access to public services and also that of control and power over these services' (1987: 565), as well as providing an opportunity to question the pattern of the development of rural space. On occasion, campaigns can succeed in keeping schools open, as in Llandinam and Llangurig in Mid Wales in 2004, but even when unsuccessful, they can provide the stimulus for further collective action as groups set up new communal spaces to replace the loss of the school, or shift their attention to other perceived threats to the community.

Difference and Discrimination in the Countryside

The two previous examples have focused on the mobilization of rural residents against actions by external agents, including government and corporations, that are perceived to threaten aspects of rural life. A 'politics of the rural' also engages with social policy, however, in respect of the treatment of minority groups within the countryside and the question of how rurality is contested through the inclusion or exclusion of groups who do not conform with the norms of the dominant rural discourse. Historically, rural communities have been discursively constructed as places of stability, coherence and solidarity, yet the other side of this construct is that they have also been places of exclusion and intolerance. Discrimination within rural communities on the basis of race, sexual orientation, gender, culture and lifestyle are well documented (see, for example, Chakraborti and Garland 2004; Cloke and Little 1997; Milbourne 1997). Moreover, as the effect of such discriminatory practices was to reinforce the power and control of the dominant rural elites, inequalities of this kind were of little concern to the traditional rural politics and received little attention from the farm unions and other established lobby groups. Indeed, they were often complicit, as in the systematic discrimination against black farmers in the United States (Sheppard 1999; Woods 2005b), and in the exploitation of migrant agricultural workers (Mitchell 1996).

As the power of the traditional rural elites has declined, so growing efforts have been made to recognize and promote diversity and tolerance in the countryside. National social policies have played a key role in this, with programmes to tackle racism and homophobia, to enforce equal opportunities and to engage with marginalized groups. Progressive rural advocacy groups, such as the Rural Coalition in the United States, have also been active in trying to improve conditions and change attitudes, as have individuals within rural communities, often in-migrants. Efforts to confront explicit discrimination and abuse have gained wider support and acceptance, but attempts to address more subtle forms of discrimination and exclusion have on occasion proved more contentious, especially when they are directed at particular local traditions. Susan Smith (1993) documented one such case in the small town of Peebles in rural Scotland, where complaints about latent racism led the Beltane Festival committee to ban customary 'golliwog' costumes from the annual fancy-dress parade. The decision provoked a fierce reaction from some local residents, with the argument that the 'golliwog' is an offensive and stereotyped representation of black people, out of place in modern society, being dismissed as outside interference, tinkering with tradition and an attempt to impose alien urban values on a rural community.

The politicization of seemingly benign rural traditions arises in part because of the significance of 'stability' to conventional discourses of the rural community. This includes not only temporal stability – the sense of unchanging values and practices connecting back to a simpler, purer age – but also geographical stability. Rural identity is defined by a rootedness to place, by a belonging to land and locality, by an understanding of spatial boundaries and by an appreciation and respect of property. The discursive conventions of rural life can therefore be disturbed by transient populations, whose mobility threatens the spatial order of the countryside, especially if other aspects of their behaviour or lifestyle are non-conforming with rural norms. During the 1980s and 1990s a particular example of this arose around the treatment of 'new age travellers' (NATs) in the British countryside. The travellers are people from a range of backgrounds who have rejected modern, consumerist society and adopted a semi-nomadic lifestyle that is mainly performed in rural space. Traveller culture is strongly influenced by their own discourse of the rural idyll, which emphasizes the freedom of the countryside, the slower and more peaceful way of life, and closeness to nature (Lowe and Shaw 1993; Woods 2005b). Yet, the mobility of travellers and their sometimes illegal occupation of private land brought them into conflict with some rural communities, fuelled by wilder rumours of criminal and deviant behaviour. The Criminal Justice and Public Order Act introduced by the British government in 1994 responded to the concerns of the rural establishment with measures to control and regulate the movement of travellers. As Halfacree (1996) demonstrates, contributions to the parliamentary debates on the Act emphasized the perceived threat of travellers to rural communities and their way of life:

> The new age travellers displayed some dreadful antics: they invaded peaceful countryside, decimated peaceful villages, went on the rampage and had raves lasting two or three days, showing a total disregard for the area. (British Member of Parliament, quoted by Halfacree 1996: 62)

> It is the nomadic transgressions of the NATs which most threaten the complacent spatiality of the rural idyll. NATs – with their 'alternative' lifestyles, 'alternative' cultures, 'alternative' spatialities – trespass against the 'idyllic' rural social representation. (Halfacree 1996: 55)

At the same time, the British government had an obligation to uphold the human rights and welfare entitlements of the travellers. In an attempt to meet this obligation while also controlling the movement of travellers, the Caravan Sites (Amendment) Act 1993 required local authorities to provide temporary and permanent sites on which travellers could reside legally. Yet, identifying and developing such sites has become an additional source of conflict, with local residents mobilizing to oppose the designation of sites which they perceive as threatening the peace and safety of the countryside (Woods 2005a; see also Sibley 2003).

Opposition to travellers' camps unites two strands of the 'politics of the rural': a concern with the appropriateness of particular practices and presence of particular groups within rural space, and Mormont's original framing of the 'new rural question' as 'questions concerning the specific function of rural space and the type of development to encourage within it' (1987: 562). The connection is also made in conflicts around the accommodation of transitory immigrant groups in rural space, including both hostels for migrant workers and reception centres for refugees seeking political asylum. The latter issues became a significant focus for political mobilization in parts of the British countryside in the early years of the twenty-first century as, against a background of public anxiety over rates of immigration, the government adopted a 'dispersal strategy' to spread refugees around the country while their applications for asylum were processed. In particular, plans to construct a number of purpose-built reception centres in rural locations were met with local opposition, notably at the two 'trial' centres at Newton in Nottinghamshire and Bicester in Oxfordshire. In both cases local residents formed action groups to oppose the proposals, with support from the local councils and from groups such as the Campaign to Protect Rural England (CPRE). As Hubbard (2005) describes, opposition to the centres drew on a range of arguments including compliance with planning policies, the impact on the landscape and the appropriateness of the local infrastructure. Local residents also expressed concerns about crime and safety, playing on the widespread (but inaccurate) media representation of the asylum-seekers as 'illegal immigrants'. However, as Hubbard demonstrates, underlying the protests was the implicit (and sometimes explicit) argument that both the asylum-seekers and the reception centres were 'out of place' in the countryside. Emotively worded projections of villages being 'swamped' by gangs of bored, wandering migrant men, counterpoised the 'otherness', 'foreignness', masculinity and mobility of the centre residents, and their perceived need to find activities to occupy themselves, with an image of the settled, tranquil, coherent and self-resourceful rural community:

> Nobody knows the backgrounds of these people – whether they have criminal records or are violent or abusive or will abscond. During the day they will have little to do but wander round the villages in groups which will be intimidating for adults, traumatic for the elderly and turn children's play spaces into no-go areas. (Oxfordshire resident, quoted by Hubbard 2005: 11)

> Has anybody actually come to look at the area that this is being inflicted on? It's not some run-down place where nobody and nothing will come to any harm. It is a beautiful part of the British countryside full of hard-working law-abiding and tax-paying people. Have you really considered how much asylum-seekers and local people will suffer, the asylum-seekers will hate being isolated from civilisation, they will be denied the support they most need as it will be too far away. (Nottinghamshire resident, quoted by Hubbard 2005: 13)

The product of these arguments was, as Sibley notes, to suggest that 'a rural area, particularly a wealthy one, is no place for poor people of a different ethnicity – asylum-seekers should be accommodated in cities' (Sibley 2003: 228). Yet, significantly, this was done by evoking the deeply embedded cultural myth of the isolated and unsuspecting rural community vulnerable to invasion and terrorization by the unknown threat from outside, be it the marauding raiding part of history, the wolves and monsters of folklore, the socialist agitators of early twentieth-century propaganda, or the new age travellers and asylum-seekers of today. In this way, issues of the development of asylum reception centres or travellers' camps, or of initiatives to combat rural racism or homophobia, continue to return to questions about the meaning of rurality and rural identity.

Conclusion

The examples discussed above demonstrate the extent to which the 'politics of the rural' permeates across the contemporary political agenda. The restructuring of rural society and economy that has fragmented the discursive homogeneity of rural space has had, as Mormont (1987) first observed, a political consequence in reframing the 'rural question' around issues of the meaning and regulation of the 'rural'. This has been most evident in conflicts over the development of rural space, from new roads and housing to wind-farms, and in the campaigns of hunters to defend their sport and of farmers to protect the model of the family farm. However, the 'politics of the rural' is not restricted to these contexts. Issues about the provision of public and private services to rural communities, about the maintenance of rural infra-structure, and about the treatment of different social groups within rural society, all cannot be separated from questions about the meaning and regulation of rurality, such that the 'politics of the rural' extends into all areas of social policy – into education, health, transport, social services, family policy, equality and so on. The adoption by some governments of 'rural proofing' to some extent reflects this, seeking to evaluate the impact of pro-posed policies on rural communities and to make adjustments if appropriate. Yet, at the same time, rural proofing misses the point. The point is that there is no single, objective entity called the 'rural' that reacts in a clear and uniform way to different external pressures. Rather, different individuals and different groups have very different ideas about what it means to be rural, about the appropriate character and components of a rural community, and about the values that are important to rural life. Indeed, the 'politics of the rural' is as much about an internal conflict within the countryside as it is about a struggle by rural interests against external threats and challenges.

Moreover, to follow Mormont's representation of a transition between an 'old' and a 'new' way of framing the rural question, or to redescribe this as a transition from 'rural politics' to a 'politics of the rural', is not to suggest that the meaning of rurality was not contested before the mid-1980s, nor that the industrial politics of agriculture are not still relevant. It is, however, to suggest that the terms and conditions of rural political engagement have changed. That 'rural identity' has become a key rallying point for political activists as they seek to defend and promote the countryside, as they imagine it. As this new social movement gathers momentum – fragmented and con-tradictory though it may be – it poses challenges both for the way in which the rural is governed, and for the ways in which the making and contesting of policies affecting the countryside are examined by researchers.

References

Argent, N. and Rolley, F. (2000), Lopping the branches: bank branch closure and rural Australian communities. In B. Pritchard and P. McManus (eds), *Land of Discontent: The Dynamics of Change in Rural and Regional Australia*, Sydney: UNSW Press, pp. 140–68.

Bailey, J. (2003), Statement of the Center for Rural Affairs on LB 556 to the Education Committee of the Nebraska Legislature, 24 February 2003. Available at: www.cfra.org/resources/Testimony/LB556_testimony.htm (accessed 14 July 2003).

Browne, W. P. (2001), *The Failure of National Rural Policy: Institutions and Interests*, Washington, DC: Georgetown University Press.

Castells, M. (1977), *The Urban Question*, Cambridge, MA: MIT Press.

Castells, M. (1978), *City, Class and Power*, London: Macmillan.

Chakraborti, N. and Garland, J. (2004), *Rural Racism*, Cullompton, UK: Willan Publishing.

Cloke, P. (1989), State deregulation and New Zealand's agricultural sector, *Sociologia Ruralis*, 29: 34–48.

Cloke, P. and Le Heron, R. (1994), Agricultural deregulation: the case of New Zealand. In P. Lowe, T. Marsden and S. Whatmore (eds), *Regulating Agriculture*, London: David Fulton, pp. 104–26.

Cloke, P. and Little, J. (1990), *The Rural State*, Oxford: Oxford University Press.

Cloke, P. and Little, J. (eds) (1997), *Contested Countryside Cultures*, London and New York: Routledge.

Cocklin, C. and Dibden, J. (2002), Taking stock: farmers' reflections on the deregulation of Australian dairying, *Australian Geographer*, 33, 1: 29–42.

Countryside Alliance (2004), Rural Services, Countryside Alliance website. Available at: www.countryside-alliance.org.uk (accessed 25 October 2005).

Doremus, H. and Tarlock, A. D. (2003), Fish, farms, and the clash of cultures in the Klamath basin, *Ecology Law Quarterly*, 30: 279–350.

Edwards, B. and Woods, M. (2004), Mobilizing the local: community, participation and governance. In L. Holloway and M. Kneafsey (eds), *Geographies of Rural Cultures and Societies*, Aldershot: Ashgate, pp. 173–98.

FAO (2004), *The State of Food and Agriculture 2003–04*, Rome: Food and Agriculture Organization.

Geddes, R. (2003), *The Structure and Effect of International Postal Reform*, American Enterprise Institute for Public Policy Research. Available at: www.aei.org (accessed 25 October 2005).

Halfacree, K. (1996), Out of place in the countryside: travellers and the 'rural idyll', *Antipode*, 29: 42–71.

Halpin, D. (2003), The collective political actions of the Australian farming and rural communities: putting farm interest groups in context, *Rural Society*, 13: 138–56.

Halpin, D. (2004), Transitions between formations and organizations: an historical perspective on the political representation of Australian farmers, *Australian Journal of Politics and History*, 50, 4: 469–90.

Halpin, D. and Guilfoyle, A. (2004), Attributions of responsibility: rural neo-liberalism and farmers' explanations of the Australian rural crisis, *Rural Society*, 14, 2: 93–111.

Herbert-Cheshire, L. (2000), Contemporary strategies for rural community development in Australia: a governmentality perspective, *Journal of Rural Studies*, 16: 203–15.

Herbert-Cheshire, L. (2003), Translating policy: power and action in Australia's country towns, *Sociologia Ruralis*, 43, 4: 454–73.

Hubbard, P. (2005), 'Inappropriate and incongruous': opposition to asylum centres in the English countryside, *Journal of Rural Studies*, 21: 3–17.

INSEE (1998), *Les Campagnes et leurs villes*, Paris: INSEE.

Knickerbocker, N. (2002), 57 public schools threatened with closure, *Teacher Newsmagazine*, May/June 2002. Available at: www.bctf.ca (accessed 14 July 2003).

Lapping, M. B., Daniels, T. L. and Keller, J. W. (1989), *Rural Planning and Development in the United States*, New York: Guilford.

Leyshon, A. and Thrift, N. (1994), Access to financial services and financial infrastructure withdrawal: problems and policies, *Area*, 26: 268–75.

Lowe, R. and Shaw, W. (1993), *Travellers: Voices of the New Age Nomads*, London: Fourth Estate.

Magnusson, W. and Shaw, K. (eds) (2003), *A Political Space: Reading the Global through Clayoquot Sound*, Minneapolis: University of Minnesota Press.

Midgley, J. (2005), Financial inclusion, universal banking and post offices in Britain, *Area*, 37: 277–85.

Milbourne, P. (ed.) (1997), *Revealing Rural 'Others': Representation, Power and Identity in the British Countryside*, London: Pinter.

Milbourne, P. (2004), *Rural Poverty*, Abingdon: Routledge.

Mitchell, D. (1996), *The Lie of the Land: Migrant Workers and the California Landscape*, Minneapolis: University of Minnesota Press.

Mormont, M. (1987), The emergence of rural struggles and their ideological effects, *International Journal of Urban and Regional Research*, 7: 559–75.

Murdoch, J. (1997), The shifting territory of government: some insights from the Rural White Paper, *Area*, 29: 109–18.

Murdoch, J. and Marsden, T. (1994), *Reconstituting Rurality*, London: UCL Press.

National Center for Education Statistics (NCES) (1997), *Statistical Analysis Report: Characteristics of Small and Rural School Districts*, Washington, DC: NCES.

Newby, H., Bell, C., Rose, D. and Saunders, P. (1978), *Property, Paternalism and Power: Class and Control in Rural England*, London: Hutchinson.

NUPGE (2003), *Privatization and Closure Threaten Canada's Rural Post Offices*, National Union of Public and General Employees website. Available at: www.nupge.ca (accessed 25 October 2005).

Pickvance, C. (1995), Marxist theories of urban politics. In D. Judge, G. Stoker and H. Wolman (eds), *Theories of Urban Politics*, London: Sage, pp. 253–75.

Postcomm (2003), *Post Office Networks Abroad*, London: Postal Services Commission.

Pritchard, B. (2000), Negotiating the two-edged sword of agricultural trade liberalisation: trade policy and its protectionist discontents. In B. Pritchard and P. McManus (eds), *Land of Discontent: The Dynamics of Change in Rural and Regional Australia*, Sydney: UNSW Press, pp. 90–104.

Pritchard, B. and McManus, P. (eds) (2000), *Land of Discontent: The Dynamics of Change in Rural and Regional Australia*, Sydney: UNSW Press.

Radio National (1996), *Bush Politics*, Transcript of Background Briefing Programme, broadcast 22 September 1996, Australian Broadcasting Corporation.

Randall, C. and Gregoriadis, L. (2000), Barclays faces the wrath of rural England, *Daily Telegraph*, 17 March 2000.

Ribchester, C. and Edwards, B. (1999), The centre and the local: policy and practice in rural education provision, *Journal of Rural Studies*, 15: 49–63.

Robinson, G. (1990), *Conflict and Change in the Countryside*, Chichester: Wiley.

Rothwell, N. (1997), Rural alliance brings bush out of a dark age, *The Weekend Australian*, 11–12 October: 11.

Sheingate, A. D. (2001), *The Rise of the Agricultural Welfare State*, Princeton, NJ: Princeton University Press.

Sheppard, B. O. (1999), Black farmers and institutionalized racism, *The Black Business Journal*. Available at: www.bbjonline.com (accessed 5 November 2003).

Sibley, D. (2003), Psychogeographies of rural space and practices of exclusion. In P. Cloke (ed.), *Country Visions*, Harlow: Pearson, pp. 218–31.

Skillern, P. (2002), When your bank leaves town, *Shelterforce Online*, issue 126. Available at: www.nhi.org/online/issues/126/bankclosings.html (accessed 25 October 2005).

Smith, M. J. (1993), *Pressure, Power and Policy*, Hemel Hempstead: Harvester Wheatsheaf.

Smith, S. J. (1993), Bounding the borders: claiming space and making place in rural Scotland, *Transactions of the Institute of British Geographers*, 18: 291–308.

Tonts, M. (2000), The restructuring of Australia's rural communities. In B. Pritchard and P. McManus (eds), *Land of Discontent: The Dynamics of Change in Rural and Regional Australia*, Sydney: UNSW Press, pp. 52–72.

Walker, G. (1995), Social mobilization in the city countryside – rural Toronto fights a waste dump, *Journal of Rural Studies*, 11, 3: 243–54.

Warner, M. and Hefetz, A. (2003), Rural–urban differences in privatization: limits to the competitive state, *Environment and Planning C: Government and Policy*, 21: 703–18.

Winter, M. (1996), *Rural Politics*, London and New York: Routledge.

Woods, M. (1998), Advocating rurality? The repositioning of rural local government, *Journal of Rural Studies*, 14: 13–26.

Woods, M. (2003a), Conflicting environmental visions of the rural: windfarm development in Mid Wales, *Sociologia Ruralis*, 43: 271–88.

Woods, M. (2003b), Deconstructing rural protest: the emergence of a new social movement, *Journal of Rural Studies*, 19: 309–25.

Woods, M. (2005a), *Contesting Rurality: Politics in the British Countryside*, Aldershot: Ashgate.

Woods, M. (2005b), *Rural Geography*, London: Sage.

Woods, M. (2006), Political articulation: the modalities of new critical politics of rural citizenship. In P. Cloke, T. Marsden and P. Mooney (eds), *Handbook of Rural Studies*, London: Sage, pp. 457–71.

Wunderlich, G. (2003), *American Country Life: A Legacy*, Lanham, MD: University Press of America.

2

Rural Movements in Europe: Scandinavia and the Accession States

Vanessa Halhead

Factors Promoting the Growth of Rural Movements

The participation of local civil society is a key factor in rural development. With the decline of the command and welfare state models, in which the state and its institutions played a very strong role in meeting the needs of society, the importance of *social capital* as a force for action has received increasing emphasis. Likewise, the reduction in *local democracy*, resulting in part from the increasing centralization and scale of local administration, has become an issue, leading to a growing interest in concepts of *participatory democracy*. At the same time, the rural areas of Europe have been experiencing often severe decline, resulting from the decreasing importance of agriculture (especially for employment) in the rural economy, the forces of the EU internal market, the globalization of markets, increasing cultural and economic urbanization and trends in rural–urban migration, especially of young and educated people.

In most Western and Eastern European countries, agriculture is now a relatively minor player in the rural economy. In Finland, for instance, the number of active farms fell from 225,000 in 1980 to 90,200 in 1998 (Ministry of Agriculture and Forestry 2000). In Denmark, the number of farms fell from 130,000 to 60,000 in the same period. During its early years of independence, in the early 1990s, Estonia reported a loss of approximately three-quarters of its agricultural jobs. These factors have contributed to the depopulation of rural communities, to imbalanced age structures, regional inequalities and the loss of rural services, which, in turn, have reinforced the negative trends. This process has occurred at different times in the different countries. In the old industrial countries, it began in the nineteenth century, in the less industrialized Nordic countries in the 1960s, and in the newly independent countries of Eastern Europe in the 1990s. In all European countries, the trends are continuing, though with differing regional characteristics and disparities.

One response to such processes of rural decline has been manifested in the growth of the rural and village movements in Europe since the 1970s. The formation of these rural movements was not only a response to rural decline *per se*, but to the inadequate responses of governments and the EU to this decline – a development which has been mirrored in the Eastern European countries since their independence in the early 1990s. The EU policy response, in common with that of most governments, has been to focus on the role of agriculture, while giving little recognition to the huge structural changes taking place in the rural economy and society or to the special characteristics of rural areas.

The Development of the Rural Movements

Rural movements have developed through a number of interlinked processes in Europe. Those in the Nordic and Eastern European countries developed from an early Finnish model, with some mobilization by the PREPARE[1] Programme. Movements in Western Europe arose independently but have developed connections through the medium of international networks, principally the PREPARE Network, the Nordic Network, *Hela Norden Ska Leva* (HNSL), the earlier Trans-European Rural Network (TERN) and the recently formed European Rural Alliance (see box 1).

Box 1

Chronology of the formation of the rural movements

1970s – The first village action groups formed in Finland and Sweden
1976 – Finnish 'Village Action 76' Programme
1976 – Danish village movement *Landsforeningen af Landsbysamfund* (LAL)
1979 – Dutch Association of Small Towns and Villages *Landelijke Vereniging voor Kleine Kernen*
1980 – Rural Voice in England (no longer active)
1981 – Finnish village movement started – 1997 *Suomen Kylätoimin-ta ry* (SYTY)
1982 – Scottish Rural Forum (no longer active)
1987 – Action with Communities in Rural England (ACRE)
1989 – Swedish Popular Movements Council for Rural Development *Folkrorelserådet*
1989 – Trans-European Rural Network (TERN) (no longer active)
1990 – Wales Rural Forum
1990 – Irish Rural Link
1991 – Northern Ireland Rural Community Network
1992 – Estonian movement started – 1997 *Kodukant*
1993 – Portuguese Association for Rural Development (ANIMAR)
1997 – Danish Council of Rural Districts *Landdistrikternes Fællesraad (LDF)*
1998 – Hungarian Rural Parliament *Vidék Parlamentje*
1999 – PREPARE Programme started
2000 – Slovakian Rural Parliament *Vidiecky Parlament na Slovensku*
2001 – Icelandic movement *Landsbyggdin Lifi*
2002 – Polish Rural Forum *Forum Aktywizacji Obszarów Wiejskich*
2002 – Lithuanian Rural Communities Union *Lietuvos Kaimo Bendruomenių Sąjunga*
2003 – Slovenian Rural Development Network *Društva za Razvoj Slovenskega Podeželja*
2003 – The PREPARE Network
2004 – Latvian Rural Forum *Latvijas Lauku Forums*
2005 – European Rural Alliance formed

The five within-country movements documented below are indicative of broader characteristics and patterns of development within Europe. The case studies were compiled from a research visit to each country. This involved travel to different regions and meetings with the key people involved in each movement, as well as representatives of government, academics and non-governmental organizations, at national, regional and local levels. The questions asked in each country followed a common format, to enable comparison. The key topics investigated were the national and international context, history of development, key players involved, organization, management and funding, activities, costs and benefits, achievements and challenges, relationships to others and future plans. Discussions were also held with many of the other national movements and networks, and several pan-European and national events were attended.

Finland

The first of the current rural movements, and the model for many others, started in Finland in the 1970s. Stimulated by rural decline in much of Finland in the 1960s and 1970s, rural communities began to take matters into their own hands, forming village committees to tackle local development. This process began as a spontaneous action in isolated villages, and the threads of this dispersed energy were pulled together in 1976, by Professor Lauri Hautemaki of the University of Helsinki, with his launch of the project 'Village Action 1976' (T. Hyyrylainen, University of Helsinki, pers. comm. 2003). This project was an unusual example of community mobilization led by universities. The project advocated the idea of Finnish Village Action, and advocated the use of special tools for the development of rural areas, different from those suitable for urban areas. Foremost among these was the development of *village committees* to harness the increasingly scarce human resources of the rural areas, to provide coordination and to focus on the development of the village as a whole. The formalization of these committees into legally constituted *village associations*, able to handle funds, was also advocated. A small number of early village committees had already been formed in 1965. Following the period of mobilization, by 1990 there were 3,000, and by 2003, 3,935 village committees were recorded, including 2,200 village associations (Village Action Association of Finland 2003).

The first national structure – The Finnish National Organization for Village Action – was established in 1981. This was an association of mostly national NGOs with a rural focus, but did not actually include the village associations. This was seen, at the time, as the best way to engage the interests of the larger NGOs in supporting village action. However, this structure was replaced in 1997 with the current national 'Village Action Association of Finland' (Suomen Kylatoiminta ry – SYTY), which more closely reflected the 'bottom–up' nature of the village movement. It has a membership of 133 organizations, including all 19 regional village associations, and 58 Local Action Groups,[2] together with the main regional and national rural organizations.

In 1989, the first regional village association was formed in Lapland, with the aim of helping these particular villages to overcome their geographical isolation. As villages recognized the increasing importance of the regional level in national and EU policy, regional associations came to be established throughout Finland. The final three regional associations were formed in 2000, thus completing a pattern of 19 regional village associations, reflecting the country's statutory regional administrative structure.

This tiered structure has shaped the approach adopted by many subsequent rural movements elsewhere: the principle being to form village associations at each level of government, thus enabling civil society in the rural areas to link more effectively with the statutory authorities. The existence of legally constituted associations provides a vehicle through which disparate rural communities can be accessed and through which planning and project implementation can be carried out.

The Finnish movement also initiated and developed the practice of village planning. This is now an integral part of the village movements in several countries, with 'nested' plans produced at village, regional and national levels. The planning process enables villages to prioritize and organize their activities more effectively. Local village plans shape regional plans for villages which, in turn, shape the national plan. At each level, the aim is both to provide an agreed agenda for the work of the associations and to influence the statutory plans produced by the authorities. Finland exemplifies the potential of this approach, its 'National Village Action Programme' constituting one of the main inputs into the government's 'Rural Policy Programme' (Ministry of Agriculture and Forestry 2001). Indeed, Finnish village action was awarded the Right Livelihood prize in 1992 and the UN Friendship Award in 1995.[3]

> Village action is local, self-initiated development work carried out by village residents to strengthen the livability, comfortability and village identity in their own home region. Village action gathers residents together regardless of profession, age, gender, political view, leisure activities or whether one is a permanent resident, newcomer or leisure resident. Village action represents local democracy and local initiative at its best. (Village Action Association of Finland 2003)

Sweden

The Finnish model was influential in the development of a similar movement in Sweden during the 1980s, which was also in response to rural decline and depopulation, especially in the north of the country. A further reason for action in this case was the amalgamation of the traditional local municipalities into larger districts in the 1970s. As in Finland, individual villages started to form associations in advance of any national movement. In the Swedish case, however, there was early mobilization through a government-supported campaign, thanks to Sweden's participation in the European Council's Campaign for Rural Europe in 1987.

The Swedish movement is now the largest and most highly developed in Europe – and it is also the only movement to receive significant government funding. The movement has assisted the formation of over 4,000 village associations, with 100,000 people directly involved. Local and regional groupings of village associations have been formed, and the whole movement is coordinated and supported by a national association, *Folkrörelserådet* (the Popular Movements Council – PMC), established in 1989. In addition to the village representatives, the PMC has 53 national NGOs as members of its Council. The PMC provides practical support to the local actors, develops programmes for rural development and aims to influence policy. Its biennial *Rural Parliament* involves over 1,000 village representatives, and provides a direct voice to the government.

> The Village Action Movement is an expression of people's desires to engage in collective values as well as an expression of their ability to find new solutions – to reclaim the initiative. Organized collectively in democratic associations, the people develop and uphold their local communities. (Herlitz 2001a)

Denmark

The rural movement in Denmark developed concurrently with, but independently of, the Finnish movement. It has its own character, but parallels to the other movements are strong. The movement was rooted in rural decline (in particular in the decline of agricultural employment since the 1960s), but also in the 1970 reform of local government, which replaced 1,388 parish municipalities with 275 much larger units. Furthermore, the rise of the Danish movement has been attributed in part to an influx of educated urban migrants in the 1970s (Svendsen 2004), who sought to re-establish 'the rural way of life' and traditional values. There was recognition that agriculture could not support these rural areas and that there was a need for a new rural development model, relevant to the post-industrial age. The movement was initiated by individuals, and the early mobilization – as in the Finnish case – was undertaken by one man, Carsten Abild: 'I see the creation of the Village Association as a form of popular movement which builds upon a knowledge that we are not satisfied just by living a materialistic way of life for ourselves. Instead we should focus more on togetherness with others and creating satisfactorily intelligible societies where the individual can thrive' (Abild 1977).

The first national organization, the Danish Village Association (*Landsfore-ningen af Landsbysamfund* – LAL), was established in 1976 to support village action. The movement has not established regional-level organizations, nor has it actively mobilized the formation of village associations, as in the Finnish model. However, it has built on the strong development of local civil society in Denmark, which has been a feature since the time of Grundtvig in the nineteenth century (Thaning 1972). LAL has no paid staff and is run by its board members; it undertakes a wide range of projects to support village action, and lobbies government on behalf of rural communities.

Internal disagreements led to the formation of a breakaway organization in 1978, the Villages in Denmark Association (*Landsbyer i Danmark* – LID) – also village-focused, but not so far on the scale of LAL. Attempts to gain government funding for this movement in 1995 led to the formation in 1997 of a *third* organization, the Council of Rural Districts (*Landdistrikternes Fællesraad* – LDF). This is in effect a *rural forum* of national-level rural NGOs, and is the only part of the movement to receive public core funding. LDF is a strategic body, working closely with the government to provide a focus on the diverse interests of rural development. These three organizations together tackle the work of the single organizations in other countries.

Estonia

The first steps in forming the Estonian movement, *Kodukant*, were taken in 1992, shortly after independence, by interested individuals working with regional rural development. The motivating force was the rapid rural decline experienced immediately following independence, when agriculture failed to meet the demands of the market economy, shifting the national focus from the rural to the urban population. The process for establishing the movement began with pilots in two Estonian counties, which were twinned with two Swedish counties. Thus the Swedes were able to provide guidance and support, enabling Estonians to learn from their experience. The result was a model based on the Swedish and Finnish concept of a *village action movement*.

Early development focused on the growth of county-level associations, and there are now independent county associations in all 15 Estonian counties. The process of mobilizing village associations has taken place largely through the activities of these county associations. The national organization Kodukant was established in 1997, with a board formed from the 15 county associations (comprising village and other local rural groups) and a number of other rural NGOs. In this way, the movement is very much owned by and responsive to its rural communities. This is supported by a process of strategic planning at village, regional and national levels, shaping the work and providing a basis for lobbying. A biennial *Rural Parliament* creates a platform for raising the rural profile and speaking to government. Kodukant is now an active partner in supporting the growth of rural movements in other parts of Eastern Europe.

> Kodukant has been essential to the development of our villages; without it we would not have had the confidence, information, contacts or organization to proceed effectively. (Soometsa village leader, pers. comm. 2003)

Slovakia

The Slovak Rural Parliament is one of the most recent manifestations of the new wave of rural movements in Eastern Europe. The factors promoting the growth of the movement are common to other Eastern European countries, in which independence precipitated a sudden and massive decline in agriculture and public support to rural areas, and a resultant out-migration to urban centres. As elsewhere, the response of government to the problems of the rural areas was perceived as inadequate and the focus on agricultural policy too strong. In addition, the prospect of joining the EU focused attention on preparing rural areas to influence and benefit from EU programmes. The development of civil society in Slovakia had, during the 1990s, been the focus of US aid, supporting the growth of many rural NGOs – though these were uncoordinated and lacked the profile to influence policy.

The early growth of the rural movement in Slovakia was supported by Sweden.[4] The Slovak Rural Development Agency of the Ministry of Agriculture took the initiative in 1994 to organize an annual Rural Forum to enable exchange between the many rural organizations. This led, in 2000, to the establishment the Slovak Rural Parliament as a national constituted organization. This is now well established and has made significant progress in establishing regional associations in four of the eight Slovak administrative regions. There are no village associations, due to the structure of municipalities at the village level. Instead, the movement has concentrated on supporting the formation of partnerships at micro-regional level, and has initiated a network of 48 Communication and Information Centres around the country, to service the 'grassroots' of the movement. Attention is now turning to influencing government policy on rural areas (Halhead and Guiheneuf 2004).

> Rural problems have a strong relationship to problems in the country as a whole; however, there are big disparities between life in rural and urban areas. Rural areas are so big, with so many players, that we now realize we need support from each other. It is important to have the support of the local people and civic society behind you. The strength of the Rural Parliament is their wide support within the rural community. It is difficult for the government to ignore this. (J. Tvrdonova, head of the Slovak Rural Development Agency, pers. comm. 2003)

Characteristics of these Rural Movements

At a gathering of rural movements in May 2004[5] a rural movement was defined as 'a linking of rural people and interests who wish to create change in rural areas by working together'. Critically, a rural movement must ensure ownership by the rural people, with other organizations taking a supportive role. Rural movements arise because people show the capacity to take their own lives into their own hands. In turn, the rural movements enable rural people to take action. The main characteristics of the movements can be summarized as follows:

* *Structured* – organized and networked at local, regional, national and international levels.
* *Locally focused* – rooted in the village and owned and run by village people.
* *Supportive* – mobilizing, networking and supporting action for local development.
* *Informed* – connected with good information dissemination.
* *Coordinated* – working with a clear common purpose achieved by strategic planning.
* *Influential* – undertaking advocacy to shape local, regional, national and EU policy.
* *International* – internationally connected through a common network.

Structured

The structural characteristics of the rural movements fall into two broad categories: the 'bottom–up' *village action movement* and the more 'top–down' *rural forum* of national and regional organizations (Halhead 2005).

A village movement is an organizational expression of local village action for rural development. It is a way of bringing together the people actively involved at the most local level of rural society, and supporting their efforts at regional and national levels. It is mobilizing rural communities to address their own futures, to influence local and national policy and to build local, national and trans-national rural networks.

The rural forum is a mechanism for providing a coordinated response to the needs of rural development, on the part of the many organizations that, individually, represent aspects of the wider rural sector. The key roles of a rural forum are to develop a cooperative and integrated approach, and to work with government to address rural issues.

A key feature is the structuring of the movements at each administratively significant level – local, regional and national. This is particularly evident in Finland, Sweden and Estonia. It provides a logical mechanism to connect civil society and to link it to the governmental system. It reduces the complexity that is inherent in community groups and NGOs, and helps them to cooperate more efficiently. The concept of a *Rural Parliament*,[6] or biennial national gathering of all rural interests, villages, NGOs and authorities, has been well developed by Sweden, and implemented also in Estonia and Slovakia. This provides a voice for rural communities and a focus for national strategy-making.

> The national association was formed in order to integrate sectoral interests, at local and national levels, to strengthen the involvement of village people and to bring their interest groups together. If we wanted to get support for these village groups we needed a body that was fighting for this at national level. (E. Uusitalo, chairman of the Village Action Association of Finland, pers. comm. 2003)

The structure of each movement reflects the national context in which it operates, the objectives and values of its initiators, the process by which it was mobilized, its age and maturity. Each movement displays its own characteristics, but there is a difference of emphasis between the Nordic movements and those of East and West Europe.

The Nordic movements are principally *village action movements* and have arisen from the village level, or have focused on mobilizing this level. This reflects the Nordic culture of participatory democratic values and the long traditions of volunteer work within local communities. The concept of the Rural Parliament originated in Sweden and has similarities to the old Norse concept of the *Ting*, or 'parliament', based on the principle of participatory democracy.

The movements being established in Eastern Europe, with the exception of Estonia, and also those that have been established in the UK, are based more on the model of the *rural forum*, or network of organizations. An important focus of these movements has been on linking the activities of the rural NGOs and providing a focus for influencing policy. The establishment of a 'grassroots' level and connections to these movements has proved to be more problematic.

Locally focused

> The home place is important to people – we need to know where we came from and our history, to know where we are going. (Jani village leader, presentation to conference workshop, Estonia, 2003)

The movements that can be classified as *village movements* are strongly rooted in the notion of the 'village' or 'homeplace'.[7] The village is closely connected to historical, cultural and social roots. It goes back into the earliest history of the rural areas and has, at different times, been a local administrative unit. In Slovakia the village is still the local authority, the result of a popular reaction against the communist imposition of a larger administrative unit, which removed the historical autonomy of the village. The traditional connections between people and place are strongly respected in all of the movements. This applies not only to the village level, but also to the parish and county levels.

The President of Estonia, speaking at the Estonian Rural Parliament in August 2003, referred to the spirit of Estonia's villages having kept alive the Estonian national identity and culture during many centuries of occupation: 'The heart of Estonian culture and economy has been a village. It started to flourish again when Estonians mastered their state and land again. Like in a real heart, our most precious principles and values were fixed there' (Rüütel 2003).

By the same tradition, the concept of the village movement is that it belongs to the rural communities. It embodies the spirit and values of the villages and is driven by a passion to retain rural life and traditions. It is a voice and marketplace for rural people and a uniting force for the many dispersed rural communities. Most importantly, it is 'bottom–up', owned by the rural people and a source of great pride to them, and is run with evident energy and enthusiasm, by many hundreds of rural people. It is also respected by national and local government for its success in mobilizing the rural communities.

The formally constituted village associations, promoted initially by Finland, have been found to be an effective model for enabling rural development, but take time to mobilize. After 30 years Finland and Sweden have 4,000 each, after 10 years Estonia has 400. They have been found, through research, to evolve as they move forward and grow in confidence and capacity. This process is described (E. Uusitalo, chairman of the Village Association of Finland, pers. comm. 2003) as the 'first generation' of working with cultural, social and environmental projects, the 'second generation' of taking on aspects of local service delivery, and the 'third generation' of undertaking business creation and economic development. As the achievements of the active villages become known, so more villages follow suit.

The idea of the village association builds on the human tendency to support the local 'tribe' and to feel allegiance to something that they themselves own and have created. (Jani village leader, presentation to conference workshop, 2003)

Supportive and informed

The movements undertake a wide range of activities in support of rural communities. These focus on building the capacity of the villages to become organized, plan their priorities, raise and manage funds, undertake projects, and link with other villages and organizations. This work is mostly carried out by the regional associations, whose staff and boards are trained by the national associations. Denmark lacks a regional structure, so it attempts to do this from a national level. Production and dissemination of information is an essential pillar in this support and network service. Each country has a range of information tools by which it achieves this: newsletters, websites, information days and training. In Slovakia a network of local Communication Centres has been established, which are the focus for the support and information services.

We are not willing to regard economic values as more important than the quality of life. We don't believe in development through centralized structures for decision-making and services. Instead we believe that people should control their own lives. (Village Action Association of Finland 1995)

Coordinated

A notable feature of the established movements is the level of strategic thought that has gone into their organization. In the most developed movements, not only are they structured at each significant level, they also undertake strategic planning at each of these levels. This is used to drive the activities of the movements at local, regional and national levels, and also to influence statutory policy at these levels. This system is particularly well developed in Finland, where the National Village Plan forms an important foundation for the development of the national Rural Policy Programme.

Village action has organized into local, regional and national activity, and international cooperation is increasing. Each level has its own responsibilities and each is needed to promote village development. This is recognized in the programme, where there are responsibilities for each level. (Village Action Association of Finland 2003)

Influential

An increasingly important role for the movements is advocacy to shape local, regional, national and EU policy. They perform a unique function in opening up the views and needs of small rural communities to the distant policy-makers. A central focus of all movements is to promote integrated policies which better reflect the changing circumstances of rural areas, and their diverse character and needs, and to modify the traditional focus on agriculture. This is a skilled job, requiring experience, knowledge, connections and credibility; hence it is one of the later activities to develop. It is, however, a critical role in achieving the aim of integrated rural policy, and is a high priority for all the movements. The Finnish movement is probably the most successful to date in its achievements, though all see the need to strengthen their capacity for advocacy.

> The relationship between the state and the local level is that the state is like a giraffe, looking down from a great height – it does not see the details at local level. So the state needs the villages. It is important to recognize and work with the village identity from the inside. (Kodukant 2003a)

International

International links are an important feature of all the movements. Since the start, the movements have networked and helped each other. This has enabled the transfer of experience and avoidance of mistakes. It has also increased the confidence and status of the movements, both at home and in the EU. Linked in a common European network, the national village movements are now actively working to influence EU policy for the next programme period, after 2006. The formation in 2005 of the European Rural Alliance will provide a formal platform through which to address the wider needs of rural areas in an EU context.

Impact of the Rural Movements

Developing rural capacity and civil society

The movements are a tool for promoting endogenous development and play a critical role in promoting rural identity within the wider society and increasing the confidence and pride of rural communities through giving them a voice and supporting the rural heritage. A key part of this process is building formal structures through which small and scattered communities can both address their own development in a more integrated and effective way, and can network with similar communities to address mutual needs and wider issues. Village associations have, in some countries, been created to help fill the vacuum left by the loss of traditional local municipalities; they also build on the historical affiliation to place. Coupled with the development of organizational structure, the movements also provide training to enable the associations to be effective planners and deliverers of rural development. This is a civil system for meeting the needs of rural areas, which the state is unable to meet.

Building participatory democracy

The weakening of local democracy due to administrative centralization has been very noticeable in the rural areas, especially in Scandinavia, where local democratic traditions have been among the strongest in the world. The effect of the two reorganizations in Sweden in 1952 and 1974 was the loss of 2,200 local municipalities in just 22 years. This sudden 'democratic deficit', coupled with the long history of local direct democracy, was undoubtedly a major factor in the subsequent growth of the Village Movement. 'When society "left", the inhabitants formed village action groups to work for the development of their community' (Herlitz 2001a). The rural movements are one force that is working in the opposite direction, not through the formal democratic system, but by mobilizing the organization and involvement of local people and transferring their issues, needs and ideas into the formal statutory processes of policy-making. This has been referred to in Sweden as 'place-based democracy' (Herlitz 2001a).

Increasing social capital

All movements are seeking to increase the participation of civil society in the planning, decision-making and implementation of rural development. Village action plays a critical role in building local confidence, pride, relationships, capacity and integration. This is building on the long-established traditions of village action, which are part of all rural areas, and providing a new framework and focus for this within the context of modern society. The importance of social capital in supplementing reduced public resources and services is recognized in all countries, and is an incentive for government support. The loss of rural population, the weakening of local democracy and the welfare state, and the transition to a monetary economy have affected all rural communities adversely. The village action movement provides inspiration and motivation to build the social capital to ensure sustainability of the rural community. The many creative ideas and solutions to local problems become common property as part of a collective movement. These can be traded for external funding and translated into contracting local service delivery. At a further stage of development, it has been recorded that villages become their own economic development agents.

The activities of the Village Action Groups in Sweden were surveyed in 1996 (Herlitz 1996). It was calculated that for the year 2003, the groups were responsible for 4.4 million hours of volunteer work per year, corresponding to €72 million per year. They also invest €22 million of their own capital per year (Herlitz 2001a). A similar survey in Finland in 2002 found that over 40,000 people were directly involved in the movement, and that 1.6 million volunteer hours per year were invested, totalling €16 million worth of volunteer time. Some €3.2 million in independent funding and €31 million in public project funding were raised by the village associations per year, and 8,000 development measures per year had been implemented, 2,600 village halls/community centres had been constructed or repaired and 1,000 village plans produced. In total, they calculated over 2.5 million Finns were assisted by village development work (Village Action Association of Finland 2003).

The Village Action Movement is an expression of people's desires to engage in collective values as well as an expression of their ability to find new solutions – to reclaim the initiative. Organized collectively in democratic associations, the people develop and uphold their local communities. (Herlitz 2001a)

Developing cooperation

The movements play an important role in creating synergy between villages and NGOs so that they avoid competition and increase their mutual capacity to meet rural needs. This was noted in Slovakia as a key reason for the establishment of the Rural Parliament: 'A significant development of civil society in the rural areas took place following independence, with many civil groups and organizations being established, at local, regional and national levels. However, there was no mechanism for networking these or for developing a more coordinated and strategic approach to rural development' (J. Tvrdonova, head of the Slovak Rural Development Agency, pers. comm. 2003).

It is also apparent that the rural movements utilize the principles of a trade union in the development of a strong and grassroots membership, able to exert influence in advocacy with the authorities: 'Collective power is an impressive device. Organization into a true social mass movement is the uppermost challenge for rural developers' (Salomaa-Santala 2003).

Influencing change

All movements aspire to influence policy, at all levels, through advocacy and partnership. The impact of the movements on policy development has not, however, been measured in any of the countries. By linking many rural organizations they provide a useful partner for government. The strategic planning process, developed by some movements, is a potentially important tool. In Finland this has succeeded in directly influencing national policy, though elsewhere ministries and regional authorities expressed the view that the movements were not effective lobbyists. All movements expressed dissatisfaction with the responsiveness of government, and the difficulties of advocacy. All also expressed their concerns about compromising neutrality through receipt of government funding, though all are seeking to gain this. Though notable achievements can be seen, these are still considered to be much less than is required. However, there is recognition of the potential importance of the movements, as shown by the attendance of the President and Prime Minister, respectively, at the Estonian and Swedish Rural Parliaments. Only in Sweden has the government played a strongly supportive role, through provision of funding, manpower and practical support. In Finland, the close connection to rural policy, through the role of the chairman, is a notable exception. There is also a growing link between the rural movements and the EU, based on the perceived need for an effective, integrated rural voice in Brussels. This has had recent success in influencing EU policy.

Future Directions

As the trends of rural decline continue, the need for a countervailing force increases. At the same time, the pressure for change in EU and national policies towards rural areas is showing signs of success, and it is likely that there will be moves towards a more integrated approach to rural policy. However, this will require continued pressure from rural lobbies, other than the agricultural lobby. Rural movements are now strongly placed to take on this role.

The role of civil society in rural development is likely to increase as the welfare state decreases. Therefore, the role of rural movements in mobilizing, organizing and networking the greater potential of civil society is of increasing importance. This has already been recognized by some national ministries.

The relationship between such movements and government requires consideration. All the movements have identified the need to become more effective in advocacy. They are seeking to become 'partners' with government, rather than adversaries, yet the need to retain independence and the ability to act in an adversarial capacity are critical to fulfilling an effective function in representing the needs of civil society.

The networking of rural movements to share experience offers the possibility of both increasing the speed of their development and of perfecting the structures and processes they employ. Each movement displays strengths and weaknesses which can serve as lessons to others. There is no need for each painfully to learn the best solutions, when this can be done through collective effort. The similarities between the rural areas and national contexts of each country are far greater than the differences; and such similarities should only increase through wider membership of the EU. It is therefore often quite appropriate to think that there might be similar solutions for different countries.

An outstanding problem for all of the movements lies in resourcing all their efforts in a sustainable way – rather than by continuing to rely on volunteer labour to the extent that they currently do. The value of this activity requires greater recognition from governments. Recent statistics provided by the Finnish Village Action Association, for instance, show the extent of its contribution to society (see section on 'Increasing social capital', above). This requires to be documented in all countries.

There is the wider question of the extent to which European society wishes to accept the inevitability of the further urbanization of its society and cultures, and the consequent effect on its rural communities. It is, after all, the central issue that the rural movements stand for. Government is, by definition, remote from the rural villages. It cannot have the detailed knowledge needed to build rural communities. It must trust rural people to do that, by providing the most supportive and appropriate frameworks and policies. This is the great strength of the rural movements – they gather rural people together and provide a clear forum with which governments can work, at all levels. It is a model deserving of recognition and support.

Notes

1. The PREPARE Programme (Pre-Accession Partnerships for Rural Europe) was launched in 1999, as an initiative of European NGOs and government officials supporting the 10 pre-accession countries in rural cooperation. The PREPARE

Programme has focused on constructing partnerships between rural actors to strengthen civil society and promote multinational exchange in rural development. 'It aims to strengthen civil society in rural areas; and to promote dialogue, trust, confidence and cooperation between local actors, governments and all stakeholders of rural development, at all geographic levels' (PREPARE 2004); in short, to enable rural civil society to become a respected partner with government. This it aims to do through 'country-specific national programmes', promoting dialogue and cooperation between the different rural actors. PREPARE has thus supported the development of national programmes in Slovenia, Poland, the Czech Republic, Latvia, Lithuania, Bulgaria and Romania.

2. Finland has 'mainstreamed' the LEADER approach to cover the whole of rural Finland.
3. Friends of the UN 'Creating Common Unity', 50th Anniversary Awards.
4. Officials of the Swedish rural development agency, Glesbydgsverket, were seconded to Slovakia for one year to assist in the development of rural partnerships.
5. Swedish Rural Parliament, 2004.
6. The term 'Rural Parliament' was first used by the Swedish village movement to describe their biennial rural gathering.
7. The name chosen for the Estonian village movement Kodukant ('homeplace').

References

Abild, C. (1977), article in Landsbyen, 1: 3.
Bond, S. (2000), Local Mobilization in the Swedish Countryside, Folkrörelseråde Hela Sverige Ska Leva, Sweden.
Halhead, V. (2005), The Rural Movements of Europe, Brussels: Forum Synergies.
Halhead, V, and Guiheneuf, P. Y. (2004), Rural Development in Europe: New Actors, New Demands: European Networks of Associations, France: Geyser.
Herlitz, U. (1996), Status report to the Landsbygdsriksdag, March.
Herlitz, U. (1999), The Village Action Movement in Sweden – Local Development – Employment – Democracy, Folkrörelseråde Hela Sverige Ska Leva, Sweden.
Herlitz, U. (2001a), Local Level Democracy in a Historical Perspective in Sweden, University of Gothenburg, Sweden.
Herlitz, U. (2001b), Village Movements. In Rural Development Lessons from the North, Arkleton Centre for Rural Development Research, University of Aberdeen.
Kodukant (2003a), Village workshop report to the Estonian Rural Parliament, August.
Kodukant (2003b), The 5th Estonian Rural Parliament, August 2003, Report of proceedings, Estonia: Kodukant.
Kodukant (2003), Strateegia 2003–2008, Estonia: Kodukant.
Ministry of Agriculture and Forestry (2000), Agriculture in Finland, Helsinki.
Ministry of Agriculture and Forestry (2001), Countryside for the People Rural Policy Programme for 2001–2004, Helsinki.
PREPARE (2004), Website. Available at: www.preparenetwork.org.
Rantama, E. and Vaatainen, E. (1997), Village Action Movement in Finland: the power of human cooperation. In Lifelong Learning in Europe.
Ringer, S. (2004), Wealth and decay, Times Literary Supplement, 13 February.
Rüütel, A. (2003), President of the Estonian Republic, Speech to the Estonian Rural Parliament, August.
Salomaa-Santala, R. (2003), Rural contract and political commitment, the keys to rural development. In Maaseutu Plus, Village Action Association of Finland, Loimaa Kirjapaino, Finland.
Svendsen, G. (2004), The right to development: construction of a non-agriculturalist discourse in rurality in Denmark, Journal of Rural Studies, 20, 1: 79–94.

Thaning, K. (1972), *NFS Grundtvig*, Copenhagen: Det Danske Selskab.

Uusitalo, E. (2003a), Local development in Finnish rural policy. Paper to the International Rural Network Conference, Inverness.

Uusitalo, E. (2003b), *The Organization of Rural Policy in Finland*, Finnish Ministry of Agriculture and Forestry, Rural Policy Committee.

Village Action Association of Finland (1995), Internal report, Loimaa Kirjapaino, Finland.

Village Action Association of Finland (2003), *All the Power of a Small Village, National Village Action Programme, 2003–2007*, ed. T. Perheentupa, Loimaa Kirjapaino, Finland.

3

Market-based Governance and the Challenge for Rural Governments: US Trends

Mildred E. Warner

Introduction

Around the world, enthusiasm for market-based approaches to government, especially privatization and decentralization, is growing. Little research has specifically addressed the challenge to rural governments of this market-based approach. Why the silence on rural impacts? What is the importance of rural local government in the 21st century? Should we worry about differential effects, if they exist? This chapter addresses these questions drawing from data in the United States covering the period 1992–2002. We find rural areas are not favoured by either of these trends – privatization or decentralization. Policy-makers should be concerned about the uneven impacts of such market-based approaches and what this may mean for rural policy in general.

Market Approaches to Government and Rural Competitiveness

Privatization and decentralization are both trends that promote competition as a source of governmental efficiency (Tiebout 1956; Savas 2000). Shifting from state to market via the privatization of local government service delivery, and shifting from national to local levels of provision via decentralization, are designed to increase local voice and local control over service delivery (Bennett 1990). Technical efficiency is enhanced by linking service delivery and revenue-raising so that fiscal equivalence (you get what you pay for) is reached. US local governments, as part of a federal system, have some of the highest levels of local government autonomy in revenue-raising and service delivery responsibility of any country in the advanced industrialized world (Conlan 1998). This autonomy encourages efficiency, fiscal responsibility and com-petition among local governments (Musgrave 1959; Oates 1998). However, while there is little doubt that fiscal federalism encourages productive efficiency, there is considerable concern about whether it also promotes allocative efficiency (Prud'homme 1995). Decentralized and privatized systems require a level of technical capacity, both managerial and financial, to ensure that efficiency is reached. They further require a level of citizen engagement to ensure government accountability.

US local governments are perhaps in the best position to be successful under decentralized systems because of a long history of autonomy in a federal system (Musgrave 1959; Conlan 1998). Property taxes, which are by and large controlled locally, account for the major source of local government revenue. Communities can select their tax and expenditure levels according to local preference – much as Charles Tiebout described in his model of competitive local government (1956). The theory of Public Choice argues that this creates a healthy competition that keeps costs down and limits overproduction in the public sector. It also focuses local government on economic development rather than redistributive priorities (Peterson 1981; Schneider 1989; O'Connor 1973).

This developmental focus has benefits and costs. One of the costs is the emergence of a destructive competition as local governments compete with each other to attract economic development through tax breaks that undermine the public infrastructure basis for long-term economic sustainability (Donahue 1997; Conlan 1998). Although meta analysis of research shows that investments in public infrastructure have a more positive impact on economic development than tax breaks (Bartik 1996), the most popular policies among local governments in the US continue to be tax breaks (Lynch 2004; Warner 2001a).

Those concerned with allocative efficiency point out that under this competitive local government system there are winners and losers. Places with economic development have stronger tax bases and more revenue to invest in further development. This virtuous cycle is contrasted with a vicious cycle in places that have weak economic development, limited tax bases, and limited capacity for investment. Under decentralization we find the places most likely to be caught in these vicious cycles are high-poverty rural and inner-city areas (Warner and Pratt 2005). Reeder and Jansen (1995) labelled these places as poor governments and showed how poor governments are associated with poor places. If government is to play a countercyclical role, then decentralization undermines the possibility for redistribution.

Under globalization, many geographers have heralded the resurgence of the city, as local governments can engage directly with global economic forces to promote their own economic competitiveness (Brenner 1999; MacLeod 2001; Swyngedouw 1997). The nation state, weakened relatively by global power and local resurgence, becomes less focused on redistribution and more focused on promoting growth (Brenner 2004). But what does this portend for rural places which are not growth centres? Will they continue to capture national interest? National rural policy has traditionally been justified by an equity-based redistributive strategy which views the nation's role as equalizing the inequalities of market-based economic development (Edwards 1981; Hansen et al. 1990; Brown and Warner 1991). At a minimum, national investment was used to promote equality in basic infrastructure through programmes to ensure that electricity (Tennessee Valley Authority, Rural Utilities Service, rural electric cooperatives), telephones, highways (interstate highway system, and Federal transportation aid) and water systems (through the Rural Community Assistance Program) were extended to all parts of the country. But the new technological advances in telecommunications have met with no such federal commitment and many rural areas are literally off the grid for fibre optics and cable for high-speed internet (Grubesic and Murray 2004).

Support for regional policy in the United States has waned in recent decades. In the 1980s, Reagan promoted a 'new federalism' designed to pass responsibilities, but not revenue, to local governments (Nathan and Lago 1990). As states and localities complained of unfunded mandates, the Clinton Administration responded by allowing more state and local control over policy determination, particularly in areas like welfare entitlement and service levels. Design and entitlement levels in basic programmes like health care, welfare and job training now have substantial state and local variation (Weinstein 1998; Powers 2000). Michael Katz (2001) has termed this the 'price of citizenship', noting that this creates a variegated landscape of resources and benefits that accrue to citizens based on where they live. The role of the subnational regional government becomes more important under decentralization, and in the US research has found state aid to be redistributive (Johnson et al. 1995; Reeder and Jansen 1995; Warner 2001b). However, rural researchers worry about the decreased emphasis on rural areas (Brown and Swanson 2003; Lobao et al. 1999).

Privatization may offer a partial solution to this retreat of federal government involvement. Private providers could potentially offer rural areas the economies of scale they lack at the local government level. Certainly, as Clean Water Act standards rise and rural local water systems become fully depreciated, the technical needs of meeting rising environmental standards, and the financial reinvestment costs to replace deteriorated public systems, might be well met by private providers. Indeed, one of the goals of the General Agreement on Trade in Services, currently under negotiation, is to expand foreign private investment opportunities in basic local government services such as water (Gerbasi and Warner forthcoming; Appleton 1994).

Rural residents in the United States are used to relying more heavily on private suppliers for many services which might be publicly provided in more urban places. Thus one would expect strong public opinion in favour of private delivery. However, recent research focusing on the transaction costs of contracting points to the need for strong managerial capacity, the ability to structure the market to ensure competition among alternative suppliers, and the need for monitoring to ensure service quality and attention to public values (Sclar 2000; Nelson 1997; Lowery 1998; Hefetz and Warner 2004; Brown and Potoski 2003). Whether rural areas have the capacity to manage private markets for service delivery is an empirical question.

The overall concern is that these competitive approaches to basic local government services delivery will undermine both the political and economic basis for redistribution. Privatization and decentralization encourage a privatized view of public services and the revenue streams to support them (Frug 1999). If rural areas are disadvantaged under both systems, then the prospects for rural development dim as we look forward to the new century.

This paper uses national survey and census data to assess how rural areas are faring under privatization and decentralization. Results show rural areas are disadvantaged under both systems, and this disadvantage both results from and creates structural impediments to market competitiveness for rural areas.

Data: Local Government Restructuring by Metro Status

This analysis is based on data from two sources: the International City/ County Management Association (ICMA) surveys of alternative service delivery, and the United States Census of Government Finance files. Each of these surveys is administered quinquennially and this analysis includes data from the 1992, 1997 and 2002 surveys. The ICMA surveys are conducted every five years and cover all counties with more than 25,000 population and cities over 10,000 population. In addition, a sample is drawn from one in eight cities and counties from 2,500 to 9,999 population and from those under 2,500 (total sample frame in 1997: 4,952). Roughly a third of all governments contacted respond (31 per cent for 1992, 32 per cent for 1997 and 24 per cent for 2002). Cities (which include villages, towns and townships) vastly outnumber counties, but counties are more heavily represented among the rural respondents. Of the roughly 1,200 to 1,400 responding governments in any given year, roughly 350 are non-metropolitan. We use a repeated cross-section analysis to preserve sample size.

Governments are differentiated by metro status according to the following criteria. First, rural–urban continuum codes developed by the US Department of Agriculture distinguish municipalities by metropolitan and non-metropolitan status. Non-metropolitan municipalities are further differentiated as adjacent or non-adjacent to a metropolitan county. For municipalities within metropolitan counties, we differentiate core metropolitan municipalities from outlying suburban municipalities using Office of Management and Budget criteria. Core cities have 40 per cent of their residents working in the central city of the Metropolitan Statistical Area and employment residence ratios of at least 0.75. All other metropolitan cities are classified as outlying–suburban.

The ICMA surveys measure direct public provision and six alternative forms of service delivery (for-profit, non-profit, inter-municipal cooperation, franchises, subsidies and volunteers) for 64 different services in seven broad areas: public works and transportation, public utilities, public safety, health and human services, parks and recreation, culture and art, and support functions. The surveys also measure government managers' responses to a range of managerial and structural factors believed to be motivators or obstacles to alternative service delivery. We supplement these factors with socio-economic and government expenditure data drawn from the City/ County Data Book, based on Census of Population and Housing for 1990 and 2000 and the Census of Government Finance files for 1992, 1997 and 2002.

Although the Census of Government includes all governments and thus could be a better data source for analysing rural governments, it has undergone considerable structural revision from survey to survey, making trend comparisons difficult. In addition, the Census of Government does not cover as broad a range of services. Only 14 services were consistently measured in all three years and three of these are rarely provided by rural municipalities: airports, public transit and hospitals. Nor does the Census cover as broad a set of service delivery alternatives. Contracting out is the only service delivery alternative measured by service in 1992 and 1997, and inter-municipal cooperation was only differentiated by service in the 2002 survey. Many governments in the US Census of Government provide no data about service provision. Although the ICMA sample size is much smaller, the greater consistency in survey design, and greater coverage of services and service delivery alternatives, make it a better source for comparing rural and urban service delivery patterns over time.

Figure 1 shows the average use of the three major forms of public service delivery, differentiated by rural, outlying suburban and metro core places. The top set of graphs in figure 1 shows that rural governments' use of for-profit privatization has dropped dramatically since 1997. Rural areas tracked suburban and metro trends from 1992 to 1997 (albeit at a much lower level), increasing their levels of for-profit provision by almost a third (from 12 to 16 per cent of service provision on average). However, they diverged after 1997, dropping back down to 12 per cent, while suburban use levelled off at 20 per cent and metro use of privatization rose to almost meet the suburban level (19 per cent). These data suggest that rural areas explored privatization but could not compete well in market-based approaches. The levelling off in suburban and metro areas suggests that privatization has limited scope even in urban areas. Indeed, overall trends in use of privatization over the 20-year period from 1982 to 2002 show that 1997 is the peak year and privatization never exceeds more than 20 per cent of local government service delivery in the US.

Inter-municipal cooperation is the next most common form of alternative service delivery but it has been on a downward trend since 1992. The drop in cooperation is most significant for suburbs (from 20 to 13 per cent), which appear to be substituting privatization for inter-municipal cooperation. Metro core places exhibit a similar drop although their cooperation level is lower to start with due to large internal economies of scale. For rural areas, by contrast, use of cooperation was stable from 1992 to 1997, prompting the suggestion that rural areas might depend more on a cooperative public market of intergovernmental contracting than the competitive private market of for-profit privatization (Warner 2003). But the 2002 data do not continue this trend. From 1997 to 2002 rural use of cooperation drops significantly from 15 to 11 per cent. Suburban use of cooperation remains the highest of all three metro groups for the entire period. As in the case of for-profit contracting, suburban areas are the most favoured by inter-municipal cooperation.

The final graph shows direct public service delivery declines for suburban places in 2002 after a slight increase in 1997. Metro areas show a steady drop in public delivery. But rural places exhibit a dramatic increase in direct public delivery, rising from 60 to 66 per cent of all service delivery. This return to public delivery, after experimentation with privatization, provides additional indication of problems with access to alternative market forms of service delivery – especially for rural communities.

Figure 1

Rural–urban differences in service delivery patterns

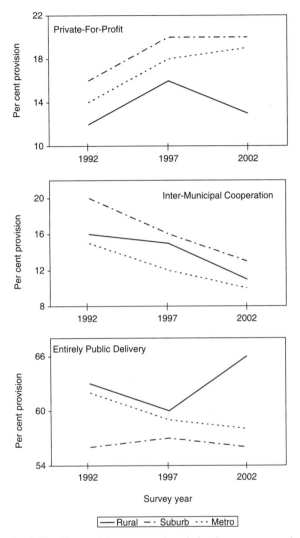

Source: International City/County Management Association (1992, 1997, 2002).

Modelling: Structural or Attitudinal Constraints?

What explains this divergent behavior of rural municipalities: structural or attitudinal constraints? Rural areas may lack the structural characteristics to be attractive market players. They are higher-cost and offer a smaller, less

Figure 2

Trends in US local government expenditure patterns by metro status, 1992–2002

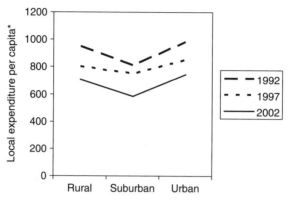

*Deflated 1992 = 100.

Source: Census of Government Finance Files (1992, 1997, 2002) for municipalities responding to ICMA Survey of Alternative Delivery (1992, 1997, 2002).

attractive market for potential private providers (Reeder and Jansen 1995; Warner and Hefetz 2003). Suburbs, by contrast, have lower costs and offer a larger market. Some argue that limited managerial capacity or opposition might reduce use of privatization (Niskanen 1971; Savas 2000). Table 1 compares the service delivery pattern of local governments as well as differences in managerial and structural factors that may be important in the restructuring decision. Differences in subgroup means and their Duncan multiple range rankings[1] for metro core, rural and suburban governments are compared for all three years. A discriminant analysis model is used to test whether rural municipalities can be distinguished from metro core and suburban municipalities based on service delivery characteristics. In addition, the model controls for structural and attitudinal variables outlined below.

Structural explanation: market attractiveness

Will rural municipalities be attractive markets for private suppliers? Previous research has found suburbs to be the most favoured (Warner and Hefetz 2002), and problems with supply of private providers in both rural (Kodrzycki 1994) and urban areas (Hirsch 1995). Theory and prior empirical analysis suggest a U-shaped cost curve with high costs for rural areas with low density (the cost of sparsity), and for urban areas with high density (the cost of congestion) (Reeder and Jansen 1995; Warner 2001b). Figure 2 uses average per capita expenditure data from the Census of Government Finance and clearly shows this U-shaped cost curve. Rural municipalities' expenditures are almost as high as metro core places on a per capita basis, even though they provide a much smaller range of services. Although there has been a

Table 1

Subgroup means with Duncan rankings, US cities and counties

Variable	Survey 1992			Survey 1997			Survey 2002		
	Rural	Suburb	Metro	Rural	Suburb	Metro	Rural	Suburb	Metro
Service delivery options*									
% entirely public[1]	63[b]	56[a]	62[b]	60[a]	57[a]	59[a]	66[b]	55[a]	58[a]
% private for-profit[2]	12[a]	16[b]	14[a]	16[a]	20[b]	18[b]	12[a]	20[b]	19[b]
% cooperation[1]	16[a]	20[b]	15[a]	15[b]	16[b]	12[a]	11[a]	13[b]	11[a]
% private non-profit[1]	5[a]	4[a]	6[b]	5	4[a]	6[c]	4[a]	4[a]	7[b]
Management & attitudinal variables									
Opposition index[1]	.13[a]	.17[b]	.24[c]	.16[a]	.17[a]	.26[b]	.13[a]	.15[a]	.22[b]
Council-manager[1] (1 = mgr, 0 = not)	.53[a]	.67[b]	.67[b]	.46[a]	.68[b]	.65[b]	.42[a]	.68[c]	.50[b]
Government attitude index[1]	.53[a]	.67[b]	.80[c]	.52[a]	.62[b]	.85[c]	.45[a]	.53[b]	.71[c]
Monitoring index[1]	.24[a]	.38[b]	.41[b]	.23[a]	.37[b]	.46[c]	.25[a]	.38[b]	.49[c]
Structural variables									
Per capita income, 1989[2]	11,228[a]	17,548[c]	13,880[b]	11,256[a]	17,299[c]	13,776[b]	13,241[a]	20,206[c]	16,098[b]
% poverty, 1989[2]	17.3[c]	7.8[a]	14.4[b]	17.4[c]	7.6[a]	14.4[b]	15.6[c]	7.7[a]	14.5[b]
Provision level (# services provided)[1]	41[a]	41[a]	45[b]	33[a]	33[a]	40[b]	35[a]	34[a]	40[b]
% in public administration, 1989 (civilian)[2]	4.8[b]	4.2[a]	4.9[b]	5.0[b]	4.3[a]	5.0[b]	3.5[b]	3.1[a]	3.3[ab]
State aid, $ per capita, dfl 1992 = 100[3]	190[b]	130[a]	180[b]	180[b]	150[a]	200[b]	155	116[a]	178[b]
State rules index[1]	.20[a]	.25[b]	.31[c]	.15[a]	.18[a]	.26[b]	.14[a]	.16[a]	.23[b]
Local exp. $ per capita, dfl 1992 = 100[3]	950[b]	810[a]	980[b]	800[ab]	750[a]	850[b]	707[b]	582[a]	743[b]
N	358	750	306	390	714	303	278	512	241

Duncan post hoc ranking of subgroup means, based on $\alpha = .05$; a = lowest, c = highest. F test found all variables significantly different ($P < .05$) by metro status, except for '% entirely public' 1997.

*As percentage of provision level.

Sources: [1]International City/County Management Association, Profile of Alternative Service Delivery Approaches, Survey Data (1992, 1997, 2002), Washington, DC: ICMA. [2]City/County Data Book, based on Census of Population and Housing (1990, 2000), Charlottesville, VA: University of Virginia. [3]US Bureau of the Census (1992, 1997, 2002).

steady decline in real expenditures per capita since 1992, the U-shaped cost curve has persisted. High costs would be a deterrent to both for-profit private providers and to neighbouring municipalities. Market solutions are voluntary, and rural areas are less attractive to alternative providers. Suburbs, because of their lower costs and larger market (large number of municipalities in each region), provide an excellent market for both privatization and inter-municipal contracting.

Higher poverty and lower income should also reduce the attractiveness of rural areas to market providers. Data from the US Census of Population and Housing conducted in 1990 and 2000 show that per capita income is relatively flat in real terms over the time period but always lowest for rural areas and highest for suburbs. Similarly, percentage poverty is highest for rural areas and lowest for suburbs, although poverty drops slightly for rural areas in the 2000 Census (see table 1).

Government policy can play a redistributive role, helping to reduce the negative impact of the rural structural deficits. Although US local governments rely primarily on locally raised revenues (property taxes, sales taxes and user fees), state aid is the second most important source of revenue for local governments. (Federal aid to place, at less than 3 per cent of total revenue, has dropped so much under decentralization, that it ceases to be significant for many local governments.) State aid, after rising slightly for suburban and metro areas from 1992 to 1997, dropped to below 1992 levels in real terms by 2002. State aid, which was higher for rural areas (than metro or suburbs) in 1992, at $190 per capita, has dropped steadily over the 10-year period and is now only $155 in real terms.[2] Although rural areas still receive more state aid per capita than suburbs, they now receive less than metro core areas, as the attention is focused on promoting urban growth centres over lagging rural areas.

Rural economies remain relatively dependent on governmental employment (Singleman and Deseran 1993). The percentage of rural employment in public administration dropped significantly from 5 per cent in 1997 to 3.5 per cent in 2002, but rural areas continued to have higher dependence on public employment than their suburban or metro core counterparts.

A state rules index is based on local government managers' attitudes about the impact of state limits on taxation and state rules encouraging inter-governmental financing on their restructuring decisions. The importance of these state rules drops over the three time periods, and in each time period a lower percentage of rural governments reports that state rules are a factor in their decision to restructure.

Attitudinal explanation: managerial capacity and opposition

A second explanation for limited rural privatization could be managerial or attitudinal constraints. Although rural areas tend to be pro-market, they may lack the managerial capability to manage market contracts. But limited capacity could encourage rural areas to outsource services to the private sector. We see in table 1, however, that rural areas have service provision levels similar to suburbs. Governments with a professional, appointed manager and an elected council are assumed to have more managerial capacity. While two-thirds of suburbs have this council–manager form of government, less than half of rural municipalities do, and the number is dropping. This reflects the high cost of professional managers and their short supply. The drop in council–manager form of government in metro core areas reflects the rise in use of elected executives to manage both the political and managerial concerns that arise in more complex and heterogeneous metropolitan areas (Hambleton 2002).

Rural areas are less likely to have opposition to privatization. The opposition index is constructed from five ICMA survey questions that ask managers to identify factors important in their decision to restructure: internal opposition from employees, department heads and elected officials, restrictive labour agreements and external opposition from citizens.[3] Opposition is highest for metro core municipalities and lowest for rural areas. Opposition shows a slight rise for rural areas in 1997, with the rise in privatization, but it is always lower for rural areas than for suburbs or metro places.

Government attitudes to reducing costs of service production are measured by two ICMA survey questions: Has the government 'studied the feasibility of alternative service delivery'? and is it 'motivated to decrease costs'? Concern about costs is highest among metro core places which have the highest average expenditures. Suburbs, which are most likely to be in a competitive Tiebout-style market competing with their neighbours to attract mobile residents, are next, and rural areas are lowest.

To ensure savings from the contracting process requires an external monitoring system.[4] Metro core areas show the highest levels of monitoring – a reflection of their more heterogeneous service demands and the complexity of urban service delivery systems. Yet, even though metro monitoring levels have increased over the 10-year period, less than half the governments monitor their contracts. This may help explain why privatization levels have not grown dramatically: performance management systems have not evolved to the level required to support higher levels of contracting. The level of contract monitoring is lowest for rural areas. Suburbs have moderate levels of monitoring that have not risen with a rise in contracting. They face a more competitive market of private service providers and may be able to rely more on competitive market pressures among alternative providers to ensure efficiency gains.

Analysis

Building upon a discriminant analysis first conducted by Warner and Hefetz (2003) for the 1992 and 1997 surveys, this chapter adds the 2002 data to look at differences over time. The discriminant analysis determines if there are differences by metro status in use of alternative service delivery mechanisms (public delivery and contracting to for-profit, inter-municipal or non-profit providers). Structural factors of market attractiveness (expenditure, income, poverty, state aid and state rules), as well as managerial factors (professional managers, opposition, governmental attitudes and monitoring) are included.

Discriminant analysis determines which variables discriminate maximally among fixed categories (metro status in this case). The analysis produces

43

functions (one fewer than the number of fixed categories) which are analogous to regression equations except that only the predictor variables are random.[5] The discriminant analysis shows that local government restructuring behaviour can be differentiated by metro status. Interestingly, the factors cluster into groups that distinguish structural from managerial factors. For the 1992 and 1997 (and to a lesser extent 2002) models, the first function captures most of the structural variables and shows a strong correlation between high income, low poverty and high privatization – suggesting that privatization is primarily driven by the market attractiveness of a place. These structural variables explain from 82 to 86 per cent of the variance in all three of the model years (see table 2).

Managerial variables, which cluster as government attitude, monitoring, opposition, state rules and council–manager, explain 14–18 per cent of the variance. Rural areas rank highest on the structural function and lowest on the managerial function in all three models, suggesting that structural factors are more critical in differentiating rural restructuring than managerial factors. Classification results show suburban places are most likely to be classified correctly (72–74 per cent of the time), whereas metro and rural are correctly classified 55–58 per cent of the time. When misclassified, metro and rural places are more likely to be confused with each other than with suburban places. These results suggest it is structural market constraints, not managerial attitudes, that explain differences in the levels of privatization by metro status.

Changes in the variable clustering over the three model years show state aid and local expenditure clustered with the structural variables in both 1992 and 2002, but clustered with managerial variables in 1997. Recall from figure 2 that the U-shaped expenditure curve showed fewer expenditure differences by metro status in 1997. State aid was rising for suburbs and metro core areas from 1992 to 1997, which could have given managers more flexibility. Another shift was percentage employment in public administration, which became part of the structural function for 1997 and 2002, as its importance for rural areas relative to other places grew.

The level of for-profit and total public service delivery clustered with the structural variables for the first two time periods, but became more of a managerial choice in 2002, and the management function rose in its explanatory power to 18 per cent. However, rural places continued to rank lowest on the managerial function (centroid value of −0.31 to −0.46, while the suburban value was near zero, and the metro value near +0.50) (see table 3). While suburban managers may be able to exercise more managerial discretion in their choice of privatization, rural areas still appear to be driven primarily by structural market attractiveness constraints (+0.82 for rural compared to −0.78 for suburbs).

Discussion

From 1992, when the book *Reinventing Government* by Osborne and Gaebler was first published (and widely read by local officials), to 1997 we see a significant increase in experimentation with privatization. But the levelling off in 2002 for suburban and urban areas, and the precipitous drop for rural

Table 2

Discriminant function structure: 1992, 1997 and 2002

	1992		1997		2002	
	Function 1 Structural factors	Function 2 Managerial factors	Function 1 Structural factors	Function 2 Managerial factors	Function 1 Structural factors	Function 2 Managerial factors
% Poverty 1989	+		+		+	
Per capita income 1989	−		−		−	
% Entirely public	+		+			−
% Private for-profit	−		−			+
State aid, per capita	+			+	+	
Local government expenditure per capita	+			+	+	
Government attitude index		+		+		
Opposition index		+		+		+
Monitoring index		+		+		+
Service provision level		+		+		+
State rules index		+		+		+
% private non-profit		+		+		+
Council–manager		−		−	−	
% Cooperation		+			−	
% in public administration 1989			+		+	
Per cent variance explained	86.1	13.9	83.4	16.6	81.8	18.2

*Largest absolute correlation between each variable and any discriminant function.

45

Table 3

Centroid values by metro status

	1992		1997		2002	
	Function 1 Structural factors	Function 2 Managerial factors	Function 1 Structural factors	Function 2 Managerial factors	Function 1 Structural factors	Function 2 Managerial factors
Rural	.95	−.31	.94	−.35	.82	−.46
Suburban	−.66	−.06	−.73	−.07	−.78	−.09
Metro	.49	.51	.51	.60	.71	.58

areas, suggest problems with the market. Unlike the United Kingdom and Australia (which had compulsory competitive tendering), privatization was not required of local governments in the United States. Recognizing that privatization is not a one-way street, the 2002 survey of the International City/County Management asks specifically why local governments have brought previously privatized services back in-house. The answers dealt primarily with problems with service quality (73 per cent) and lack of cost savings (51 per cent). Political concerns ranked much lower in the list of reasons (22 per cent) (Warner and Hefetz 2004).

Cost studies of privatization are difficult to find. George Boyne (1998) in his meta analysis of such studies from the US and Europe demonstrated that one could not conclude that privatization saves money. Before and after comparisons are hard to find, model specification is poor, and coefficients range from positive to negative to non-significant. This is reflected in the case study data which show both successes and failures (Sclar 2000; Savas 2000). A more recent meta analysis of privatization and costs in water distribution and waste collection finds little evidence of cost savings, especially in the more recent studies (Bel and Warner forthcoming).

For rural areas, one of the main challenges may be lack of market access. Rural areas are less attractive to private for-profit providers, and they have less managerial capacity to engage in market forms of service delivery. Williamson (1996) points out that internal production (hierarchy) will be preferred to contracting when there is high uncertainty, high costs of contracting (including search costs) and lack of competitive markets. These reasons may explain the drop in use of for-profit contracting among rural places.

Although privatization among local governments has levelled off and is actually dropping for rural governments, privatization remains an important political project at the national level. The Workforce Investment Act of 1998, for example, specified that local governments should use private providers for workforce development services (Hipp and Warner 2006; King 1999). For many rural areas this proved difficult and undermined any potential for competition, since there were too few jobs to accommodate all the welfare leavers, and private employment training providers were concentrated in the cities and suburbs where the jobs are (Weber *et al.* 2002).

Support for privatization is one of the goals of the new generation of free trade agreements. These agreements are negotiated by national governments but have critical impacts on local government authority over service delivery (Warner and Gerbasi 2004). Beginning with the North American Free Trade Agreement (NAFTA) between the US, Canada and Mexico, passed in 1995, we see a new set of market governance arrangements which may further weaken local government authority.

In order to use market approaches to public service delivery, local governments must be able to negotiate and monitor contracts and have access to a common dispute resolution mechanism should disagreements arise (Gerbasi and Warner forthcoming). However, the arbitration mechanism used under NAFTA is private, not subject to any public accountability or Freedom of Information Act rules, and open only to nation states and private foreign investors (Greider 2001). NAFTA reinterprets government action as potential barriers to trade, and local laws regarding residency requirements, local purchasing requirements or bonding fall outside the narrow cost and quality criteria deemed appropriate for regulation (Schweke and Stumberg 2000). Furthermore, local governments wishing to impose regulations that respond to unique local conditions may be challenged for reducing potential foreign profit or market share. This biases the playing field further in favour of foreign investors, over rural local governments, and is likely to make it even more difficult for rural governments to achieve public service delivery through privatization.

For example, a rural town in Mexico, which refused to issue a building permit for a toxic waste facility, was required by a NAFTA tribunal to reimburse the US-based firm Metalclad for all of its investment costs in building construction (Tysoe 2001).

The US was recently challenged for allowing the State of California to regulate MTBE, a gasoline additive that had contaminated many local community water supplies, because reducing MTBE was not the 'least trade-restrictive' approach to protecting ground water. The Canadian manufacturer, Methanex, argued that controlling the thousands of underground storage tanks across the state would be less trade-restrictive (although more costly and less effective in protecting the public health) (Lazar 2000). Although the Canadian case recently failed (US Department of State 2005), neither the State of California nor its affected municipalities were allowed to be party to arbitration proceedings about their own laws.

Even at the national level we are beginning to see some challenges to public subsidy for rural delivery under NAFTA. United Parcel Service, a private US package delivery company, is challenging the Canadian Royal Post's implicit subsidy of rural package delivery by having packages travel in the same conveyances as its letter service. UPS is asking that the implicit subsidy be abolished, or that UPS packages have equal access to the Royal Post trucks and planes for its packages (IISD 2001). Canada, as a large rural country, has a public interest in maintaining communication connections as part of building a national sense of community. While Europe does not have house-to-house mail delivery, in the US and Canada the tradition of rural free delivery and government-supported post offices in *every* rural town has helped to link rural towns scattered across the frontier (Sclar 2000). UPS is challenging a traditional government service and a public decision to subsidize rural areas.

These new free trade agreements make clear that the only criteria on which services can be judged are cost and quality. To create a level playing field there can be no subsidies for public providers that are not extended also to foreign private investors. Although most challenges are still under arbitration, they raise concerns about the ability to retain subsidies for rural service delivery.

The General Agreement on Trade in Services (GATS), currently under discussion, expands the list of covered services to include many public services – education, environmental management, business services, etc. (Appleton 1994; GATS 1995; Gerbasi and Warner forthcoming). However, it is doubtful that opening public service markets to foreign private competition will widen the supply of alternative private deliverers for rural areas, given their higher costs. In fact, such agreements may actually narrow the range of public services that rural areas now receive. So we may be faced in the future with a double challenge – rural areas, less attractive to private suppliers, will enjoy fewer private services, and any subsidies to ensure continued public service delivery (a form of delivery that is growing in rural communities) may be challenged by those same private suppliers who choose not to serve rural communities.

Cost pressures in the last decade have led to the closure of many basic services in rural communities – hospitals, bus and air services are particularly notable. Increasingly, rural areas are becoming disconnected from the wider society at a time when telecommunications offer the possibility that rural areas might have a new economic role that could overcome the disadvantage of distance. But without public investment to ensure critical extension of telecommunications infrastructure, and lack of profit to encourage private investment, rural areas get left behind. Basic local government services are key to quality of life in rural areas, but higher costs, and lower ability to engage alternative market forms of provision, and declining national interest in investments to ensure distributional equity, put rural areas at a triple disadvantage.

Conclusion

These trends do not bode well for rural local governments. Increased pressure to be competitive will not, in itself, improve the competitive position of rural governments. As the logic of economic competitiveness and efficiency trumps concerns with local voice and cross-jurisdictional equity, we can expect more and more rural places to be left behind. Decentralization works best in contexts where inequality across jurisdictions is low. But in the US we see increasing spatial inequality within regions, in part as a result of decentralization itself (Dewees *et al.* 2003; Johnson *et al.* 1995; Warner and Pratt 2005). Similarly, privatization works best in medium-sized suburbs which enjoy both market competition and managerial talent to manage private providers. Rural areas in the US are not favoured by either of these trends. Furthermore, the new free trade rules privilege foreign investors and market access over citizen voice and local government authority.

Does the capacity and competitiveness of rural governments matter for development in the twenty-first century? As attention is directed more towards global competitiveness based on investment in centres of growth, the ability to achieve equity and provide basic services in rural areas will become more difficult. There are limits to the applicability of decentralization and privatization, and trends data from the last decade in the United States suggest those limits may have been reached.

Acknowledgements

This work builds on earlier work with Amir Hefetz. Funding for this research was provided in part by the US Department of Agriculture National Research Initiative Grant # NYC-121524.

Notes

1. The Duncan multiple range method tests the hypothesis that one subgroup mean is significantly larger than another. Group means are clustered and ranked based on a 0.05 significance level.
2. State aid and local government expenditures in 1997 and 2002 are deflated using the GDP Implicit Price Deflator for state and local government expenditures. 1992 = 100 is the base year (Economic Report of the President 2005).
3. This index and the other indices used in this paper are created by summing positive responses to component questions and dividing by the total number of questions in the index. $\Sigma f_i / N$, where $f = 1$ if checked yes to question and 0 if not, and $i = 1, 2, \ldots N$ for questions.
4. The monitoring index includes citizen satisfaction, costs and contract compliance.
5. Logistic regression is not appropriate in this case because regression requires the dependent variable to be random and our dependent variable, metro status, is a fixed category.

References

Appleton, B. (1994), *Navigating NAFTA: A Concise User's Guide to the North American Free Trade Agreement*, Rochester, NY: Carswell Thomson Professional Publishing.

Bartik, T. J. (1996), *Growing State Economies: How Taxes and Public Services Affect Private Sector Performance*, Washington, DC: Economic Policy Institute.

Bel, G. and Warner, M. E. (forthcoming), Challenging issues in local privatization. Under review at *Environment and Planning C: Government and Policy*.

Bennett, R. (1990), Decentralization, intergovernmental relations and markets: towards a post-welfare agenda? In R. Bennett (ed.), *Decentralization, Local Governments and Markets: Towards a Post-welfare Agenda*, Oxford: Clarendon Press, pp. 1–26.

Boyne, G. A. (1998), *Public Choice Theory and Local Government: A Comparative Analysis of the UK and the USA*, New York: St Martin's Press.

Brenner, N. (1999), Globalization as reterritorialization: the re-scaling of urban governance in the European Union, *Urban Studies*, 36, 3: 431–51.

Brenner, N. (2004), *New State Spaces: Urban Governance and the Rescaling of Statehood*, Oxford and New York: Oxford University Press.

Brown, D. L. and Warner, M. E. (1991), Persistent low-income nonmetropolitan areas in the United States: some conceptual challenges for policy development, *Policy Studies Journal*, 19, 2: 22–41.

Brown, T. L. and Potoski, M. (2003), Managing contract performance: a transaction costs approach, *Journal of Policy Analysis and Management*, 22, 2: 275–97.

Brown, D. and Swanson, L. (2003), *Challenges for Rural America in the Twenty First Century*, University Park, PA: Penn State University Press.

City/County Data Book (1994), Regional Economic Information System, Charlottesville, VA: University of Virginia. Available at: http//fisher.lib.Virginia.EDU/ccdb/

Conlan, T. (1998), *From New Federalism to Devolution: Twenty Five Years of Intergovernmental Reform*, Washington, DC: Brookings Institution Press.

Dewees, S., Lobao, L. and Swanson, L. (2003), Local economic development in an age of devolution: the question of rural localities, *Rural Sociology*, 68, 2: 182–206.

Donahue, J. D. (1997), *Disunited States*, New York: Basic Books.

Economic Report of the President (2005), Chain-type price indexes for gross domestic product, 1959–04. Government consumption expenditures and gross investment/State and Local, Washington, DC: United States Government Printing Office, p. 219, table B-7.

Edwards, C. (1981), The bases for regional growth. In L. R. Martin (ed.), *A Survey of Agricultural Economics Literature: Economics of Welfare, Rural Development and Natural Resources in Agriculture 1940s–1970s*, Minneapolis: University of Minnesota Press.

Frug, G. E. (1999), *City Making: Building Communities without Building Walls*, Princeton, NJ: Princeton University Press.

General Agreement on Trade in Services (1995), Official Text. World Trade Organization. Available at: www.wto.org/englis/tratop_e/serv_e/gatsintr_e.htm.

Gerbasi, J. and Warner, M. E. (forthcoming), Privatization, public goods and the ironic challenge of free trade agreements, *Administration and Society*.

Greider, W. (2001), The right and US trade law: invalidating the 20th century, *The Nation* (15 October).

Grubesic, T. and Murray, A. (2004), Waiting for broadband: spatial competition and the growth in advanced telecommunications services in the United States, *Growth and Change*, 35, 2: 139–65.

Hambleton, R. (2002), The new city management. In R. Hambleton, H. Savitch and M. Stewart (eds), *Globalism and Local Democracy: Challenge and Change in Europe and North America*, New York: Palgrave Macmillan.

Hansen, N., Higgins, B. and Savoie, D. (1990), Regional economic development policies and programmes in the United States: a critical overview and implications for the future. In *Regional Policy in a Changing World*, New York: Plenum Press.

Hefetz, A. and Warner, M. E. (2004), Privatization and its reverse: explaining the dynamics of the government contracting process, *Journal of Public Administration Research and Theory*, 14, 2: 171–90.

Hipp, M. and Warner, M. (2006), Market forces for the unemployed? Training vouchers in Germany and the US. Unpublished paper, Department of City and Regional Planning, Cornell University, Ithaca, NY.

Hirsch, W. Z. (1995), Factors important in local governments' privatization decisions, *Urban Affairs Review*, 31, 2: 226–43.

International City/County Management Association (1992, 1997, 2002), *Survey of Alternative Service Delivery*, Washington, DC: ICMA.

International Institute for Sustainable Development (IISD) (2001), *Public Rights, Public Problems: A Guide to NAFTA's Controversial Chapter on Investor Rights*, Canada: World Wildlife Fund.

Johnson, K. M., Pelissero, J. P., Holien, D. B. and Maly, M. T. (1995), Local government fiscal burden in nonmetropolitan America, *Rural Sociology*, 60, 3: 381–98.

Katz, M. B. (2001), *The Price of Citizenship: Redefining America's Welfare State*, 1st edn, New York: Metropolitan Books.

King, C. T. (1999), Federalism and workforce policy reform, *Publius – The Journal of Federalism*, 29, 2: 53–71.

Kodrzycki, Y. K. (1994), Privatization of local public services: lessons for New England, *New England Economic Review* (May/June): 31–46.

Lazar, L. (2000), Dispute resolution: secret corporate weapon? *Journal of Global Financial Markets* (Winter). Available at: www.sachnoff.com/publications/articles/nafta.htm.

Lobao, L., Rulli, J. and Brown, L. A. (1999), Macro-level theory and local-level inequality: industrial structure, institutional arrangements, and the political economy of redistribution, 1970 and 1990, *Annals of the Association of American Geographers*, 89, 4: 571–601.

Lowery, D. (1998), Consumer sovereignty and quasi-market failure, *Journal of Public Administration Research and Theory*, 8, 2: 137–72.

Lynch, R. G. (2004), *Rethinking Growth Strategies: How State and Local Taxes and Services Affect Economic Development*, Washington, DC: Economic Policy Institute.

MacLeod, G. (2001), New regionalism reconsidered: globalization and the remaking of political economic space, *International Journal of Urban and Regional Research*, 50, 2: 804–29.

Musgrave, R. A. (1959), *The Theory of Public Finance*, New York: McGraw Hill.

Nathan, R. A. and Lago, J. R. (1990), Intergovernmental fiscal roles and relations, *Annals American Academy of Political and Social Science*, 509: 36–47.

Nelson, M. A. (1997), Municipal government approaches to service delivery: an analysis from a transactions cost perspective, *Economic Inquiry*, 35 (January): 82–96.

Niskanen, W. (1971), *Bureaucracy and Representative Government*, Chicago: Aldine-Atherton.

Oates, W. E. (1998), *The Economics of Fiscal Federalism and Local Finance*, Northampton, MA: Edward Elgar.

O'Connor, J. (1973), *The Fiscal Crisis of the State*, New York: St Martin's Press.

Osborne, D. E. and Gaebler, T. (1992), *Reinventing Government: How the Entrepreneurial Spirit is Transforming Government*, Reading, MA: Addison-Wesley.

Peterson, P. E. (1981), *City Limits*, Chicago: University of Chicago Press.

Powers, E. T. (2000), Block granting welfare: fiscal impact on the States, *Economic Development Quarterly*, 14, 4: 323–39.

Prud'homme, R. (1995), The dangers of decentralization, *The World Bank Research Observer*, 10, 2: 201–21.

Reeder, R. and Jansen, A. (1995), *Rural Government – Poor Counties, 1962–1987*, Washington, DC: USDA, ERS, Agriculture and Rural Economy Division.

Savas, E. S. (2000), *Privatization and Public–Private Partnerships*, Chatham, NY: Chatham House.

Schneider, M. (1989), *The Competitive City: the Political Economy of Suburbia*, Pittsburgh, PA: University of Pittsburgh Press.

Schweke, W. and Stumberg, R. (2000), The emerging constitution: why local governments could be left out, *Public Management (US)*, 82, 1: 4–11.

Sclar, E. (2000), *You Don't Always Get What You Pay For: The Economics of Privatization*, Ithaca, NY: Cornell University Press.

Singleman, J. and Deseran, F. (1993), *Inequalities in Labor Market Areas*, Boulder, CO: Westview.

Swyngedouw, E. (1997), Neither global nor local: 'glocalization' and the politics of scale. In K. R. Cox (ed.), *Spaces of Globalization: Reasserting the Power of the Local*, New York: Guilford Press, pp. 137–66.

Tiebout, C. (1956), A pure theory of local expenditures, *Journal of Political Economy*, 64, 5: 416–24.

Tysoe, Honorable Justice (2001), In the Supreme Court of British Columbia, Between the United Mexican States and Metalclad Corporation, Reasons for Final Judgment.

US Bureau of the Census (1992, 1997, 2002), *Census of Governments: State and Local Government Finances, Individual Unit File*, Washington, DC: US Department of Commerce. Available at: http//www.census.gov/govs/www/estimate.html

US Bureau of the Census (1999), *Metropolitan Areas and Components (Metropolitan areas defined by Office of Management and Budget)*, 30 June 1993. Revised April 1999. Available at: http//www.census.gov/population/estimates/metro-city/93mfips.txt

US Department of State (2005), In the Matter of an International Arbitration under Chapter 11 of the North American Free Trade Agreement and the Uncitral Arbitration Rules Between Methanex Corporation and The United States of America, Final Award of the Tribunal. US Department of State: Washington, DC. Available at: http://www.state.gov/documents/organization/51052.pdf

Warner, M. E. (2001a), Local government support for community-based economic development. In *The Municipal Year Book 2001*, Washington, DC: International City/County Management Association (ICMA), pp. 21–7.

Warner, M. E. (2001b), State policy under devolution: redistribution and centralization, *National Tax Journal*, 54, 3: 541–56.

Warner, M. E. (2003), Local governance: from competition to cooperation. In D. Brown and L. Swanson (eds), *Challenges for Rural America in the Twenty First Century*, College Station, PA: Penn State University Press.

Warner, M. E. and Gerbasi, J. (2004), Rescaling and reforming the state under NAFTA: implications for subnational authority, *International Journal of Urban and Regional Research*, 28, 4: 853–73.

Warner, M. E. and Hefetz, A. (2002), The uneven distribution of market solutions for public goods, *Journal of Urban Affairs*, 24, 4: 15.

Warner, M. E. and Hefetz, A. (2003), Rural–urban differences in privatization: limits to the competitive state, *Environment and Planning C: Government and Policy*, 21, 5: 703–18.

Warner, M. E. and Hefetz, A. (2004), Pragmatism over politics: alternative service delivery in local government, 1992–2002. In *The Municipal Year Book 2004*, Washington, DC: International City/County Management Association, pp. 8–16.

Warner, M. E. and Pratt, J. E. (2005), Spatial diversity in local government revenue effort under decentralization: a neural network approach, *Environment and Planning C: Government and Policy*, 23, 5: 657–77.

Weber, B., Duncan, G. J. and Whitener, L. A. (2002), *Rural Dimensions of Welfare Reform*, Kalamazoo, MI: W. E. Upjohn Institute for Employment Research.

Weinstein, D. (1998), *Race to the Bottom: Plummeting Welfare Caseloads in the South and the Nation*, Washington, DC: Children's Defense Fund.

Williamson, O. E. (1996), *The Mechanisms of Governance*, New York: Oxford University Press.

4

Between Decentralized Planning and Neo-liberalism: Challenges for the Survival of the Indigenous People of Kerala, India

Darley Jose Kjosavik and Nadarajah Shanmugaratnam

The term *decentralization* is often used to refer to the disaggregation and delegation of political, economic and administrative powers and responsibilities to a wide range of institutions and actors – local and regional governments, parastatal agencies, NGOs, local resource use groups, cooperatives, community-based organizations and private enterprises. In the current development policy discourse, decentralization has become more explicitly articulated and prescribed as a market-led process and a part of the larger reform of rolling back the state and privatizing and liberalizing the economy. This decentralization is closely associated with destatization, which involves reallocation of tasks performed by the state to non-governmental and private agencies, a redefinition of the public–private divide and a shift from government to governance (Jessop 2002). Destatization, while clearing the way for privatization to move ahead, is supposed to enhance the freedom of civil society and enable it to play an active role in development, especially in providing certain social services that markets fail to deliver and promoting the expansion of a market economy. Thus civil society is regarded as the source of necessary non-market alternatives to the state in order to develop and sustain a market economy.

The Indian state of Kerala is an interesting case to examine the experiences of decentralization under two successive governments with opposing ideological leanings. The neo-liberal prescription was adopted in 2001 by the newly elected Congress Party-led government in Kerala, where the outgoing government led by the CPI(M) (Communist Party of India–Marxist) had been implementing a home-grown state-led programme of decentralization since 1996. The result was conflict and tension between the two divergent approaches in this highly politicized state in which two coalitions, one led by the CPI(M) and the other by the Congress, have been wielding power alternately through democratic elections. The Left coalition had introduced its new policy of decentralized planning when it regained power in 1996 and had been actively implementing it through a 'People's Planning Campaign' (PPC). In line with the policy of the central government, the newly elected Congress-led government adopted a neo-liberal approach to development and decentralization, with little role for the state bureaucratic and political actors in mobilizing people for planning and implementing projects at the local level, which inevitably meant making amendments in the programme institutionalized by the previous government. Not surprisingly, this situation led to controversies over the different approaches to decentralization in Kerala, and one of the areas of concern was how these would affect the poor and marginalized groups. Kerala has been known for its positive achievements in social development through radical reforms (Franke and Chasin 1994). It is also well known that these reforms and their implementation were state-led. Indeed, Kerala went through a process of social democratization under Communist Party-led governments after 1957 within the parliamentary democratic framework of India until the central government decided to adopt structural adjustment as a national policy in 1991.[1]

This policy shift had more serious implications for Kerala than for any other state in India, because this state had gone furthest with state-led development. Thus the withdrawal of the state from social and economic sectors was more complicated and bound to lead to more problems here than in the other Indian states. Among the affected groups were those that did not have the resources to participate in the emerging competitive market economy. Signs of new social exclusion were becoming visible among the indigenous communities and other resource-poor groups. The radical reformist Kerala model had been to a large extent inclusive of the indigenous people (*adivasis*), despite many shortcomings (Kjosavik and Shanmugaratnam 2004).

In this chapter, we look at how the previous government's decentralized planning and the policy shift of 2001 have affected the state's indigenous people as a group that has historically suffered exclusion and been identified in post-independence times as 'Scheduled Tribes' entitled to affirmative action and inclusion.[2] In fact, the Indian constitution has special provisions to protect groups such as Scheduled Tribes from social injustice and exclusion. From a careful reading of the various Articles of the Constitution that deal with these provisions, it would seem reasonable to believe that the authors of the constitution did envisage a direct role for the state to enforce these provisions. The question now is whether the provisions can be met by the current policy, which is premised on destatization and liberalization.

Fieldwork for the study was conducted in Poothady *panchayat*, Wayanad district, in the highlands of northern Kerala, as part of a larger study on indigenous peoples which involved several field visits from August 1998 to December 2003 (see Kjosavik 2004, 2005a, 2005b, 2006; Kjosavik and Shanmugaratnam 2004, forthcoming). Indigenous people (*adivasis*) constitute 1.01 per cent of Kerala's 31.8 million population. Wayanad district has the highest percentage of *adivasi* population in Kerala (15 per cent of the total district population and 35 per cent of the total *adivasi* population of Kerala). The rationale for selecting Poothady *panchayat* was that the three major indigenous communities of Wayanad – *Kurumar* (traditionally agriculturists), *Paniyar* (traditionally agrestic slaves/bonded labourers) and *Kattunaicker* (traditionally hunters and gatherers), who had different socio-economic histories, inhabit this *panchayat* area in substantial numbers. The data were collected through in-depth interviews and group discussions. The interviewees and resource persons included individuals of different political persuasions. Secondary data sources were also relied upon. In the next section, we discuss the decentralized planning in Kerala and its implications for indigenous communities. This is followed by an analysis of the emerging trends in Kerala's development in the context of neo-liberal policies and their consequences for indigenous people. We then analyse the recent trends in decentralized planning in the changing political context with reference to *adivasi* communities. We conclude by highlighting that the policy change in 2001 has not been favourable to the indigenous communities as regards their development and empowerment.

Decentralized Planning in Kerala

The Constitution of India was amended in 1992 to provide a legal basis and a mandate for the states to devolve power to the *panchayats* (democratically elected bodies at subregional levels). In accordance with these amendments, the government of Kerala, led by the Congress coalition, passed the Kerala *Panchayat Raj* Act in 1994. Kerala accepted the three-tier *panchayat* system proposed by the central government and elections were held in 1995 to establish elected bodies at the village level (*grama panchayat*), block level (block *panchayat*) and district level (*jilla panchayat*). In 1996, when the Left coalition was returned to power in the state, it undertook fiscal and administrative decentralization,[3] which represented a major step toward democratic decentralization.

The authors of Kerala's decentralized planning rejected the neo-liberal position that regarded the state and civil society as binary oppositional categories. They also rejected the theoretical framework of the new social movements, in which an autonomous civil society is positioned against the state and the market as well as the romantic visions of civil society as non-hierarchical and non-exploitative.[4] Instead, it would seem that the massive people's planning campaign (PPC) for decentralized development initiated by the Left coalition was more in line with the 'state-in-society' approach of Migdal *et al.* (1994), where state and society mutually shape each other (see also Véron 2001). Rather than treating state and society as two conflictual/ antagonistic spheres, the emphasis is on state–society relations (Törnquist 1999; Fox 1997) and on strategic engagement and disengagement between different factions of the two (Stokke and Mohan 2001). This perspective acknowledges the existence of a multiplicity of links between actors within the state bureaucratic and political systems and actors in civil society. Such a conceptualization of state–society relations is helpful in grasping the proactive potential of both the state and civil society to engage each other.

Evans (1995) developed the concept of 'embedded autonomy' to understand state–society relations in a developmental state. The bureaucratic apparatus in a developmental state is expected to have a certain kind of autonomy arising from a sense of corporate coherence. At the same time it differs from the Weberian ideal type that is insulated from society. In a developmental state, the bureaucracy is 'embedded in a concrete set of social ties that binds the state to society and provides institutionalized channels for the continual negotiation and renegotiation of goals and policies' (Evans 1995: 12). This combination of autonomy and connectedness, Evans calls embedded autonomy. While the connectedness in general may be with the entrepreneurial class within a society, Evans highlights Kerala as a variant in that the connectedness is with the working rather than the entrepreneurial class. We stretch the concept of embedded autonomy to gain a more nuanced understanding of state–society relations in Kerala in the context of the decentralized planning introduced by the Left coalition and the later decentralization programme of the Conservative coalition. In our view, the case of Kerala shows that embedded autonomy is mediated by changes in political power within a parliamentary democratic framework. This has to do with the fact that Kerala has a functioning parliamentary democratic system in which political power shifts between the Left and the Conservatives through the electoral process. While it is true that the reformist agenda instituted by the Communist Party-led government in 1957 set the stage for the policies of future governments, Left or Conservative, the dynamics of embeddedness tend to vary with the government in power. It could be said that the connectedness to the peasants, working class, indigenous communities, women and other marginalized groups is stronger when a Left coalition government is in power, and it shifts in favour of the entrepreneurial and landed classes when a Conservative coalition takes over. The dynamic nature of embeddedness could help understand the differential experience of indigenous people's development through decentralized planning under different regimes.

The democratic decentralization through PPC in 1996 was clearly an instance of the state's engagement with civil society, initiated by the Left forces within the state. This instance has to be distinguished from the historical mass mobilization by civil society to engage the state in Kerala in the late nineteenth and early twentieth centuries.[5] From the late 1930s, however, the mobilization of Kerala's civil society to engage the state has largely been led by the Leftist political parties and Left-leaning individuals. After the Communist Party formed the first government in Kerala in 1957,[6] state–society relations had thickened owing to the institutionalization of various rights and reforms demanded in the mass struggles. Therefore, it was no coincidence that when the Left coalition formed the government in 1996 they initiated a form of re-engagement with civil society through the PPC to address development issues posed by the new policy regime. This moment of re-engagement required the Communist Party to make a shift from its traditional stance of democratic centralism to democratic decentralization.

The Left coalition government started addressing questions of growth and equity by renewing its earlier programmes aimed at expanding the material production base with the support of mass movements, and at the same time defending the redistributive gains from the past. Substantial fiscal and executive powers were devolved to the elected local bodies. It devolved about 35–40 per cent of the Plan funds to the *panchayats* for the implementation of development programmes formulated with the people's participation. A massive campaign, involving state agencies and bureaucrats, non-governmental organizations, trade unions, other civil society organizations and activists, was organized to provide training for elected representatives, resource persons and local people in project formulation and implementation.[7] Significant institutional reforms and procedural innovations were adopted so as to enable people's participation at the grassroots level. This extensive mass mobilization actively mediated by the state has had a positive impact on the *adivasis*' participation in the political, economic and social realms. Transparency was built into the process to pre-empt possible corruption and nepotism. It was also widely seen as a mass resistance movement against ongoing liberalization and structural adjustment policies. The prescription for rolling back the state was disregarded by the Left government in 1996, on the grounds that it did not leave space for building the state–society synergy necessary to achieve growth with equity.

The successes and failures of Kerala's decentralized planning have been much debated (see Das 2000; Chathukulam and John 2002; Mohanakumar 2002, among others). The vision for Kerala's decentralized planning was an economic policy that emphasized self-reliance and a broadening of the domestic market (Patnaik 2001). This was not consistent with the neo-liberal economic agenda of the central government. Such a situation was bound to place serious constraints on the project of decentralization as envisaged by the Left; the state being an integral part of the Indian economy and polity. Moreover, Kerala's decentralization had been beset with conflicts between the then-ruling Left front and the opposition Congress coalition. There were also conflicts within the government – between the bureaucracy that largely resisted decentralization and the proponents of decentralization represented by politicians of Leftist persuasion and some committed bureaucrats. Gurukkal (2001) alleges that the conflict of interests within state and within civil society delimited the radical objectives of decentralized planning in spite of the Leftist agenda of effecting changes in the existing structural distribution of power. Kerala has a highly politicized civil society, which had been the prime mover of the state's achievements in social development. Civil society in Kerala has been understood as a heterogeneous and contested terrain where mass organizations have also been engaged in organized political action to achieve collective goals such as radical land reforms, workers' rights, enhancement of public entitlements, women's rights and environmental protection.

The decentralized planning initiated by the Left-wing government had been actualized through the PPC, where the state acted in partnership with civil society at various levels. With the introduction of Robert Putnam's conception of social capital as located in networks of associations and organizations residing in depoliticized local spaces and places – that is, in civil society (Putnam 1993) – and its co-optation by the World Bank, 'over-politicization' of civil society has been highlighted as the major cause of all the developmental ills of Kerala (Tharamangalam 1998). As regards decentralized planning, Tharakan (2004) holds that over-politicization led to major failures. On the other hand, it has been argued that the reformists within the CPI(M) had focused more on 'de-politicizing' the local space than on 're-politicizing' it and this had led to major failures (Törnquist 2004). Our contention is that the highly politicized civil society has been both enabling and constraining at the same time, as regards the PPC. It is the politicization of Kerala's civil society that made the PPC possible in the first place. Contestational politics and conflicts of values and ideologies are essential elements of democracy. We would argue that it was through politicization, including the inevitable party politicization in a multi-party democracy, that Kerala's marginalized and excluded groups gained whatever bargaining power they have *vis-à-vis* the dominant groups. While it may be true that the PPC could have achieved more if the differences between political parties had been minimized – which in any case is a counterfactual condition – the so-called 'over-politicization' cannot be considered a criticism of the PPC *per se*.

Indigenous Communities in Decentralized Planning

While controversies over the decentralized planning approach abound, our task here is to analyse the ways in which decentralized planning contributed to the socio-economic and political empowerment of the *adivasis*. Participatory approaches, though advocated in development programmes for indigenous peoples, have seldom been practised in Kerala. For example, the *adivasis'* participation in poverty reduction programmes implemented under the Integrated Tribal Development Programme had been very low. This is a major reason for the ineffectiveness of various tribal development programmes implemented by the state (Vijayanand 1997). The embedded participation of *adivasis* in the socio-economic and political processes is important to enable them to take control of their development, and the decentralized planning introduced through the PPC provided a meaningful participatory space for them. This was ensured by the reservation of 10 per cent of the seats in the local bodies for indigenous communities. Funds were earmarked for them by creating a tribal sub-plan (TSP) at the local level. While the overall transfer of state funds to the local bodies was only 36 per cent, 75–80 per cent of the total TSP funds were devolved (Isaac 2001). Depending upon the size of the *adivasi* population and the extent of their deprivation, the local bodies had the flexibility to decide on the share of funds to be allocated for programmes for these communities. Accordingly, in six *grama panchayats* and four block *panchayats* the share of the TSP and special component plan for scheduled castes exceeded 50 per cent of the total allocation – the real flow of funds to the weaker sections reached a record high in 1997–8 (Isaac and Franke 2002). Several safeguards were included to reduce corruption and misuse of funds, such as ensuring greater participation of *adivasis* in the campaign, and setting up special subject groups in the *grama sabhas*[8] and development seminars to discuss special issues related to the development of *adivasis*. A task force chaired by an elected representative of indigenous people had the responsibility for overseeing the drafting of projects under the TSP. Individual beneficiary projects were encouraged rather than infrastructural projects; if infrastructural projects such as irrigation were to be implemented, the condition was that at least 51 per cent of the beneficiaries had to be *adivasis*. These stipulations were intended to ensure that the funds allocated for the *adivasis* would in effect be used for addressing their specific development concerns. Projects for drinking water, housing and sanitation were emphasized. In the production sphere, the emphasis was on vegetable cultivation, as it could be practised in small parcels of land, and animal husbandry, as fodder could be obtained from the neighbouring forests and plantations and the summer rice fallows could be used for grazing. Schemes for employment training for *adivasi* men and women were also prioritized in many regions.

Apart from these tangible benefits, perhaps the most important achievement as far as the *adivasis* were concerned was their empowerment. The various platforms that were created, mandated and institutionalized by the PPC provided space for advocacy and agency of the indigenous peoples. Their participation in the *grama sabhas*, development seminars and other project-planning and decision-making bodies was fairly high. Mobilization by NGOs and political activists played a major role in this. The institutions were designed in such a way as to enable the participation of all sections of the population, particularly the marginalized communities such as *adivasis* and oppressed castes. In the first year of decentralized planning (1996) the participation rate of the Scheduled Castes (SC) and Scheduled Tribes (ST) in the *grama sabha* was lower than that of the general population (Chaudhuri and Heller 2003). However, in the second year (1997) there was a dramatic increase. This increased participation was due to certain procedural changes that were intended to facilitate participation and increase the transparency of fund targeting. Large-scale training programmes targeting these groups were also undertaken in addition to increased mobilization by the CPI(M) and the People's Science Movement (KSSP) (*ibid.*).

The participation of elected members of *adivasi* communities in the local bodies, and as presidents in 10 per cent of the local bodies, ensured that the community's voices were heard in matters of decision-making not only at the local level but at the higher levels as well. In Poothady *panchayat* of the Wayanad district, where our field study was conducted, we encountered an *adivasi* population articulating and addressing their development issues with enthusiasm. The Left coalition had a majority in the *panchayat* body during 1996–2001, while in the period 2001–5 the Conservative coalition dominated. About 18.5 per cent of the population of this *panchayat* belonged to *adivasi* communities. Of the 14 elected representatives, two were from indigenous communities – a woman and a man.[9] A study of the pattern of allocation of funds in this *panchayat* revealed that the development issues of the *adivasis* had received priority. The fund allocation for the TSP in 1998–9 was 35.5 per cent of the total funds. It increased to 42.5 per cent in 1999–2000, and in 2000–1 the allocation was 36 per cent.[10] This had significant positive implications for the development of *adivasis*, given that their community constituted only 18.5 per cent of the overall population. It was an indication that the *panchayat* had given priority to issues of equity. Housing, sanitation, drinking water, agriculture and animal husbandry were the projects that received priority as regards *adivasis*. Discussions with the elected representatives of the *adivasis* revealed that the total number of houses built during the four-year period from 1997–8 to 2000–1 was much higher than that of the total number of houses built for the *adivasis* of the *panchayat* during all the previous years since the formation of Kerala State in 1956. House construction and other project works were undertaken by the 'beneficiary committees', which provided them with employment opportunities. The quality of the works was also claimed to be much higher. Projects for self-employment targeting men and women were helpful in mitigating the unemployment problem to a certain extent. The mandatory allocation of at least 10 per cent of the *panchayat* funds for women's development projects helped promote women's participation in the *grama sabhas* as well as in project planning and implementation. Discussions with the *panchayat* president and other representatives revealed that there was a high level of participation of the indigenous communities in *grama sabhas* and development seminars. The educated youth among the *adivasis*, supported by activists from various political parties, NGOs and community-based organizations, played a major role in facilitating informed participation of the *adivasis* in the planning and implementation process. The PPC had seen a revival of the indigenous communities' spirits. As an *adivasi* woman elected representative put it: '*The process has been empowering and enlightening, and all the more, it provides us with a possibility of tackling the problems of our communities based on our priorities.*'

Neo-liberal Policies and Kerala's Development: Emerging Trends

With the implementation of neo-liberal policies, the central government has adopted serious cuts in public spending. This has impacted on government spending in the states as well, due to reduced fund transfers from the centre. State governments have been advised to reduce social sector expenditure, mainly in education, health and the public distribution system (PDS).[11] The transfer of funds to the states is currently being linked to the extent to which the state has reduced its social sector expenses. This has clearly created a dilemma for Kerala. Moreover, the non-plan funds transferred to the state – which were already lower than those of other states (George 1999) – have been further reduced, leaving Kerala to fend for itself in the social sector. The PDS of the state had been in part supported by the central government. Its withdrawal has negative implications for a state like Kerala, which imports more than 70 per cent of its food grains from other regions of India. The fact that 97 per cent of the population had until now been covered by the PDS exacerbates the problem.

The state's agricultural sector has been directly affected by the new policies. The opening up of the sector has resulted in a severe crash of the agricultural product market. In the fiscal year 1999–2000, Kerala incurred a loss of about US$800 million, and in 2000–1 the loss was around US$1,300 million (GoK 2001). The removal of quantitative restrictions on imports under the liberalized regime has been pointed out as the major reason for the fall in prices of agricultural commodities (GoK 2001). For example, imports of rubber more than tripled during the period from 1998–9 to 2001– 2. As about 18 per cent of the cultivated area is under rubber crop, this trend is detrimental to Kerala's agricultural economy. Moreover, the increased withdrawal of input subsidies and low investments in irrigation and other infrastructure have grave consequences for the farm sector. The agricultural economy of Kerala is dominated by perennial cash crops that have a relatively long productive life.[12] They require heavy initial investments and take several years of gestation before yielding returns. This constrains the farmers' ability to respond to market price signals by switching instantly from one crop to another. Moreover, because information about prices is incomplete, unpredictable and often delayed, the farmers are not in a position to adjust their annual outputs.

Subrahmanian and Azeez (2000) argue that liberalization has not resulted in any structural change in Kerala's industrial sector. The new markets, actors and rules involved in the new phase of globalization have strong negative consequences for Kerala, as it is historically integrated into the world market as an exporter of primary goods (Parayil and Sreekumar 2003). Terms of trade that favour manufactured goods at the expense of primary commodities or that are unfavourable to certain export crops and in favour of certain foodgrains are bound to affect incomes and food availability (Patnaik 2001). This is particularly the case for a primary commodity-exporting region such as Kerala. Moreover, the institutionalization of workers' rights and their trade union activism have now come to be regarded as disincentives for attracting international and domestic private investments into Kerala. Ironically, the basic rights that were won through historic struggles, and the current democratic struggles for their defence, are being portrayed as obstacles to growth and development in the new policy context.

Consequences and Prospects for the Indigenous Communities

The *adivasis* constitute the most disadvantaged group of people in Kerala, with neither the resources nor the capabilities to participate in the market as equal players.[13] Our field study revealed that such a situation, in conjunction with the structural adjustment policies, is giving rise to certain trends that have serious negative impacts on the *adivasis*.

The shift in the policy regime has engendered a process of 'new' social exclusion; the *adivasis* are increasingly being pushed out of the market fringes they have been inhabiting, and simultaneously denied the nominal welfare measures and other benefits they were entitled to earlier. A substantial proportion of the funds for *adivasi* development programmes had been from the central government. With the decrease in such transfers, development and welfare programmes for the *adivasis* have been attenuated. The general welfare programmes of the state have also been diminished by the strict regulations in social spending. One hundred per cent of the *adivasi* families depended on the PDS for a major share of their basic food and fuel consumption requirements. The dismantling of the PDS – though a nominal version still exists – means that all these households now have to incur four to five times more in expenses for food and fuel, which in turn affects their capacity to spend on other basic needs; alternatively, that they must decrease their already low consumption levels of food and fuel. Our field discussions revealed that the pensions and unemployment benefits entitled to them are often not paid regularly, which means that they have to buy basic food and other requirements on credit from petty traders at high interest. During field visits we observed that the landless *adivasi* families, who constituted the majority, managed at best one meal a day. In the lean seasons, particularly during the monsoons when they have practically no employment, they are perhaps able to have one square meal every other day. The gender-specific impact of the dismantling of the PDS was evident, too. Our discussions with *adivasi* women revealed that they had often forgone meals, particularly in the lean season, for the sake of children, husbands, fathers or brothers. They drank *kanji* water, that is, water drained after boiling rice, and let the others have the rice.

The central pillars of the Kerala model are the education and health sectors. These sectors are now being progressively privatized. What does this foretell for the *adivasis*? The facilities in the state schools are deteriorating owing to decreased funding, and the *adivasis* cannot afford to send their children to expensive private schools. Because of the state's reduced spending policy, not enough teachers are employed even in the special schools for *adivasi* children. Allowances for books, school uniforms, umbrellas, and food are not disbursed in time. Such delays in payments lead to increased school dropouts. During field visits we met such dropouts. The parents told us that they could not send the children to school without books and uniforms, so they would allow them to drop out for a year and then send them back to school the following year if they got the money to buy books and other things needed for school. This is a widespread phenomenon, particularly among the landless *adivasis* of Wayanad – *Paniyar*, *Kattunaicker*, *Adiyar* and *Urali* communities.

The expenditure cuts in the health sector are even more harmful to the *adivasis*. Their dependence on state health services is near total. Decreased government spending in this sector has affected the quality of services and the government hospitals do not have the necessary equipment and medicines. The prices of medicines, including the most essential ones (vital drugs) have increased substantially following the regulations of the Trade Related Intellectual Property Rights (TRIPs) enforced by the World Trade Organization. For instance, 67 per cent of the formulations of the top-selling 73 brands in the year 2000, which constitute 20 per cent of the pharmaceutical market in India, showed a substantial price increase (Rane 2003). This has serious implications for the health status of the *adivasis*, including the health of their children. The high-priced health services operating in the private sector are beyond their reach.

The crash in agricultural prices has seriously affected employment opportunities for the *adivasis*. The limited employment opportunities they did have were in the cash crop sector, which consists of a large number of small-holdings and a few medium-sized and large plantations. Pepper and coffee are the major cash crops grown in the study area. According to the farmers (non-*adivasis*) with whom we had discussions, 'the agricultural sector is being destroyed by the new policies of the government'. For instance, in the year 2000 they received about 200 rupees per kg of pepper. The price has since then decreased to about one-third (67 rupees per kg in December 2003). A minimum price of 100 rupees per kg is required to break even. A few years ago coffee fetched more than 50 rupees per kg, but it fell to about half of that (27 rupees per kg in December 2003). The break-even price for coffee is about 40 rupees per kg. The farmers perceive this situation to be a consequence of the liberalized trade regime. Various farmers' organizations, independent as well as affiliated to political parties, are active in the study area.

The fall in prices has adversely affected the capacity of the plantations and smallholders to absorb wage labour. At the same time productivity is adversely affected owing to the high price of fertilizers and other inputs. The farmers and planters are forced to save on wage labour, in an attempt to break even. Discussions with planters revealed that to produce one kilogram of coffee the labour cost incurred is at least 25 rupees, so the coffee plantations now employ workers only for pruning and harvesting. Agronomic operations such as weeding, fertilizer and pesticide application and so on have been suspended. This has reduced the number of labour days to about one-third. 'Both workers and us are suffering', said the owner of a small coffee estate. The coping strategies adopted by the farmers have serious consequences for the *adivasis* as their employment opportunities are closely linked to the perennial cash crop sector in the highlands. The state-owned plantations, which are supposed to provide employment for the *adivasis* are also following the same strategy (discussions with plantation management and workers).[14] Either way, it is a no-win situation for the *adivasis*. The coffee prices were so low that the income did not even pay for employing workers to harvest the produce. In many places farmers entered into an arrangement with the workers: the workers who harvested the coffee could have half of it instead of wages, and the other half would go to the farmer.

Changing Politics and *Adivasi* Development

The new government has introduced certain changes in the guidelines for decentralized planning, which have considerably reduced the space for people's participation. The Area Development Scheme of the pre-decentralization period was reintroduced by the new government. According to this scheme each member of the legislative assembly (MLA) is allotted a sum of 2.5 million rupees (about 25 per cent of the current annual budget of a *panchayat*) for the development of his or her constituency. This has been a long-standing demand of the MLAs – particularly those belonging to the Conservative coalition – since the beginning of decentralization. However, this scheme, which has not been integrated with the development plan for the *panchayats*, may reintroduce the space for patronage, corruption and nepotism. Given the experience with the scheme before decentralization, it is highly unlikely that projects that would benefit *adivasis* would be undertaken under this scheme.

Another major setback for the indigenous people has been the de-linking of the tribal sub-plan (TSP) from *panchayats*, and its transfer to the line department. The new government's argument for taking this decision was that the projects had not been implemented effectively under the PPC. However, many *adivasi* activists we had discussions with told us that the government's argument was contrary to the experience in many *panchayats*. They believe that the transfer of the TSP funds back to the line departments was due to pressure from the bureaucrats' lobby. Another reason given by the government was that one of the leaders of the *adivasi* groups had asked for such a de-linking. When we raised this issue, the activists pointed out that the *adivasis* were a heterogeneous group with several leaders for several organizations with leanings to different political parties. Therefore, according to these activists, the hurried de-linking without wider consultations, and purportedly based on the demand from one *adivasi* leader, cannot be justified. The following statement by a *panchayat*-level official corroborates these arguments:

> 'The bureaucrats in the line department felt emasculated without much funds for tribal development at their disposal. The Left government antagonized the bureaucracy by taking away funds from their control. The Congress government is now giving more recognition and importance to the bureaucracy. The return of the TSP funds to bureaucratic hands was part of this new bureaucrat–politician collusion.'

One avowed rationale for decentralization raised by proponents of all political persuasions is to reduce bureaucratic control over resources. However, what is happening in Kerala at present seems to be a progressive 'recentralization' of the devolved powers and resources. The de-linking of the TSP from the *panchayat* would, undoubtedly, result in a substantial reduction in the funds available for the programmes for *adivasis*, because there would be no room for flexibility, as there was in the case of the *panchayat* funds. We have seen earlier that six *panchayats* had allocated more than 50 per cent of their total funds for the TSP. In Poothady *panchayat*, on average, up to 42.5 per cent of the total funds had been used for projects for *adivasis*, although they constitute only about 18.5 per cent of the population. The de-linking would also increase the space for corruption and take away much of the space for the *adivasis* to participate in the development processes at the local level, as well as decision-making at higher levels. It would also undermine the role of the elected representatives of the indigenous communities.

Our last field visit in December 2003 revealed that many of these fears were being realized. Discussions with *panchayat* members and *panchayat*-level bureaucrats revealed that, within six months of the TSP funds being transferred to the line department, it became clear that the department was in no position to implement all the projects. Consequently, the *Panchayat* Presidents' Association – with the support of other *panchayat* functionaries, elected members, indigenous people and activists, and the opposition political parties – demanded that the TSP funds should be transferred back to the *panchayats* so that projects could be efficiently implemented. The government partially gave in to the popular pressure and transferred 50 per cent of the TSP funds back to the *panchayats*, while 50 per cent was retained with the line department. The *panchayats* are fighting for full TSP funds. Caught between these struggles are the *adivasis*. Kerala's decentralized planning was intentionally named *Janakeeyasoothranam* (People's Planning) by its pioneers, to underline the importance of people's participation at the grassroots level. The new government has renamed it *Kerala Vikasana Padhathi*, meaning Kerala Development Programme. According to an *adivasi panchayat* member, the change in name itself symbolized an undermining of the people's role in decentralized planning.

The Leftist government, before it lost the election, had established *oorukkoottams*, that is, special and separate assemblies of *adivasis* in each settlement, facilitated by trained *adivasi* activists.[15] It was a strategy to further enhance the participation and effectiveness of the planning and implementation of development projects. It was mandatory that the *oorukkoottam* met every six months for project discussions, beneficiary selection based on preferential points, formation of beneficiary committees to implement projects, and so on. The institution of *oorukkoottam* now remains only in form; the meaning and content have changed, as an *adivasi* activist relates:

> '*The oorukkoottam meeting has now become a ritual. Earlier, the potential beneficiaries of projects were given marks [points] at the meeting openly by the participants. But now, the marks are already given to the beneficiaries prior to the meeting and these are just read out in the meeting. This promotes corruption and partisan politics.*'

This shows that the transparency that was built into the procedures of project formulation, implementation and beneficiary selection is clearly being undermined. Some of the *adivasis* pointed out that the concept of 'beneficiary committee' has lost its meaning. Now most of the projects are implemented by government agencies, NGOs, contractors and so on. This means more space for corruption, wastage and undue time lag in project implementation. Earlier, a substantial share of the funds required for various projects was contributed by the beneficiary committee, in the form of labour or land, and in some cases cash. This was conducive to the implementation of more projects with less contribution from the government. Cost-sharing has now taken a different form, with much heavier demand on the beneficiaries. Moreover, employment opportunities for the beneficiaries and locals have been reduced as they have to compete with 'outsiders': '*The ownership of the projects is lost from our hands*', an *adivasi* activist said.

The beneficiary committee's role has become nominal, even in the case of general (non-*adivasi*) projects. According to the revised rules, projects with an estimated cost of less than 50,000 rupees can only be implemented by beneficiary committees. The more expensive projects are to be implemented by contractors or other government agencies. However, the beneficiaries have to make contributions in cash. For example, for drinking water projects 10 per cent of the total project cost, and for agricultural projects 20 per cent, has to be contributed in cash in advance. The project will be implemented only after this payment is made. A *panchayat* member explained:

> '*It is the poor people who are in need of these projects. How can they find such large sums? Providing labour is the only way for them to contribute. That is how the projects were implemented in the earlier set-up. But now, if the payment is not made in cash in advance the project will not be implemented. Many projects thus lapsed . . . and the government can save money.*'

The *adivasis*' cost-sharing burden has thus increased, while their income-earning opportunities have diminished substantially – a sort of 'double squeeze' for them. According to another *panchayat* member, in the new set-up the beneficiary committees are reluctant to take up projects, as they would be harassed by the government officials who are supposed to give them technical support. The *panchayat* member said:

> 'They may even give wrong measurements after project completion. This will put the beneficiary committee in trouble. It has actually happened. This is their ploy to deter beneficiary committees from taking up projects. Sometimes, the beneficiary committees entrust projects with "ben ami" contractors, and they deal with the officials in the appropriate way [paying bribe and so on] and get things done. It is sad to see how things have deteriorated.'

An *adivasi panchayat* member pointed out that 3 million rupees had been allotted to Poothady *panchayat* under TSP in the past three years, but that this was merely a paper allotment, and no money had been handed over to the *panchayat*. The *panchayat* had therefore not been in a position to implement any new projects for the benefit of the indigenous people in the past three years, but only some spill-over projects from the time of the previous government. There are also confusions about which projects are to be implemented by the *panchayats*, and which ones by the line department:

> 'There is no clarity of roles and division of responsibilities in the matter of adivasi funds and development projects even nearly three years after the amendments were made. The achievements made by the adivasis in the first five years of people's planning are now being reversed.' (*Adivasi panchayat* member)

The *adivasis* have organized under the auspices of the *Adivasi Kshema Samithi* (AKS), a Left-oriented *adivasi* organization, and are now engaged in struggles demanding the transfer of all TSP funds back to the *panchayats*, and changing some of the project implementation practices that are unfavourable to *adivasi* interests.

Inconsistency with Constitutional Provisions?

The changing politics and their consequences for the indigenous people take us to the question of how compatible the neo-liberal policy of increasing state withdrawal from social and economic sectors is with India's Constitutional provisions. As part of affirmative action, the Constitution has provided for reserving employment for the *adivasis* both in the central and state services. However, in the new policy context, the government has adopted a strategy of non-recruitment, or minimum recruitment to state services, with negative consequences for *adivasis*. It is unlikely that the increasing privatization of services and other economic activities will have a significant positive impact on the *adivasi* communities as regards employment, because the affirmative action policy of job reservation is not applicable in the private sector. Moreover, the *adivasis'* chances of competing in the open job market are seriously constrained because of their low educational levels and lack of the skills demanded by the market, such as technical and social skills, and lack of the right social and political connections.

The Constitution sees the state as a major player, in both the social and the economic arena, but under the new policy regime this particular role for the state has been drastically reduced. The socio-economic entitlements the *adivasis* had gained through state involvement in implementing the Constitutional provisions are now being gradually eroded. Market-led development is unlikely to help them retain or expand their entitlements; rather, it will disentitle them, if the current trend is anything to go by. The withdrawal of the state from these sectors would thus be inconsistent with the Constitutional safeguards extended to indigenous communities (Scheduled Tribes) and other marginal groups such as the Scheduled Castes. For example, Article 275 of the Constitution provides for grants-in-aid to states for promoting the *adivasis'* welfare:

> Provided that there shall be paid out of the Consolidated Fund of India . . . to enable that State to meet the costs of such schemes of development as may be undertaken by the State . . . for the purpose of promoting the welfare of the Scheduled Tribes in that State. (p. 160)[16]

Article 46 states:

> The State shall promote with special care the educational and economic interests . . . of the Scheduled Castes and the Scheduled Tribes, and shall protect them from social injustice and all forms of exploitation. (p. 28)

Article 335 provides for job reservation in central and state services:

> The claims . . . of the Scheduled Castes and the Scheduled Tribes shall be taken into consideration . . . in the making of appointments to services and posts in connection with the affairs of the Union or of a State. (p. 199)

Our contention is that these Constitutional provisions can be effectively implemented only with the active intervention of the state both in the economic and social sectors. The radical policies of the Kerala model in the post-independence period facilitated an inclusive development, which enabled the *adivasis* to make gains, albeit limited, in education, health care, employment and social security. Their institutionalized participation in development and political processes became possible only with the implementation of decentralized planning in 1996. However, they did not have sufficient time to improve their asset base in material terms or to catch up on human development for the new generation to face the impact of the neo-liberal policies. With the Congress-led government's policy on decentralized planning since 2001, the *adivasis* have increasingly lost control over the limited development resources they had at the local level. The vulnerability of these communities has been increasing, which is particularly disadvantageous to the younger generation, owing to the lack of opportunities for high-quality education and health care. The long-term human development of the younger generation will be adversely affected, leading to the intergenerational reproduction of poverty and deprivation.

Conclusion

In this chapter we have critically examined the emerging trends in decentralization and neo-liberal policies and their implications for indigenous communities in Kerala. The decentralized planning implemented by the Leftist government in 1996, through the PPC, was an attempt to make the development process more inclusive of the marginal groups such as indigenous communities and to contain the 'new social exclusion' that had started setting in. We have dealt with the means by which the PPC had envisaged and institutionalized the inclusion of the indigenous communities. In the vision of decentralization followed by the Leftists, the state had a direct role in empowering the people at grassroots level. The negative effects of liberalization, particularly in the agricultural sector, have diminished the employment opportunities for the *adivasis*, and the increased withdrawal of the state, particularly from the social and economic sectors, has contributed to further marginalization of this community. The amended decentralization, introduced by the Congress government in 2001, resulted in a decreased role and space for the state bureaucracy in mobilizing people for planning and implementing projects at the local level. At the same time, the bureaucracy intervened in ways that undermined the powers of the local bodies. We have argued that shifts in political power impact on the embedded autonomy of the state, and that the change of government in 2001 had led to a shift more favourable to the entrepreneurial class and less favourable to the marginalized communities in general and *adivasis* in particular.

The new environment created by the government, being supposedly free-market-friendly, is quite unfavourable to the participatory decentralized planning envisaged by the former Leftist government. We have discussed how, by making certain amendments to the radical provisions of the original decentralized planning, the present government has to a large extent reversed the control over resources and decision-making powers that were extended to local bodies by the former government, thus undermining the transparency, accountability and improved governance fostered by the PPC. These changes have also reduced the space for indigenous people's participation and increased the power of the bureaucracy. Such measures have adversely affected the indigenous people's agency and their chances of defining their own development priorities. The changes have not opened up new spaces for community initiatives either; rather, the opposite seems to be happening, owing to the increased socio-economic and political exclusion. The *adivasis* are now caught in the dynamics of Kerala's politics and the larger neo-liberal politics. These communities, vulnerable even when the state played an active role in the social and economic sectors, will be even more vulnerable if the current situation persists.

Postscript

The results of the elections to the local governments and State Assembly were out as this paper was being finalized. The Left coalition won more than 90 per cent of the local bodies in the local government elections held in

September 2005. In the State Assembly elections held in April 2006 they obtained a comfortable majority of 70 per cent of the seats (98 out of 140). It will be interesting to see how this latest change of government will affect decentralization.

Acknowledgements

We thank David Simon and Knut Nustad for critical comments on an earlier draft of this paper.

Notes

1. We have described the Communist Party-led institutional reforms in Kerala as social democratic in the sense that these reforms were designed within the framework of the Indian Constitution (see Kjosavik and Shanmugaratnam 2004). The communists, while preaching radical socialist transformation, were actually practising distributive and democratic reforms within a developing capitalist world order.
2. See Kjosavik and Shanmugaratnam (forthcoming) for an account of the historical exclusion of indigenous peoples from their resources.
3. The administrative decentralization, particularly the redeployment of administrative staff, has been incomplete due to the organized resistance – overt and covert – from the employees' trade unions (see Das 2000; Isaac 2001).
4. See Mohan and Stokke (2000), and Harris *et al.* (2004).
5. See Tharakan (1998) for an account of early social movements in Kerala.
6. The State of Kerala was established in 1956 and the Communist Party formed the first state government following the elections in 1957.
7. Isaac (2001) and Isaac and Franke (2002) are first-hand accounts of the people's campaign for decentralized planning in Kerala.
8. *Grama sabha* is the assembly of people from each ward in the *panchayat*. The *grama sabha* meets every six months to discuss various issues related to the planning and implementation of projects.
9. In Poothady *panchayat*, out of the 14 elected representatives 5 are women.
10. The figures are calculated from the Project Reports of Poothady *panchayat* for the relevant years.
11. A network of outlets for supplying food grains, fuel and other basic necessities at subsidized prices to low-income categories of people, including the *adivasis*.
12. See also Jose and Shanmugaratnam (1993).
13. See Kjosavik and Shanmugaratnam (2004) for an account of the processes by which *adivasis* were marginalized in the wage labour market, and Kjosavik and Shanmugaratnam (forthcoming) for the historical processes of their alienation from land and forest resources.
14. In Irulam village, two such plantations are currently under occupation by the indigenous people, as part of the larger struggle for land. See Kjosavik (2004) for a study of the *adivasi* land struggles in Kerala.
15. See Isaac (2001).
16. The Constitution of India, as modified up to 15 April 1967 (Delhi: The Manager of Publications, 1967).

References

Chathukulam, J. and John, M. S. (2002), Five years of participatory planning in Kerala: rhetoric and reality, *Economic and Political Weekly*, 7 December: 4917–26.

Chaudhuri, S. and Heller, P. (2003), The plasticity of participation: evidence from a participatory governance experiment. Paper presented to the Norwegian Association for Development Research (NFU) Annual Conference – Politics and Poverty, Oslo, Norway, 23–24 October.

Das, M. K. (2000), Kerala's decentralized planning: floundering experiment, *Economic and Political Weekly*, 2 December: 4300–3.

Evans, P. (1995), *Embedded Autonomy: States and Industrial Transformation*, Princeton, NJ: Princeton University Press.

Fox, J. (1997), How does civil society thicken? The political construction of social capital in rural Mexico. In P. Evans (ed.), *State–Society Synergy: Government and Social Capital in Development*, IAS Research Series no. 94, Berkeley: University of California Press.

Franke, R. W. and Chasin, B. H. (1994), *Kerala: Development through Radical Reform*, New Delhi: Promilla.

George, K. K. (1999), *Limits to Kerala Model of Development*, Trivandrum: Centre for Development Studies.

GoK (2001), *White Paper on State Finances*, Trivandrum: Finance Department, Government of Kerala.

Gurukkal, R. (2001), When a coalition of conflicting interests decentralizes: a theoretical critique of decentralization politics in Kerala, *Social Scientist*, 29, 9–10: 60–76.

Harris, J., Stokke, K. and Törnquist, O. (2004), Introduction: the new local politics of democratization. In J. Harris, K. Stokke and O. Törnquist (eds), *Politicizing Democracy: The New Local Politics of Democratization*, Basingstoke: Palgrave Macmillan, pp. 1–28.

Isaac, T. M. T. (2001), Campaign for democratic decentralization in Kerala, *Social Scientist*, 29, 9–10: 8–47.

Isaac, T. M. T. and Franke, R. W. (2002), *Local Democracy and Development: The Kerala People's Campaign for Decentralized Planning*, New York: Rowman and Littlefield.

Jessop, B. (2002), *The Future of the Capitalist State*, Cambridge: Polity Press.

Jose, D. and Shanmugaratnam, N. (1993), Traditional homegardens of Kerala: a sustainable human ecosystem, *Agroforestry Systems*, 24, 2: 203–13.

Kjosavik, D. J. (2004), Contested frontiers: re-imagining *adivasi* land rights and identities in highland Kerala, South India. Paper presented to the 11th World Congress of Rural Sociology, Trondheim, Norway, 25–30 July.

Kjosavik, D. J. (2005a), In the intersection of class and indigeneity: the political economy of indigenous people's development in Kerala, India. PhD Thesis, Aas, Norway: Norwegian University of Life Sciences.

Kjosavik, D. J. (2005b), Re-claiming land rights: the politics of place and *adivasi* identity in highland Kerala, India. Paper presented at the NFU Annual Conference –Transforming Landscapes of Poverty – Resources, Rights and Conflicts, 20–21 June, Aas, Norway.

Kjosavik, D. J. (2006), Articulating identities in the struggle for land: the case of the indigenous people (*adivasis*) of highland Kerala, South India. Paper presented at the International Symposium – At the Frontier of Land Issues: Social Embeddedness of Rights and Public Policy, 17–19 May, Montpellier, France.

Kjosavik, D. J. and Shanmugaratnam, N. (2004), Integration or exclusion? Locating indigenous peoples in the development process of Kerala, South India, *Forum for Development Studies*, 31, 2: 231–73.

Kjosavik, D. J. and Shanmugaratnam, N. (forthcoming), Property rights dynamics and indigenous communities in highland Kerala, South India: an institutional-historical perspective, *Modern Asian Studies*.

Migdal, J. S., Kholi, A. and Shue, V. (eds) (1994), *State Power and Social Forces: Domination and Transformation in the Third World*, Cambridge: Cambridge University Press.

Mohan, G. and Stokke, K. (2000), Participatory development and empowerment: the dangers of localism, *Third World Quarterly*, 21, 2: 247–68.

Mohanakumar, S. (2002), From people's plan to plan sans people, *Economic and Political Weekly*, 37, 16: 1492–7.

Parayil, G. and Sreekumar, T. T. (2003), Kerala's experience of development and change, *Journal of Contemporary Asia*, 33, 4: 465–92.

Patnaik, P. (2001), Alternative paradigms of economic decentralization, *Social Scientist*, 29, 9–10: 48–59.

Putnam, R. (1993), *Making Democracy Work: Civic Traditions in Modern Italy*, Princeton, NJ: Princeton University Press.

Rane, W. (2003), Have drug prices fallen? *Economic and Political Weekly*, 1 November: 4640–2.

Stokke, K. and Mohan, G. (2001), The convergence around local civil society and the dangers of localism, *Social Scientist*, 29, 11–12: 3–24.

Subrahmanian, K. K. and Azeez, A. (2000), *Industrial Growth in Kerala: Trends and Explanations*, Working Paper no. 310, Trivandrum: Centre for Development Studies.

Tharakan, P. K. M. (1998), Socio-religious reform movements: the process of democratization and human development: the case of Kerala, South-West India. In L. Rudebeck and O. Törnquist (eds), *Democratization in the Third World: Concrete Cases in Comparative and Theoretical Perspective*, London: Macmillan.

Tharakan, P. K. M. (2004), Historical hurdles in the course of the people's planning campaign in Kerala, India. In J. Harris, K. Stokke and O. Törnquist (eds), *Politicizing Democracy: The New Local Politics of Democratization*, Basingstoke: Palgrave Macmillan, pp. 107–26.

Tharamangalam, J. (1998), The perils of social development without economic growth: the development debacle of Kerala, India, *Bulletin of Concerned Asian Scholars*, 30, 1: 3–34. Available at: http://csf.colorado.edu/bcas/kerala/kertheri.htm (accessed 6 February 2003), pp. 1–21.

Törnquist, O. (1999), *Politics and Development: A Critical Introduction*, London: Sage.

Törnquist, O. (2004), The political deficit of substantial democratization. In J. Harris, K. Stokke and O. Törnquist (eds), *Politicizing Democracy: The New Local Politics of Democratization*, Basingstoke: Palgrave Macmillan, pp. 201–45.

Véron, R. (2001), The 'new' Kerala model: lessons for sustainable development, *World Development*, 29, 4: 601–17.

Vijayanand, S. M. (1997), People's Participation in Poverty Reduction Programmes: A Case Study of the Integrated Tribal Development Project (ITDP), Attappady. MPhil thesis, Trivandrum: Centre for Development Studies.

5

Child Health in Rural Mexico: Has Progresa Reduced Children's Morbidity Risks?

Maria C. Huerta

Introduction

Poor health in early life has negative consequences that can result in long-term disadvantage. Children with ill health tend to miss more days of school and perform worse in school, both of which are associated with adverse achievements later in life. In developing countries, diarrhoea and acute respiratory infections are still the two leading causes of child mortality and remain among the most common childhood diseases. Furthermore, rural, more isolated communities tend to have restricted access to basic services, which increases the likelihood and perhaps the severity of these diseases. Poor children growing up in these settings are at risk of experiencing frequent and severe episodes of illness because they are highly exposed to the factors associated with catching infectious diseases.

Progresa – Mexico's main anti-poverty programme – aims to shift the odds of disadvantage by promoting and supporting parents' investments in education, health and nutrition. The Programme is based on the philosophy that investing in human capital can set the grounds for breaking the inter-generational transmission of poverty. Progresa's intervention includes a set of activities aimed at improving child health and related health care behaviours. The research reported in this chapter was designed to examine whether or how far Progresa reduces the morbidity rates of its beneficiary children.

Background to the Research

Child health

The literature on child health suggests that children's health status is not only linked to future health outcomes, but also to educational achievements, accumulation of human capital, employment opportunities, earnings and social status (Case *et al.* 2004). There is evidence from both developed and developing countries that children's health status is positively associated with family's socio-economic background (Singer and Ryff 2001; Case *et al.* 2002;

Burgess *et al.* 2004; Gwatkin *et al.* 2004). Children from poorer backgrounds, especially those in remote rural areas, are more likely to have poor health outcomes because they have limited access to health care and are more exposed to the hazards associated with ill health. Therefore, it is believed that child health plays a decisive role in the transmission of poverty intergenerationally and over the life course (Wolfe and Behrman 1982; Mata 1995; Case *et al.* 2004).

In developing countries, children living in impoverished environments are likely to catch infectious diseases because they are exposed to a complex interplay of risk factors (e.g. poor diet, inadequate feeding and hygienic practices, unhealthy environments, restricted access to health services), which make them less resistant to disease. In addition, the severity and duration of an infection depends on prior nutritional status and the diet consumed during the recovery period (Scrimshaw 2003). Inadequate nutrition makes children from deprived settings more susceptible to frequent and severe illnesses, which can hinder their growth and development.

Despite some progress over the last decade,[1] diarrhoea and acute respiratory infections (ARI) are still the two leading causes of child mortality in developing countries and remain among the most common childhood diseases. In Mexico, despite notable achievements on child mortality over the last decade,[2] the number of child deaths due to diarrhoea and respiratory infections remains high, exceeding 6,500 deaths per year (Zedillo 2000). These child deaths are concentrated among the poorest segments of the population. Moreover, children from disadvantaged groups who survive these diseases are more likely to be undernourished and ill during their infancy and preschool years.

Like many other countries, social progress in Mexico has been unequally distributed between rural and urban areas. Although in both settings there have been improvements, progress in rural localities started later and proceeded at a slower rate. In recent years the urban–rural gap has begun to diminish, but considerable differences still prevail. For instance, rural children are more than twice as likely to be malnourished during their first five years of life (31.7 per cent versus 11.6 per cent in urban areas[3]).

Progresa's benefits geared to child health

Progresa is one of the main strategies the Mexican government has implemented to reduce the health disparities. It is a nationwide anti-poverty programme whose main objective is to improve the basic capabilities of the poorest and most vulnerable families in the country. The Programme has an integral approach. It gives benefits in three areas that are closely linked to each other: education, health and nutrition. It is believed that the positive link between these components should reinforce the effect that each component could have separately, and thus the impact should be multiplied.

Progresa started operating in August 1997 and its coverage has increased throughout several phases. At the end of 2004, *Oportunidades'* coverage had reached 5 million households; that is, 20 per cent of all households in the country were receiving benefits from this Programme (see table 1). At present, it operates in 31 of the 32 Mexican states,[4] in more than

73

Table 1

Progresa's coverage and budget, 1997–2004

Year	Municipalities	Localities	Families	Scholarships	Budget (millions pesos)[2]	% GDP[2]
1997	358	6,357	301,262	344,457	465.8	0.01
1998	1,750	40,711	1,930,032	1,719,090	3,398.5	0.09
1999	2,155	53,215	2,306,325	2,338,957	6,890.1	0.15
2000	2,166	53,232	2,476,430	2,485,323	9,586.9	0.17
2001	2,310	67,539	3,116,042	3,325,524	12,393.8	0.21
2002	2,354	70,520	4,240,000	4,355,927	17,003.8	0.27
2003	2,360	70,436	4,240,000	4,577,009	22,331.1	0.33
2004	2,429	82,973	5,000,000	n.a.	25,324.3	0.35
Total[1]	2,436	1,999,391	22,268,916	8,932,936	–	–

Notes: [1]Total refers to the national number of municipalities, localities, households and number of children of school age (6–19 yrs old); *Source:* INEGI (2001). [2]*Source:* Fox (2004).
Source: Programa de Desarrollo Humano Oportunidades (http://www.progresa.gob.mx).

2,000 municipalities, and over 80,000 localities. The budget allocated to this Programme in 2004 was approximately 2,200 million US dollars, equivalent to 0.35% of GDP (Fox 2004). From 1997 to 2002, 100% of its budget came from the Mexican government. However, from 2002 onwards it has been receiving an additional 10% from the Inter-American Development Bank.

Progresa gives a set of monetary and in-kind benefits that vary according to the demographic characteristics of each family. The Programme aims to improve access to medical treatment by promoting: regular visits to the health centre; health care practices through monthly educational sessions; and children's nutritional status through a monetary grant for food consumption and nutritional supplements.

Children, as well as other family members, must attend the health centre on a regular basis according to a schedule based upon their age (see table 2). In their first two years of life children are expected to have visited the health centre eleven times. Regular medical attention during the most vulnerable period of children's growth should facilitate the early detection and treatment of illness or growth failure. At the same time, these numerous visits should have a positive impact on maternal health care behaviours since they may raise mothers' awareness of the importance of preventive measures, such as vaccinations and growth surveillance.

Health care givers, mainly mothers, attend monthly educational sessions at the nearest health centre. These sessions are provided by health personnel and include 25 different themes on education and promotion of health, the great majority of which are related to child health (see table 3). Moreover, there are specific sessions aimed at improving the recognition and treatment of diarrhoea and respiratory infections.

Table 2

Health check-up schedules for children under 5 years old

Age group	Number of visits	Purpose
0–4 months	Three visits: (1) at 7 days old, (2) at 28 days old, and (3) at 2 months old	• Monitor growth, weight and height
4–23 months	Eight visits: at 4, 6, 9, 12, 15, 18, 21 and 23 months	• Immunizations; • Monitor growth, weight, and height; • Evaluate signs of illness
24–59 months	Three visits per year: one every 4 months	• Immunizations; • Monitor growth, weight, and height; • Evaluate signs of illness

Source: SEDESOL (1999).

Table 3

Educational sessions related to child health outcomes

1. New-born health care practices
2. Infant health care practices
3. Toddler health care practices
4. Breastfeeding practices
5. Vaccination scheme (immunizations child should have according to age)
6. Oral rehydration therapy (preparation and use of ORS, '*vida suero oral*')
7. Health care of children when sick with diarrhoea
8. Deworming (importance of children's and adults' deworming)
9. Acute respiratory infections (recognition and treatment of ARIs)
10. Tuberculosis (to detect when a person has TB)
11. Basic sanitation (handling litter, latrines and unhygienic animals)

In addition, beneficiary families are provided with a monetary grant (equal to about US$20[5]) for the purchase of food products. Likewise, nutritional supplements are provided to those members of the family who are at most risk of malnutrition – children between the ages of four months and two years, pregnant and breastfeeding women, and children between the ages of two and five with any signs of malnutrition. Improved nutritional status should also have an effect on children's overall health since it is associated with lower morbidity and mortality rates (Mata 1995; Scrimshaw 2003).

There have been two assessments of Progresa's performance on improving child health outcomes, but neither has examined the effect of the Programme on reducing specific infectious diseases (Gertler 2000; Gertler *et al.* 2004). Instead these studies have analysed the impact of Progresa on child health outcomes using overall illness as the dependent variable. However, due to the substantial risk of infectious diseases in poor communities, a specific focus on diarrhoea and respiratory infections is warranted. Moreover, the measure of overall illness suffered from reporting errors, making this variable a poor indicator of actual child illness.

The Research Enquiry

In this investigation, our aim was to assess whether Progresa reduced the major childhood diseases that affect children under the age of five: diarrhoea and respiratory infections. To complement these findings we also examined whether Progresa's activities reduced the gaps in health status associated with household degree of poverty.

Progresa's own main strategy of evaluation was a longitudinal survey (ENCEL from its acronym in Spanish) carried out approximately every 6 months, which collected information at both the household and individual level. The first round of data collection took place before the families started receiving their benefits (baseline), which allowed estimating with more precision the changes observed after the intervention was implemented. The survey randomly sampled treatment and control localities (320 and 186 localities, respectively) situated in rural areas of the seven states in which the Programme was initially operating.[6]

Assignment by randomization implies that prior to Programme implementation, the treatment and control localities should, on average, have similar observed and unobserved characteristics. In theory, this treatment-control design should enable rigorous testing of the effects of the intervention as the only difference between the control and the treatment groups is the presence of the Programme. An assessment of the randomness of the ENCEL sample found randomization was adequate at the locality level; however, some significant differences at the household and individual level were detected (Behrman and Todd 1999). Thus, estimates of the programme effect at the household or individual level have to be carried out controlling for any pre-programme differences.

Treatment localities were scheduled to receive benefits from the beginning of the intervention (from May 1998). Control communities did not receive benefits until a later date (from December 1999). The lagged inclusion of the control group is important because in this study the period of analysis included rounds of data collection (wave 3) during which households in the control group were beginning to receive Programme benefits.

To assess the impact of Progresa on the health and nutritional status of beneficiary families the National Institute of Public Health (INSP for its acronym in Spanish) collected additional data on a sub-sample of the ENCEL survey. This set of surveys includes three rounds: the first was carried out between August and September 1998,[7] the second one between October and December 1999 and the last survey between November and December 2000. Unfortunately, the INSP does not have information on morbidity at baseline (i.e. at wave one). Nevertheless, we use these data because they provide the best information on child morbidity.

One of the limitations of these data is that information on health outcomes may suffer from reporting errors. In preliminary analyses, we found some evidence of reporting errors, specifically for respiratory infections.[8] When interpreting the results, it is important to keep in mind that this variable might be measuring mother's perception of illness rather than illness per se.

The main outcome variables of interest are the *incidence of diarrhoeal diseases* and the *incidence of respiratory infections*. Both are binary variables, taking a value of one if a child is ill and zero otherwise. The period of reference includes those episodes that took place during the two weeks prior to the survey.

In order to isolate the intervention effect from the possible influence of other background variables, we included a set of explanatory variables at the individual, household and community level. The independent variables selected were those that previous analyses showed to be significantly different between treatment and control groups: mother's education, mother's language, access to water, distance to the health centre and region of residence. In addition, we controlled for two individual characteristics: age and sex of the child; and for variables at the locality level that could be associated with health outcomes: degree of marginality,[9] region of residence, natural disasters (flood, frost and drought) and average wage of agricultural workers. The models also controlled for some risk factors associated with these diseases: number of children under the age of five (proxy for crowding), access to w.c. (sanitation), and indoor air pollution.

Studies of domestic air pollution have found a strong and significant increase in the incidence of acute lower respiratory infections among children living in households that are exposed to indoor cooking fires (Victora 1999; Smith *et al.* 2000). In our rural study, 80 per cent of families live in dwellings without a gas stove and 60 per cent of them live in one-room dwellings. Hence, indoor smoke exposure for these children is high. To control for a possible influence of this risk factor, the models fitted for respiratory infections include two additional covariates: a dummy variable for dwellings without a gas stove, and a dummy variable for dwellings with one room only.

We looked at information on children classified as eligible to receive Programme benefits living in both treatment and control communities. We carried out most of our analyses in respect of two age categories: children aged between 0 and 23 months, and children aged between 24 and 59 months. This was to allow for the fact that the incidence of infectious diseases varies according to age and this variable could thus affect the impact of the Programme.

Methods of Analysis

We first looked at Progresa's impact on the prevalence of illness, comparing eligible children who were receiving Programme with those who were not. To assess differences between these groups, we estimated a test of equality of proportions. We then computed rough estimates of the Programme's impact by comparing changes over time between the treatment and control groups (see further, below).

Multivariate models were estimated using the information of individuals with repeated observations over time. We estimated all models for the sample

Table 4

Age at wave two by type of sample, INSP sample

Age at wave 2 (months)	Children in waves 2 and 3	Children in waves 1, 2 and 3
0–11	183	–
12–23	249	133
24–35	304	182
36–47	267	165
48–59	–	–
Total	1,003	480

Table 5

Age across time: INSP longitudinal sample with information at waves 1, 2 and 3

Age (months)	Wave 1	Wave 2	Wave 3
0–11	174	–	–
12–23	166	133	–
24–35	140	182	128
36–47	–	165	180
48–59	–	–	172
Total	480	480	480

of children with observations in waves two and three, and also for the sample of children with observations in all three waves of data collection. For the former sample, we disaggregated results by the two age groups under consideration: children aged 0–23 months and children aged 24–59 months at the time of the wave two interview (see table 4).

Table 5 presents the age of children with observations in all three waves of data collection. It can be seen that at wave two these children were aged between 12 and 47 months.[10] Hence, when comparing results, it is important to keep in mind that this group of children are between the two age categories under study (i.e. between children 0–23 months and children 24–59 months).

Our purpose was to establish whether Progresa reduced the chances of catching diarrhoea and respiratory infections, whether this effect was stronger among children who received nutritional supplements, and whether the Programme had greater effects among certain groups of the population. We estimated logit models of child illness, given that the outcome variable was binary (with a value of one if the child is ill and zero otherwise).[11]

For the first objective, we specified a model to estimate Progresa's effect on children's morbidity status, including a set of variables at the individual, household, and community level to control for differences in the outcomes which were not associated with Progresa's intervention. A second model included three additional terms to evaluate whether children receiving nutritional supplements had better outcomes than those not receiving this benefit. (For ethical reasons, health centres provided supplements to malnourished children irrespective of whether they belonged to a control or a treatment community. Therefore, children in both types of localities could receive this in-kind benefit.) To control for the fact that we did not have a baseline measure, we estimated the previous models controlling for children's anthropometric status (height for age) at time t-1. (This method is carried out only for the longitudinal sample with three observations over time since it is the only one that includes information on nutritional status at baseline.) Finally, to investigate whether the Programme had a differential effect on child morbidity according to the household's degree of poverty, we estimated the first model for three different categories of poverty (terciles of Progresa's poverty index). This approach allowed us to examine whether Progresa has had a greater influence among children from the most disadvantaged (or advantaged) groups.

Results

Descriptive results

Table 6 shows estimates of the prevalence of diarrhoea and respiratory infections for both treatment and control groups at waves two and three of the INSP survey. Estimates are given for children in all age groups (0 to 59 months), as well as for children aged between 0 and 23 months and for children aged between 24 and 59 months. This descriptive analysis corresponds to children in the cross-sectional sample, i.e. children with at least one observation over time.

In these rural localities a considerable proportion of children were reported to be ill in the past two weeks: 13.2 per cent were reported as having been ill with diarrhoea and 43.5 per cent as having been ill with some kind of respiratory infection. Furthermore, though not shown here, 47.7 per cent of children under the age of five were reported as having been ill from at least one of these diseases. The fact that almost half of eligible children in these rural localities were reported as sick suggests high levels of morbidity.

It is difficult to quantify Progresa's impact using these data, not only because we lack a baseline measure, but also because differences in background characteristics between the treatment groups could have introduced an additional bias. If we assume that all children had similar morbidity rates at baseline, as well as similar household characteristics, then the Programme's effect can be roughly estimated from the difference between groups at wave two or by the control group's change between waves two and three. These are crude estimates which, if anything, may underestimate Progresa's effect, since the treatment group at baseline was in general worse-off than the control group.

Diarrhoea

The first part of table 6 and figure 1 show that at wave two – slightly more than a year after the Programme's implementation – treatment children are

Table 6

Prevalence of diarrhoea and respiratory infections: eligible children in treatment and control groups, INSP cross-sectional sample

	Proportion sick with diarrhoea			Diff. in proportions (P > |t|²)	Proportion sick with respiratory infections			Diff. in proportions (P > |t|²)
	Wave 1	Wave 2	Wave 3	(w2 vs w3)	Wave 1	Wave 2	Wave 3	(w2 vs. w3)
All children	—	13.2	12.7	0.57	—	43.5	43.5	0.97
Control	—	16.4	13.5	0.05*	—	45.7	42.8	0.17
Treatment	—	11.2	12.1	0.41	—	42.1	44.0	0.28
P > |t|¹	—	0.00***	0.28		—	0.07*	0.54	
Children 0–23 months	—	19.6	17.7	0.28	—	44.7	43.6	0.65
Control	—	23.9	17.9	0.04**	—	45.9	42.3	0.32
Treatment	—	16.8	17.5	0.76	—	43.9	44.7	0.79
P > |t|¹	—	0.01***	0.86		—	0.57	0.45	
Children 24–59 months	—	10.0	10.1	0.94	—	42.9	43.4	0.61
Control	—	12.6	11.2	0.37	—	45.6	43.1	0.33
Treatment	—	8.3	9.3	0.45	—	41.2	43.6	0.27
P > |t|¹	—	0.00***	0.18		—	0.07*	0.84	

Note: Statistical significance: *p < 0.10; **p < 0.05; ***p < 0.01.
¹Test equality on proportions (Control vs. treatment).
²Test equality on proportions (Wave 2 vs. wave 3).

Figure 1

Proportion sick with diarrhoea: eligible children by age groups and treatment, INSP
cross-sectional sample

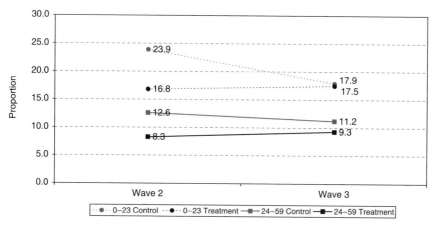

Note: Information on morbidity rates was not collected at wave 1.

significantly less likely to be ill than are the control children. In localities
receiving Progresa's benefits the prevalence of diarrhoea is 11.2 per cent, and
the corresponding prevalence in control communities is 16.4 per cent. Moreover, the differences are statistically significant for both age groups. At wave
three, however, the differences between treatment and control groups are no
longer significant. It is worth recalling that between waves two and three
some control localities were incorporated into the Programme. Hence, the
lack of differences between groups could indicate that those children in the
control localities who had started receiving benefits had managed to catch
up with their treatment peers.

If we look at changes in prevalence over time, the proportion of sick
children in treatment localities remains relatively constant between waves two
and three. In contrast, the proportion of children sick with diarrhoea in
control localities decreases during this period and this improvement is
statistically significant. These preliminary results suggest that the Programme
has a positive effect on reducing the incidence of diarrhoea, but that its
impact is stronger at the initial stage of the intervention.

Our estimates suggest the Programme reduced the prevalence of diarrhoea
by 5.2 percentage points (or 31.9 per cent lower than at baseline) for children
under the age of five. Disaggregating by age group, these rough estimates
represent a reduction of 7.1 percentage points (or 29.8 per cent lower than
at baseline) for children aged between 0 and 23 months and of 4.3 percentage
points (or 34.1 per cent lower than at baseline) for children between 24 and
59 months old.

Figure 2

Proportion sick with respiratory infections: eligible children by age groups and treatment,
INSP cross-sectional sample

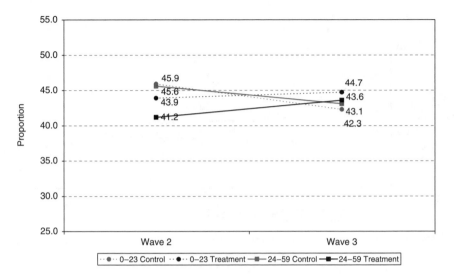

Respiratory infections

The second part of table 6 and figure 2 show that at wave two, the proportion of children sick with respiratory infections is somewhat smaller in treatment localities than in control communities, 42.1 per cent versus 45.7 per cent, respectively. This difference suggests a positive Programme effect, but not as strong as that observed for diarrhoea. However, at wave three this difference is no longer evident. Figure 2 illustrates these results. We observe a positive Programme effect only at wave two and only among older children. Regarding changes over time, there is no evidence of differences in morbidity rates between waves two and three.

Estimates of the Programme's effect indicate a reduction in the prevalence of ARI (Acute Respiratory Infection) of 3.6 percentage points (or 7.8 per cent lower than at baseline) for children between 0 and 59 months old and of 4.4 percentage points (or 9.6 per cent lower than at baseline) for children between 24 and 59 months old. We have not presented an estimate for children in the younger age group because there is no evidence of a Programme effect for this age group.

These descriptive results offer a first insight into changes over time. However, as mentioned above, it is necessary to control for factors that could be introducing important bias in these estimations. From previous analyses, we know that the INSP sample is not a fully randomized group, so we have controlled for differences between the groups using a multivariate model.

Multivariate analysis

Tables 7 to 12 present the results obtained from the different models specified for assessing Progresa's effect on diarrhoea and ARI. These tables include odds ratios, robust standard errors, the level of significance of each parameter, and the 95% confidence intervals. The odds ratios represent the change in the odds of being ill, in respect of children in the reference category, i.e. of children not receiving benefits at wave two. Hence, the reference group represents the situation that would prevail without intervention (the counter-factual situation).

The Programme's impact is estimated from comparison with the reference group and indicates the extent to which morbidity levels are better than they might have been in the absence of Progresa. The second model includes interaction terms (product of the value of two independent variables) to assess the impact of supplement 'intake' on this health outcome. In this model the interpretation of parameters is more elaborate: the parameter for *Progresa* shows the influence of living in a treatment locality at wave two; the parameter for *supplement* describes the impact of receiving this in-kind benefit at wave two (recall some non-beneficiary children received the supplement); and the interaction term (*Progresa* * *Supplement*) indicates the additional effect of living in a treatment locality and receiving supplements at wave two.

Diarrhoea

In table 7, the parameter estimates for Model 1 suggest that at wave two the odds of being ill with diarrhoea among beneficiary children are 0.68:1 – or 32 per cent lower than those of children in the control group (with a significance level of 0.04). Regarding changes over time, the parameter estim-ates for wave three indicate that the odds of being ill among children in control localities are 0.64:1 (or 36 per cent lower) at wave three compared with their experiences at wave two (with a p-value of 0.02). This result suggests that, once children living in control communities were incorporated into the Programme, their morbidity risks decreased at a somewhat similar rate to those of the treatment group during that group's first year of inter-vention. Moreover, the interaction effect of Progresa and wave three – which can be interpreted as the difference between the treatment and control groups at wave three – shows no significant differences between groups. In other words, the control children seem to catch up once they start receiving benefits. On the other hand, our estimates suggest that at wave three children in the treatment group[12] had lower morbidity levels (odds 0.45:1) than those experienced at wave two (odds 0.68:1), and lower levels than the control group at wave three (odds 0.64:1).

Figure 3 presents the predicted probabilities of Model 1. At wave two, the probability of being ill with diarrhoea among beneficiary children is 13 per cent, whereas that of non-beneficiary children is 18 per cent. The difference between the groups suggests a positive Programme effect. One year later, we observe that the probabilities decrease for both groups, but do so at a steeper rate among children in the control group. At wave three, the probability of

Table 7

Estimates of Progresa's effect on diarrhoea: longitudinal sample with observations in waves 2 and 3

| | Children 0–59 months | | | | | | | | Children 0–23 months | | | | Children 24–59 months | | | |
| | Model 1 | | | | Model 2 | | | | Model 1 | | | | Model 1 | | | |
	Odds ratios	z	P > |z|	[95% C.I.]	Odds ratios	z	P > |z|	[95% C.I.]	Odds ratios	z	P > |z|	[95% C.I.]	Odds ratios	z	P > |z|	[95% C.I.]
Progresa's benefits																
Progresa	0.68	−2.1	**	0.48 1.00	0.55	−2.4	**	0.35 0.93	0.88	−0.5		0.51 1.69	0.53	−2.5	**	0.32 0.90
	(0.13)				(0.14)				(0.26)				(0.14)			
Supplement					0.77	−0.7		0.40 1.61								
					(0.27)											
Progresa * Supplements					1.70	1.4		0.74 3.44								
					(0.67)											
Wave																
Wave 3	0.64	−2.4	**	0.44 0.92	0.61	−1.9	*	0.36 1.00	0.76	−0.9		0.41 1.44	0.52	−2.5	**	0.31 0.87
	(0.12)				(0.16)				(0.24)				(0.14)			
*Progresa * Wave*																
Progresa * Wave 3	1.02	0.1		0.61 1.71	0.81	−0.6		0.41 1.69	0.66	−0.1		0.30 1.42	1.52	1.1		0.72 3.08
	(0.27)				(0.29)				(0.26)				(0.57)			
*Supplement * Wave*																
Supplement * Wave 3					1.35	0.8		0.61 2.82								
					(0.53)											
Controls																
Individual characteristics	√				√				√				√			
Household characteristics	√				√				√				√			
Community characteristics	√				√				√				√			
Number of observations	1,988				1,988				843				1,145			
Wald chi²	81.9				89.3				47.7				75.4			
Pseudo R-sq	0.08				0.08				0.10				0.10			
Log pseudo-likelihood	−681.6				−702.5				−326.3				−357.4			

Notes: Statistical significance: *$p < 0.10$; **$p < 0.05$; ***$p < 0.01$.
Robust standard errors in parentheses.
All models include controls for individual household and community characteristics.

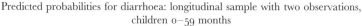

Figure 3

Predicted probabilities for diarrhoea: longitudinal sample with two observations, children 0–59 months

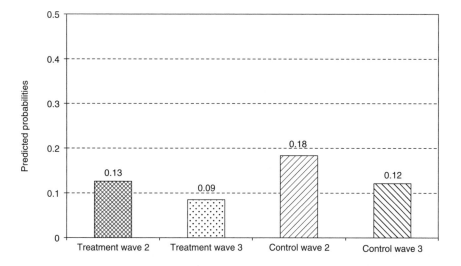

being ill with diarrhoea is 9 per cent among beneficiary children and 12 per cent among non-beneficiaries.

Results by age group show that the Programme effect is mainly due to a decrease in the morbidity risks of children in the older age category. Table 7 shows that the odds ratios corresponding to children under the age of two, though less than 1, are not statistically significant. Yet, the estimate for the treatment group at wave three (obtained from the combined effect of the different interaction terms) yields an odds ratio of 0.44:1, which is significantly different from the situation we would expect to observe without the intervention (the reference group). This suggests that Progresa's benefits – nutritional supplements and the monetary grant for food – are likely to have a larger impact on morbidity after the weaning period. Before this stage, breastfeeding protects children from exposure to infections from food products and other environmental factors.

Regarding children aged between 24 and 59 months old, the exponentiated coefficients and corresponding p-values provide evidence of an important Programme effect. At wave two, children living in Progresa localities have odds of being ill with diarrhoea of 0.53:1. At wave three, once control children receive benefits, their odds of being ill are 0.52:1. Additionally, at wave three, the treatment group presents smaller odds than those without the intervention (the reference group) (odds of 0.41:1), but this parameter is not significantly different from the odds at wave two or of the odds of the control group at wave three.

Results from Model 2 indicate that there is no evidence of a supplement effect on the probability of being ill with diarrhoea. Neither the p-values for the main effect of supplement nor its interaction with living in a Progresa locality suggest that children receiving this in-kind benefit were better off than those who did not receive it. In addition, the interaction between wave three and supplement (*Supplement * wave*) shows there is no additional effect of supplement intake at wave three. Hence, our results do not provide evidence of a positive impact on diarrhoea attributable to supplement intake.[13]

Table 8 displays the findings obtained for the longitudinal sample with complete information (observations in waves one, two and three). Estimates from children in this sample also indicate a positive Programme effect; yet, the magnitude of the odds ratios and the statistical significance of these parameters suggest larger and stronger differences between groups. However, the larger effect among children in this sample might be explained by the fact that our assessment took place when the great majority had passed the weaning period, i.e. the peak stage of diarrhoea (the children being aged between 12 and 47 months at wave two). Furthermore, some children in this sample had been exposed to the intervention during infancy, which perhaps enhanced a protective effect.

To control for possible pre-programme differences between groups we estimated Model 3 including a baseline health measure (height for age) as an additional covariate. The results from this model are quite similar to those obtained without including height for age as an explanatory variable. The odds ratios are slightly larger, suggesting smaller Programme effects once we control for this lagged health outcome. This suggests that our estimates could have slightly overestimated the Programme's effect, as a result of not having had a baseline measure.

Models 2 and 4, which include controls for supplement intake, show a pattern similar to that of the sample with two observations over time. That is, the parameter estimates for supplement intake, and the conjoint effect of Progresa and supplement are not statistically significant, suggesting no evidence of a supplement effect.

Respiratory infections

Here we obtained two consistent results (see table 9). First, it is clear from table 9 that, at wave two, children living in Progresa localities have reduced odds of illness compared with those in the control group (with odds ratios ranging between 0.83:1 and 0.50:1). Second, at wave three, beneficiary children have higher odds of being ill with ARI than those observed at wave two (with odds between 1.2:1 and 2.3:1), suggesting an increase in illness for children in the treatment group.

Estimates from Model 1 show that the odds of being ill with a respiratory infection at wave two among beneficiary children are 0.7 times (or 30 per cent lower) those of their control counterparts, and this effect is statistically significant (see table 9). On the other hand, unlike the case of diarrhoea, control children do not show significant reductions on ARI over time (as indicated by the parameter estimate of wave three). Moreover, as mentioned above, the interaction term of Progresa suggests an increase in morbidity risks at wave three for children in the treatment group. These trends are illustrated

Table 8

Estimates of Progresa's effect on diarrhoea: longitudinal sample with observations in waves 1, 2 and 3

Children 12–47 months

	Model 1				Model 2				Model 3				Model 4			
	Odds ratios	z	P > |z|	[95% C.I.]	Odds ratios	z	P > |z|	[95% C.I.]	Odds ratios	z	P > |z|	[95% C.I.]	Odds ratios	z	P > |z|	[95% C.I.]
Progresa's benefits																
Progresa	0.43 (0.13)	−2.9	***	0.24 0.76	0.32 (0.12)	−2.9	***	0.14 0.67	0.48 (0.14)	−2.5	**	0.27 0.86	0.36 (0.15)	−2.5	**	0.17 0.80
Supplement					0.91 (0.42)	−0.2		0.33 2.38					1.12 (0.54)	0.2		0.44 2.88
Progress * Supplements					1.63 (0.91)	0.9		0.56 5.55					1.36 (0.77)	0.6		0.45 4.13
Wave																
Wave 3	0.38 (0.11)	−3.4	***	0.22 0.67	0.40 (0.12)	−2.7	***	0.22 0.84	0.46 (0.13)	−2.7	***	0.26 0.81	0.50 (0.18)	−1.9	*	0.24 1.02
*Progresa * Wave*																
Progresa * Wave 3	2.22 (0.89)	2.0	**	1.02 4.78	2.05 (1.00)	1.5		0.77 5.43	1.69 (0.68)	1.3		0.77 3.74	1.82 (0.89)	1.2		0.70 4.75
*Supplement * Wave*																
Supplement * Wave 3	—				0.99 (0.55)	0.0		0.30 2.88					0.78 (0.44)	−0.4		0.26 2.39
Controls																
Individual characteristics	✓				✓				✓				✓			
Household characteristics	✓				✓				✓				✓			
Community characteristics	✓				✓				✓				✓			
HAZ_{t-1}	—				—				✓				✓			
Number of observations	967				967				893				893			
Wald chi^2	69.5				70.7				57.4				71.2			
Pseudo R-sq	0.11				0.12				0.13				0.12			
Log pseudo-likelihood	−301.2				−300.6				−229.8				−282.9			

Notes: Statistical significance: *p < 0.10; **p < 0.05; ***p < 0.01.
Robust standard errors in parentheses.
All models include controls for individual, household and community characteristics.

Table 9

Estimates of Progresa's effect on respiratory infections: longitudinal sample with observations in waves 2 and 3

| | Children 0–59 months | | | | | | | | Children 0–23 months | | | | Children 24–59 months | | | |
| | Model 1 | | | | Model 2 | | | | Model 1 | | | | Model 1 | | | |
	Odds ratios	z	P > |z|	[95% C.I.]	Odds ratios	z	P > |z|	[95% C.I.]	Odds ratios	z	P > |z|	[95% C.I.]	Odds ratios	z	P > |z|	[95% C.I.]
Progresa's benefits																
Progresa	0.70 (0.09)	−2.7	***	0.54 0.93	0.62 (0.10)	−2.8	***	0.46 0.89	0.83 (0.17)	−0.9		0.55 1.30	0.62 (0.11)	−2.7	***	0.43 0.88
Supplement					0.68 (0.17)	−1.6		1.05 2.63								
Progresa * Supplements					1.66 (0.39)	2.2	**	0.75 1.57								
Wave																
Wave 3	0.89 (0.13)	−0.8		0.66 1.16	1.10 (0.21)	0.5		0.71 1.88	1.08 (0.25)	0.4		0.65 1.63	0.77 (0.14)	−1.4		0.53 1.11
*Progresa * Wave*																
Progresa * Wave 3	1.46 (0.27)	2.1	**	1.02 2.11	1.17 (0.29)	0.6		0.40 1.08	1.18 (0.34)	0.6		0.65 2.06	1.74 (0.43)	2.3	**	1.07 2.80
*Supplement * Wave*																
Supplement * Wave 3					1.00 (0.24)	0.0		0.62 1.62								
Controls																
Individual characteristics	✓				✓				✓							
Household characteristics	✓				✓				✓							
Community characteristics	✓				✓				✓							
Number of observations	2,006				2,006				852				1,154			
Wald chi^2	90.6				97.9				45.0				77.0			
Pseudo R-sq	0.03				0.04				0.03				0.05			
Log pseudo-likelihood	−1,324.5				−1,324.4				−565.5				−748.5			

Notes: Statistical significance: *p < 0.10; **p < 0.05; ***p < 0.01.
Robust standard errors in parentheses.
All models include controls for individual, household and community characteristics.

Figure 4

Predicted probabilities for respiratory infections: longitudinal sample with two observations, children 0–59 months

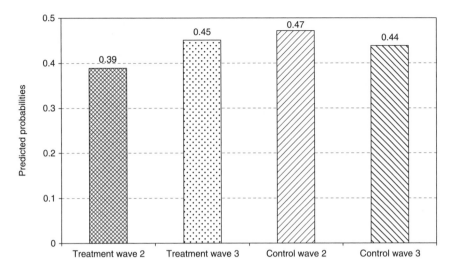

in figure 4. At wave three, the probability of being ill with respiratory infections among children in the treatment group was very similar to that observed in the absence of Progresa (as indicated by the probability among control children at wave two).

Comparing by age groups, we notice that Progresa's effect on ARI is significant only among children in the older age category. At wave two, the estimates for beneficiary children aged 24–59 months show that the odds of being ill with ARI are 38 per cent lower (odds of 0.62:1) than those of children in the control group. In contrast, the odds for children in the younger age group, despite being less than one (odds of 0.83:1), are not significantly different from those of the reference group. Hence, for this age group there is no evidence of a Programme effect.[14]

Regarding the impact of supplement 'intake' on ARI, models 2 and 4 provide some evidence of a positive effect. The odds ratio for the main effect of supplement is less than one in all models, but its p-value is significant only among the sample with complete information. It is not clear why the supplement shows a positive effect on ARI but does not show any effect on diarrhoea. If the supplement improves children's nutritional status, then it should have a positive effect on both kinds of diseases.

Impact according to household's severity of poverty

In order to examine for a possible difference in Progresa's effect according to background characteristics, we estimated Model 1 by household severity of poverty (measured using Progresa's own poverty index). We fitted these models for the sample with complete information as well as for the sample with only two observations over time; and we obtained similar results. For this reason, we only present the findings of the sample with at least two observations.

Tables 11 and 12 present our estimates for diarrhoea and respiratory infections, respectively. Note that our findings differ, depending on the outcome analysed. Whereas for diarrhoeal diseases the Programme has a significant positive effect among children in the most deprived households (first tercile); for respiratory infections the impact of the Programme is only significant among children in the mid-poverty category (second tercile). The odd result for ARI could once again reflect the fact that these data are more heavily influenced by mothers' perception of illness.[15]

It is possible that the Programme has a greater impact on children in the poorest families because, as other interventions have shown, the benefits provided are serving as a substitute for these families' lack of resources. For example, the information provided at the educational sessions might have effected greater improvements in the health care behaviours of mothers without formal education than on those of mothers who had had more years of schooling. This translates into a larger influence on the outcomes of the most disadvantaged children.

Conclusions

At baseline, child morbidity was very high in the rural localities under study. Almost half (47.7 per cent) of eligible children were reported as sick with some kind of illness during the two weeks prior to the survey. According to type of disease, 13.2 per cent were reported as ill with diarrhoea and 43.5 per cent with acute respiratory infections. These figures illustrate the poor health status of eligible children in rural areas. This is of particular concern because it is widely accepted that children with ill health are more likely to experience adverse outcomes later in life.

There is some evidence that Progresa contributes to reducing morbidity rates. After one year of Programme implementation, there was a significant positive difference between the outcomes of the treatment by comparison with the control group. In addition, two years after Programme implementation, once children living in control areas have been incorporated into the Programme, differences between the two groups are no longer evident. We find that for both the diseases under study, the Programme effect is mainly due to a decrease in the morbidity risks of children aged between 24 and 59 months. But the evidence of a Programme effect is stronger for diarrhoea than for ARI.

Regarding the incidence of diarrhoea, estimates from our multivariate models suggest that after one year of Progresa's operation, the odds of being ill with diarrhoea among beneficiary children under five are 32 per cent lower than those of their control peers. However, two years after Programme implementation we observe the control group catching up to a degree, but observe reduced improvements among the treatment group. With respect to

Table 10

Estimates of Progresa's effect on respiratory infections: longitudinal sample with observations in waves 1, 2 and 3

Children 12–47 months

	Model 1				Model 2				Model 3				Model 4			
	Odds ratios	z	P > |z|	[95% C.I.]	Odds ratios	z	P > |z|	[95% C.I.]	Odds ratios	z	P > |z|	[95% C.I.]	Odds ratios	z	P > |z|	[95% C.I.]
Progresa's benefits																
Progresa	0.55 (0.11)	−3.0	***	0.37 0.83	0.57 (0.15)	−2.1	**	0.33 0.95	0.50 (0.11)	−3.3	***	0.34 0.78	0.56 (0.16)	−2.1	**	0.32 0.97
Supplement					0.45 (0.17)	−2.2	**	0.21 0.92					0.45 (0.18)	−2.0	**	0.21 0.96
Progresa * Supplements					1.89 (0.64)	1.9	*	1.01 3.84					1.71 (0.61)	1.5		0.88 3.60
Wave																
Wave 3	0.72 (0.14)	−1.7	*	0.46 1.03	0.77 (0.20)	−1.0		0.46 1.26	0.71 (0.15)	−1.6		0.44 1.02	0.73 (0.20)	−1.2		0.41 1.20
*Progresa * Wave*																
Progresa * Wave 3	2.10 (0.55)	2.8	***	1.29 3.66	1.29 (0.46)	0.7		0.66 2.69	2.29 (0.63)	3.0	***	1.38 4.12	1.45 (0.53)	1.0		0.72 3.02
*Supplement * Wave*																
Supplement * Wave 3					1.75 (0.62)	1.6		0.85 3.40					1.81 (0.65)	1.7	*	0.89 3.64
Controls																
Individual characteristics	✓				✓				✓				✓			
Household characteristics	✓				✓				✓				✓			
Community characteristics	✓				✓				✓				✓			
HAZ_{t-1}	—				—				✓				✓			
Number of observations	974				974				900				664			
Wald chi²	50.3				55.6				49.4				66.9			
Pseudo R-sq	0.06				0.06				0.06				0.06			
Log pseudo-likelihood	−643.3				−640.5				−593.2				−461.5			

Notes: Statistical significance: *p < 0.10; **p < 0.05; ***p < 0.01.
Robust standard errors in parentheses.
All models include controls for individual, household and community characteristics.

Table 11

Estimates of Progresa's effect on diarrhoea by terciles of poverty

	Longitudinal sample with observations in waves 2 and 3											
	First tercile				Second tercile				Third tercile			
	Odds ratios	z	P > |z|	[95% C.I.]	Odds ratios	z	P > |z|	[95% C.I.]	Odds ratios	z	P > |z|	[95% C.I.]
Progresa's benefits												
Progresa	0.36 (0.15)	−2.5	**	0.17 0.83	0.84 (0.31)	−0.5		0.40 1.73	0.91 (0.13)	−0.3		0.47 1.85
Wave												
Wave 3	0.60 (0.21)	−1.5		0.31 1.26	1.02 (0.39)	0.1		0.49 2.18	0.56 (0.19)	−1.7	*	0.28 1.11
Progresa * Wave												
Progresa * Wave 3	1.61 (0.88)	0.9		0.53 4.55	0.55 (0.30)	−1.1		0.19 1.56	1.17 (0.51)	0.4		0.49 2.75
Controls												
Individual characteristics	✓				✓				✓			
Household characteristics	✓				✓				✓			
Community characteristics	✓				✓				✓			
Number of observations	567				571				690			
Wald chi^2	55.1				32.3				58.9			
Pseudo R-sq	0.14				0.08				0.11			
Log pseudo-likelihood	−179.8				−191.5				−240.6			

Notes: Statistical significance: *p < 0.10; **p < 0.05; ***p<0.01.
Robust standard errors in parentheses.
All models include controls for individual, household and community characteristics.

Table 12

Estimates of Progresa's effect on respiratory infections by terciles of poverty

| | Longitudinal sample with observations in waves 2 and 3 | | | | | | | | | | | |
| | First tercile | | | | Second tercile | | | | Third tercile | | | |
	Odds ratios	z	P > |z|	[95% C.I.]		Odds ratios	z	P > |z|	[95% C.I.]		Odds ratios	z	P > |z|	[95% C.I.]	
Progresa's benefits																
Progresa	0.82 (0.23)	−0.7		0.48	1.44	0.44 (0.12)	−3.1	***	0.24	0.71	0.92 (0.22)	−0.4		0.54	1.38
Wave																
Wave 3	1.78 (0.51)	2.0	**	0.95	3.02	0.64 (0.17)	−1.7	*	0.38	1.07	0.78 (0.20)	−1.0		0.46	1.25
*Progresa * Wave*																
Progresa * Wave 3	0.72 (0.27)	−0.9		0.35	1.51	2.77 (0.93)	3.0	***	1.45	5.80	1.44 (0.47)	1.1		0.77	2.88
Controls																
Individual characteristics	√					√					√				
Household characteristics	√					√					√				
Community characteristics	√					√					√				
Number of observations	567					600					700				
Wald chi²	64.0					69.2					0.0				
Pseudo R-sq	0.08					0.08					0.05				
Log pseudo-likelihood	−355.9					−374.2					−455.9				

Notes: Statistical significance: *p < 0.10; **p < 0.05; ***p < 0.01.
Robust standard errors in parentheses.
All models include controls for individual, household and community characteristics.

ARI, our results suggest a positive Programme effect at wave two among children aged between 24 and 59 months (odds of 0.62:1) and among children with complete information (odds of 0.50:1). Nonetheless, our estimates show important increases in the prevalence of ARI between waves two and three among children living in treatment localities. To be sure, this outcome should be treated with caution, since it is not clear whether these results reflect an increase in the actual levels of morbidity and/or reflect an increased awareness of the symptoms associated with respiratory infections.

For both the diseases under study, Progresa's impact was mainly reflected in a decrease in the morbidity risks of children aged between 24 and 59 months. The larger impact among children over two might be related to the fact that they had surpassed the weaning period, so they were at a stage when they were less susceptible to diarrhoea and other infectious diseases. The impact of supplement 'intake' shows different results according to illness. Whereas there is no evidence of a positive effect associated with supplements for diarrhoea, there is some evidence of an important influence of supplements on respiratory infections. However, due to the data constraints associated with ARI, the apparent supplement effect for this illness should again be treated with caution. With reference to the household's severity of poverty, the Programme has its greatest impact on reducing the chances of being ill with diarrhoea among children in the most deprived households. This finding suggests that Progresa's benefits are serving as a substitute for household lack of resources.

Meanwhile, the positive results observed in the first stages of the Programme have encouraged its spread into urban areas and into other countries, particularly in Latin America.[16] In 2002, Mexico's present administration transformed Progresa into a new programme named *Oportunidades*. This programme preserved the main characteristics of Progresa, but it broadened and adjusted its activities to meet the needs of the urban population.

Although we have observed some positive programme effects on child health, we believe it is important to increase the investment in preventive health measures addressed to the needs of children at an early age. Other studies have shown that resilience after the age of two is possible, but these studies have also found that this effect tends to fade away as interventions cease to operate (Myers 1992; Walker *et al.* 1996). Thus, in order to observe enduring effects, it is crucial for all the health-related activities to be sustained. The importance of the early years for influencing future achievements indicates that these programmes should augment their efforts to improve conditions for very young children.

Acknowledgements

I gratefully acknowledge the financial support received for this work from CONACYT and the ESRC Research Centre for Analysis of Social Exclusion (CASE) at the London School of Economics. I am also very thankful to Prof. John Hobcraft, Dr Wendy Sigle-Rushton, Dr Marta Mier y Teran and Dr Caroline Paskell for comments on an earlier version of this chapter. Needless to say, surviving errors remain my own.

Notes

1. Between 1990 and 2000, global trends indicate deaths from diarrhoeal diseases declined by 50 per cent (from around 3 million deaths a year to 1.5 million) (WHO 2001). In contrast, during this period, there are no accurate data to assess the performance of deaths from ARI. However, WHO's perspective is that there was a shortfall (WHO 2001). Furthermore, morbidity from these infectious diseases has remained relatively stable over time (Parashar *et al.* 2003; WHO 2003).
2. During the last decade, mortality rates related to diarrhoea decreased by 82 per cent (from 125.6 deaths per 100,000 children under the age of five to 22.1) and those attributable to ARI decreased by 61 per cent (from 115.7 deaths per 100,000 children to 44.7) (Zedillo 2000).
3. These figures include moderate and severe malnutrition according to height for age. Source: INSP, Encuesta Nacional de Nutrición, Mexico, 1999.
4. The Programme operates in all Mexican states except in the Distrito Federal.
5. For comparison purposes, throughout this thesis, we convert Mexico's currency (pesos) into US dollars using purchasing power parity rates (PPP). We use the PPP rates for Mexico published by the OECD (http://www.oecd.org/std/ppp/).
6. The states were Guerrero, Hidalgo, Michoacán, Puebla, Querétaro, San Luis Potosí and Veracruz.
7. During the sampling process, it was ensured that the INSP treatment group had not received benefits by August 1998.
8. The data show some reporting biases by household characteristics.
9. An indicator that comprises a set of dimensions associated with the exclusion process: educational level, access to basic services, quality of housing, degree of isolation among others. For further details, see CONAPO and Progresa, 1998.
10. The number of members in each cohort varies slightly across waves because the surveys were not collected at exactly the same months of the year.
11. We used a longitudinal discrete method that adjusts for the fact that some observations belong to the same individual. Stata uses the Huber/White sandwich estimator to adjust the standard errors for the fact that some observations belong to the same individual.
12. The value of Progresa at wave three is estimated by combining the main effect of living in a *Progresa* locality and *wave* of data collection, with the effect of their conjoint term (*Progresa*wave*).
13. We estimated Model 2 for both age groups under study and the parameter estimates were not significant either. Thus, we only present the findings for this model without disaggregating by age.
14. The parameter estimates for the sample with complete information show results that are consistent with those of the sample with two observations in time.
15. These findings were corroborated by running models with an interaction term between participating in Progresa and our poverty measure. The differences by severity of poverty were similar to those shown in tables 11 and 12.
16. Similar cash transfers are now operating in Honduras, Nicaragua, Brazil, Colombia, Jamaica, Chile, Ecuador, Turkey and South Africa.

References

Behrman, J. and Todd, P. E. (1999), *Randomness in the Experimental Sample of PROGRESA (Education, Health, and Nutrition Program)*, Washington, D.C.: International Food Policy Research Institute.

Burgess, S., Propper, C. and Rigg, J. A. (2004), The impact of low income on child health: evidence from a birth cohort study, *CASE Paper*, 85, London: LSE.

Case, A., Fertig, A. and Paxson, C. (2004), The lasting impact of childhood health and circumstance. *Working Papers*, Princeton, NJ: Center for Health and Wellbeing, Princeton University.

Case, A., Lubotsky, D. and Paxson, C. (2002), Economic status and health in childhood: the origins of the gradient, *American Economic Review*, 92, 5: 1308–34.

CONAPO and Progresa (1998), *Indices de Marginación, 1995*, México, D.F.: CONAPO and Progresa.

Fox, V. (2004), *Cuarto Informe de Gobierno*, Mexico, D.F.: Presidencia de la Republica.

Gertler, P. J. (2000), *Final Report: an Evaluation of the Impact of Progresa on Health Care Utilization and Health Status*, Washington, D.C.: International Food Policy Research Institute.

Gertler, P. J., Rivera Domarco, J., Levy, S. and Sepúlveda, J. (2004), Mexico's Progresa: using a poverty alleviation program incentive for poor families to invest in child health, UC Berkeley and Instituto Nacional de Salud Publica.

Gwatkin, D., Rutstein, S., Johnson, K., Pande, R. and Wagstaff, A. (2004), *Socio-Economic Differences in Health, Nutrition, and Population: 45 Countries*, Washington, D.C.: World Bank Poverty Net Library.

Mata, L. (1995), The Santa María Cauqué study: health and survival of Mayan Indians under deprivation, Guatemala. In N. S. Scrimshaw, *Community-based Longitudinal Nutrition and Health Studies: Classical Examples from Guatemala, Haiti and Mexico*, Boston, MA: UNU Press.

Myers, R. G. (1992), Relating child development to schooling and beyond. In R. G. Myers and Consultative Group on Early Childhood Care and Development, *The Twelve Who Survive: Strengthening Programmes of Early Childhood Development in the Third World*, London: Routledge in cooperation with UNESCO for the Consultative Group on Early Childhood Care and Development, pp. 209–62.

Parashar, U. D., Bresse, J. S. and Glass, R. I. (2003), The global burden of diarrhoeal disease in children, *Bulletin of the World Health Organization*, 81, 4: 236.

Scrimshaw, N. S. (2003), Historical concepts of interactions, synergism and antagonism between nutrition and infection, *Journal of Nutrition*, 133: 316S–21S.

Secretaría de Salud (2004), Infecciones respiratorias agudas, *Panorama Epidemiológico 1990–2000*, México, D.F.: Secretaría de Salud. 2004.

SEDESOL (1999), *Lineamientos Generales para la Operación del Programa de Educación, Salud y Alimentación (PROGRESA)*, Documento de Divulgación, Diario Oficial de la Federación.

Singer, B. H. and Ryff, C. D. (2001), *New Horizons in Health*, Washington, D.C.: National Academy Press.

Smith, K., Samet, J., Romieu, I. and Bruce, N. (2000), Indoor air pollution in developing countries and acute lower respiratory infections in children, *Thorax*, 55, 6: 518–32.

Victora, C. (1999), Risk factors for acute lower respiratory infections. Y. Benguigui, F. J. L. Antuñano, G. Schmunis and J. Yunes, *Respiratory Infections in Children*, Washington, D.C.: Pan American Health Organization.

Walker, S., Grantham-McGregor, S., Himes, J., Powell, C. and Chang, S. (1996), Early childhood supplementation does not benefit the long-term growth of stunted children in Jamaica, *Journal of Nutrition*, 126, 12: 3017–24.

WHO (2001), WHO's contribution to the report for the follow-up to the world summit for children. In *Preparation for the UN General Assembly Special Session on Children, September 2001*, Department of Child and Adolescent Health and Development.

WHO (2003), *World Health Report*, Geneva: World Health Organization.

Wolfe, B. L. and Behrman, J. R. (1982), Determinants of child mortality, health, and nutrition in a developing country, *Journal of Development Economics*, 11: 163–93.

World Bank (2004), *Millennium Development Goals*, Washington, D.C.: World Bank.

Zedillo, E. (2000), *Sexto Informe de Gobierno*, México, D.F.: Presidencia de la República. 2004.

6

Rurality and Social Inclusion: A Case of Preschool Education

Mark Shucksmith, Janet Shucksmith and Joyce Watt

Introduction

Social exclusion and inclusion are chaotic and contested terms, in both academic and policy circles. This chapter aims to bring some clarity to this topic by reviewing the principal ways in which the term has been used by researchers, and then by exploring these perspectives in an empirical study of the provision of preschool education in rural areas of Scotland.[1]

Publicly funded educational provision for preschool children in most of rural Scotland has always been minimal, and the pattern has been quite different to that in urban areas. Preschool education has never been a statutory service, so until very recently it flourished mainly in traditionally Labour-dominated urban areas, where it has been part of the battle against educational and economic disadvantage. In most rural areas the gap has been plugged since the 1960s by the voluntary sector, mainly the preschool playgroup movement. For example, in 1996, as a rate per 1,000 population of under-5s, in Argyll and Bute 323 children were catered for in playgroups but only 21 in state nursery schools or classes; in Highland 231 were catered for in playgroups, and 62 in nursery schools and classes; and in the Western Isles 471 children were catered for in playgroups but none at all in local authority schools or classes (Scottish Office 1998a).

The situation began to change in 1996 when the Conservative government launched a voucher scheme in four pilot areas of Scotland, offering a part-time preschool place for every child if there was available provision. In 1997 the incoming Labour government transformed the position by pledging to provide a good-quality place in preschool education for every 4-year-old in Scotland by 1998 and for every 3-year-old by 2002 where parents wanted it (Scottish Office 1998b, 1999). Funding for this was given to local authorities, who were expected to work in partnership with the voluntary and private sectors. The stated rationale for this policy was that intervention in the preschool years is the most effective means of addressing the reproduction of social exclusion across generations (Waldfogel 1998; Sparkes and Glennerster

2002). The concept of social inclusion/exclusion is therefore at the heart of this initiative.

Contested Conceptualizations of Social Exclusion

The term 'social exclusion' is often deployed loosely to cover such a broad range of meanings that its analytical clarity is dissipated (Peace 2001). Yet the term is found at the heart of political agendas in Britain and Europe: the Lisbon summit committed all EU member states to promote social cohesion and inclusion.

Burchardt *et al.* (2002) argue that recent usage of the term 'social exclusion' originated in France. At first, the term referred to those administratively excluded by the state (Lenoir 1974; Duffy 1997) but was soon extended to disaffected youth and isolated individuals living in the peripheral urban housing estates. The latter was seen also as a form of spatial exclusion. Later French and European thinking moved the focus away from administrative exclusion by the state towards a concern with unemployment and labour market exclusion (Paugam 1995), and especially to the impacts of globalization and neo-liberalism on individuals and social groups. Byrne (1999: 128) has gone further, portraying social exclusion as 'a necessary and inherent characteristic of unequal post-industrial capitalism founded around a flexible labour market'. To him, the socially excluded are a reserve army of labour in the Marxist sense, continually changing places.

These two variations, seeing social exclusion as administrative exclusion by the state or labour market exclusion through late capitalist restructuring, have been generalized further by various authors, including Commins (1993), Berghman (1995), Philip and Shucksmith (2003) and Reimer (2004). Reimer, reformulating Polanyi's (1944) three 'modes of economic integration', proposed that processes of social inclusion/exclusion operate through four systems:

1. market relations, or private systems
2. bureaucratic relations, or state administrative systems
3. associative relations, i.e. collective action processes based on shared interests
4. communal relations, based on shared identity, among family and friends networks

These 'represent four relatively coherent ways in which people organise their relationships to accomplish tasks, legitimise their actions, allocate resources, and structure their interactions. Exclusion and inclusion can occur with respect to any or all of these types of relationships, simultaneously creating both distributional and relational manifestations of the problem' (Reimer 2004: 78). One's sense of belonging in society, as well as one's purchase on resources, depends on all these systems. Reimer has seen these four systems not only as the underlying dimensions of social exclusion but also as dimensions of individuals' and communities' capacity to act

These approaches contrast with an 'American' focus on 'underclass', 'marginalization' and 'ghettoization' (Burchardt *et al.* 2002: 2). The fundamental difference lies in who is doing the excluding in these models: while 'European' social exclusion approaches tend to highlight the role of institutions and systems, or perhaps of more powerful individuals and groups in society, 'the central tenet of "the underclass" argument is that miserable conditions are self-induced – the poor do it to themselves' (Byrne 1999: 1) through their moral failings. In addition to deviant behaviour (notably drug-taking and crime) and a dependency culture, the blame is also placed on benefit systems which encourage such dependency and deviance.

A further distinct approach, deriving from the UN Development Programme, has been to conceptualize social exclusion as a lack of recognition of basic rights, or at least a 'lack of access to political and legal systems necessary to make those rights a reality' (Burchardt et al. 2002: 3). Such a perspective may be related to Marshallian citizenship, conceived as civil, political and social rights. Jordan (1996: 85) identifies a danger inherent in this perspective when he dismisses 'the analysis of poverty and social exclusion in terms of citizenship, especially within the liberal tradition' because of 'the narrow focus of this concept on individual rights and responsibilities, at the expense of interdependency and collective action'. Byrne (1999) advocates, in contrast, Teague and Wilson's (1995) 'solidaristic' conception of social exclusion and inclusion. This

> places much more emphasis on the idea of collective good and on the social duties and responsibilities of individuals. The idea that citizenship is simply some kind of legal status that confers on individuals certain rights against the state is rejected as impoverished. Individuals are regarded as only being fully enriched through social cooperation and in circumstances where they play an active role in public life and abide by community norms and rules. (Teague and Wilson 1995: 93; cited in Byrne 1999)

This focus on access to political and legal systems, and to basic education and health services, and on Marshall's 'right to participate', let alone the civil republican conception of citizenship as social cooperation and active participation, has led many to place emphasis on participation as a central element of social inclusion. Of course, exercising the right to participate is quite different from holding that right. Hayward et al. (2004: 105), for example, have noted that non-participation and peripheral participation are perfectly valid and legitimate choices exercised by community members, and 'not necessarily evidence of social exclusion or a lack of empowerment'. This reveals a basic contradiction between individualist and communitarian conceptions of social exclusion in terms of rights,[2] and this may also be related to discussions of individual and collective conceptions of social capital (Shucksmith 2000).

In this section, we have reviewed a number of different ways of conceptualizing social exclusion, the most notable of which are: (1) systemic explanations deriving from France and the EU, couched at first in terms of administrative exclusion from the state's social contract or in terms of labour market exclusion, and then generalized more comprehensively by Reimer in terms of four systems through which resources are allocated in society; (2) 'underclass' explanations deriving from the USA, which regard exclusion as self-induced within the framework of inappropriately generous welfare systems which encourage dependency; and (3) explanations deriving from the UNDP which emphasize issues of discrimination and a lack of enforced rights. A fundamental difference between these approaches is who or what is considered to be 'doing' the excluding: the system (institutions or markets), individuals themselves, or powerful elites. Another crucial axis of difference is between individualist and communitarian conceptions of social exclusion: individual rights and capabilities as against collective action and social responsibilities. The next section seeks to illuminate these perspectives further through empirical enquiry.

Preschool Education in Rural Scotland

Research on the provision and use of education services might be expected to focus on administrative aspects of exclusion by the state, while perhaps also revealing deviant morals on the part of parents who choose not to include their children in this system. However, as will be seen, many broader issues are also unexpectedly raised. This study of the provision of preschool education in rural areas of Scotland employed mixed methods, including analysis and mapping of available statistics on the distribution of preschool children and of the preschool places provided in 1998. Alongside this, a range of qualitative techniques was employed, including telephone interviews with local authority officers and providers throughout rural Scotland, and five detailed case studies which explored not only models of provision but also parents' and providers' perspectives on these issues. More details are available in Copus et al. (2000).

The statistical analysis identified a gap between the numbers of eligible preschool children and the provision of preschool places, which became systematically greater with remoteness. In school catchments beyond 15 miles from urban settlements the number of funded preschool places was less than half of the estimated number of 4-year-olds, with only 843 places for 1,757 children. While this may not affect many of Scotland's preschool children, it does lead to restricted opportunities in these remoter areas and the small numbers add to the difficulties of cost-effective provision. In rural areas within two miles of towns, children have similar choices to those in urban areas so long as a two-mile journey is considered acceptable. In the intermediate rural areas, two to fifteen miles from urban settlements, costs increase as groups become smaller, while children face lengthy journeys and parents incur considerable transport costs. Moreover, there is a risk that some children may be unable to attend because of transport difficulties and costs and because of clashes of nursery times with older siblings' school times and parents' employment. There is also likely to be less choice available. In the remoter areas, so few children may be available that groups are very small and distant, exacerbating many of the educational, social and financial costs, and making full-service flexible options or teacher input non-viable.

The telephone interviews revealed both a rapidly changing situation and a huge variation in the practices of local authorities across rural Scotland.

They differed not only in their actions but also in the principles that governed their actions, their perceptions of the nature and importance of issues such as travel and staffing, and in the ways in which they interpreted government guidelines. Some of the recent responses to the changed policy environment for preschoolers are innovative, and are geared specifically to rural areas. The sorts of new arrangements typically put in place included opening new local authority centres in towns to serve several adjacent rural communities and expecting children to travel to these; providing peripatetic outreach for a few sessions each week; and catering for preschool children within a composite first-year class at a nearby primary school. Innovations in direct provision were most necessary in areas with small numbers of preschool children, and these tended to be the remoter rural areas.

Accessing 'entitlements' in preschool education?

Both parents and providers viewed access to funded preschool education as an entitlement. The central and local states clearly have a role, along with the voluntary sector, in the provision of preschool education in rural areas. The promotion of inclusion expressed as an entitlement is a government commitment across all aspects of Scottish social policy: 'individuals and groups should not be excluded by virtue of poverty, race, gender, disability or other discriminatory aspects of lifestyle from the opportunities to which all citizens are entitled' (Scottish Office 1999). Policies for the inclusion of children from disadvantaged backgrounds in preschool education have long been taken for granted, but have largely been associated with deprived urban areas and children with 'special needs'. While the issue of how to include children from the most vulnerable families is still highly relevant, inclusion in the context of rural areas has also to consider whether rural children and families get the provision to which they are 'entitled' in terms of both physical access and quality services on the same terms as their urban counterparts.

A first question was whether children were attending groups in the areas we looked at. On our evidence, there were a very few families which did not want to take up a funded place at all. We were told that, despite persuasive arguments from primary schools and preschool leaders, these parents were adamant that children's needs were best met within their families. Barry (2002) and others have discussed the thorny issue of self-exclusion, arguing that such choices may be viewed as socially isolating but can hardly be seen as social exclusion where there truly is an opportunity to participate. Where choice is exercised in accordance with parental preferences, the choice of non-participation is not evidence of social exclusion (although it may weaken social solidarity). It is also important to note that those exercising this choice in our study areas could hardly be viewed as an underclass, and that their view that preschool children's needs are best met within families tends not to be seen as moral deviance in British society.

There were also parents who rejected the funded provision on offer because the form of provision was not what they wanted or were able to access. These included those who might have opted for a funded place but did not want the five (half-day) sessions which, in their area, was the only pattern on offer; those who, for a range of reasons, preferred a non-partnered group; and those whose basic need was for childcare and who therefore used a regular childminder and a funded place only once or twice a week. Issues arise here of the extent to which choice is itself an entitlement, and this is returned to below. Where choice is circumscribed, for example by an unmet need for childcare, can the offer of a part-time preschool place constitute entitlement?

Some parents wanted a full entitlement that was not available to them. For example, in some more remote areas fewer than five half-day sessions a week were offered to children, and in some areas, where families had no transport of their own, they had to be content with the number of sessions for which transport could be provided. Others, although they wanted funded places, had no access to them at all because of transport problems or because their overwhelming need was for childcare. Looking to the future, a number of parents doubted whether they would be able to access their full entitlement for 3-year-olds when their present preschool child (the older sibling) had started primary school because of high transport costs and the severe practical difficulties raised by the uncoordinated hours of preschool groups and primary schools. These are clear instances of social exclusion in terms of a lack of access to basic educational services, and are systemic, in terms of administrative exclusion by the state.

Obviously, issues of transport lie at the heart of problems of inclusion in service provision in rural areas. Ironically, the immediate problems in our study areas were sometimes less in the most remote areas, where personal transport was always necessary, and more in the small settlements where families could access a local shop or primary school without a car but were unable to reach preschool provision set up at some distance to service a number of small communities. Families in every area saw public transport as useless for the purpose (only one family throughout the five case study areas used it), but costs for personal transport could involve very real personal sacrifices, given the particularly high costs of fuel in rural areas, the distances and the double journeys involved. In a recent study of car ownership in rural Scotland Farrington et al. (1998) identify four groups as having significant actual or potential problems if car use/ownership is threatened by increased costs: the elderly, young mothers, job-seekers and those on low incomes. Shucksmith et al. (1996) also point out that while car ownership is higher among the rural poor than among the urban poor, car ownership/use in rural areas may in itself be a cause of deprivation because of its additional financial drain on the family's resources.

A few local authorities commissioned nursery buses to transport children from outlying areas to a central facility. In one case the local authority was willing to provide transport for those unable to provide it for themselves. There were also examples of parents themselves commissioning taxis. A fuel allowance for those who lived beyond a certain distance and who transported their own and other people's children was suggested.

Not surprisingly, parents and providers in the present study felt strongly that access to funded preschool education was an entitlement which should not be obscured by transport issues. In a climate where educational opportunities were seen as increasingly important, problems of access, particularly where the high cost of car ownership and use was the fundamental factor, would be most discriminatory against the already disadvantaged and might also be yet another factor contributing to the depopulation of the more remote areas. The importance of suitable subsidized transport cannot be overemphasized if the aims of social inclusion policies are to be met in this context.

However, while costs are important, they are not the only issue. There were many in our study who disliked the idea of very young children travelling long distances regularly without their parents. This is a matter for individual judgement but, on the evidence of the case studies, some who initially disliked the idea of the nursery bus later found that children enjoyed the journey because it was carefully planned as an integral part of the preschool group experience and was shared with adults who would spend the rest of the day with them. It has to be said, however, that some children could not cope.

A further crucial point in relation to the 'inclusion' of children is the quality of the educational service provided. Are rural children, particularly those in the most remote areas, being 'included' on the same terms and on comparable conditions to those in more populated areas or are they getting the 'second-class service' which some had predicted would be their lot (Stephen et al. 1998; Howe et al. 1998)? This debate revolves round access to professional teachers and is one to which we return below in our discussion of quality.

It is appropriate to highlight at this point the opportunities in terms of social inclusion opened up by two multi-purpose centres found in our case study areas, one in operation, another planned. These multi-purpose preschool education centres with their extended day care and their flexible hours open up employment opportunities for women and, on some models, provide opportunities for adult education as well as health and other social services. Centres such as these are not new, but existing centres are associated more with urban than with rural areas. Our research found that many parents in rural areas were sceptical about their ability to access their full entitlement for 3- and 4-year-olds while also continuing their own engagement in the labour market (a central pillar of UK welfare policy). It is ironic that attempts to improve inclusion among preschoolers should inadvertently exclude their parents from full participation in the labour market, unless these isolated instances of provision of preschool facilities embedded in wrap-around care arrangements become generally available.

In relation to preschool education in rural Scotland, then, there is no evidence to support 'underclass'-type explanations for social exclusion. Rather, it is apparent that the issues arising are systemic, relating in particular to distance, transport costs, the high costs of providing for small dispersed populations, and issues of quality of provision. These tended to be viewed by parents as features which the state had an obligation to overcome to provide their children with their entitlement to high-quality preschool education. Such views are consistent both with the UNDP conceptualization of social exclusion as a lack of access to basic entitlements, and equally with the systemic approaches, which see social exclusion in terms of spheres of integration, and administrative exclusion by the state.

Individualized and collective aspects of preschool education in rural Scotland

Quality of provision is a central issue. In an analysis of quality in preschool settings, Moss and Pence (1994) argue that defining quality is a political process, although it is sometimes treated purely as the application of scientific, managerial or professional expertise or 'consumer' preference (1994: 5). For them (1994: 172), definitions of quality in preschool education should go well beyond the consumer–producer relationship, which is essentially private and individualistic, and open up the process in an 'inclusionary paradigm' where the whole community has the chance to be involved. Here we consider 'quality' in both these senses, looking in turn at the positions of children, parents and communities.

First, we consider quality for *children*. Here there seemed to be some consensus: children should be in a safe environment which was conducive to promoting child 'care' as well as learning. Learning should be broadly based, it should be fun and free from pressure but should have a strong 'educational' component in the preschool year; children's rights to inclusion and equality should be promoted; staff should be enthusiastic, responsive to individual children's needs and should be good managers. As far as possible, preschool provision should be local and should link to children's lives and experiences outside the group. Parents recognized the importance of their children developing both personal and social skills, and indeed the isolation of children in sparsely populated areas suggested a particular need for preschool education to help develop their social and communication skills. This adds a collective dimension to their education.

There was, however, no consensus on the quality associated with some of the structural features of preschool education. There were wide variations among both parents and providers on whether using a number of groups or flexible sessions and hours enhanced or detracted from quality for children. Some argued strongly for the diversity of mixed age groups, others for dedicated time particularly for 3- and 4-year-olds. There was also uncertainty about any link between quality and group size, or quality and distance travelled: nor was there consensus on when a group became too small or too large, or on when distance travelled began to detract from the benefits of preschool education.

While most agreed in principle that preschool should link to primary education, there were varied reactions to the need for children in their preschool year to mix with their primary school peer group, although some did feel strongly about this. Perhaps most significantly, there was no consensus on the link between the employment of a professional teacher and the quality of a child's preschool experience. While most professionals and many parents linked the two strongly, some parents, particularly those whose experience was largely in the voluntary sector, thought personal qualities of commitment and enthusiasm, as they saw them reflected in the people they knew, were much more important. Again, this might be related to individualistic and collectivist conceptions of education itself. On the other hand, there were those parents also identified in the research on preschool vouchers (Stephen *et al.* 1998) who feared that rural areas might be allocated what they saw as a 'second-class' service, one bereft of teachers, and they were willing to travel long distances for the quality which they assumed teachers and a local authority service would provide.

Quality for *parents*, as they themselves saw it, was overwhelmingly about being confident to leave their child happy and secure. With that reassurance, parents had the freedom to relax and meet other commitments – to other members of the family, to employers, to other members of the community, and to themselves. Where preschool provision was the result of their own active choice, reflected their family lifestyle and coordinated with meeting other needs, parents perceived it as having 'quality' for them.

Much more debatable was the link between the quality of a group and the opportunities it provided for active parent involvement. There was plenty of the kind of evidence identified by Howe *et al.* (1998) that parents valued the social opportunities for themselves provided by preschool groups, particularly voluntary groups. It was significant, however, that many who had experienced both the voluntary and public sectors saw them as legitimately different in the ways they included parents, and they did not look to be included in local authority groups in the same way. A few parents from remote areas did, however, mention the stimulus to themselves of meeting families from other areas when they met at a preschool group in a larger, more central, location and a few also mentioned feeling cut off from their child's experiences where the child was transported by bus or by another family.

There is plenty of popular evidence, particularly from the voluntary sector, that preschool groups do play an important part in opening up social opportunities for young women in rural areas and there is also ample evidence of the power of parent involvement in urban groups. Both social networks and other forms of social capital can develop around a preschool facility. Our evidence is, however, very limited on how far parents can be or want to be involved in local authority preschool groups in rural areas. At the very least they want to know about their children and to share their own knowledge of their child with those who run the group. Because of all the practical difficulties of access, and some of the apparent assumptions about local authority preschool groups as relatively 'parent-free' zones, this may be difficult to achieve in any effective way.

Our fieldwork has shown clearly that, with the development of more 'professional' centres in rural areas, as elsewhere, the opportunities for parents to be 'included' through their involvement in preschool centres have generally diminished. This is a complex issue and again one to which we shall return below in our discussion of 'choice', where the particular implications for rural communities are discussed.

While quality for children is at the heart of preschool education and quality for parents impinges on that, quality for *communities* is a spin-off from both. In our fieldwork, few spoke directly of the contribution of preschool education to community life in rural areas but there were many implicit references to it. For example, we were told that a preschool group could be a stimulus to the community, it could encourage volunteering, it could nurture and develop management skills, it could bring different generations of adults together with children, it could provide training and employment opportunities and it could provide networks of friendship and common interests within the local community and beyond. These benefits accrue not only to the community but also to the individual. One example was the claim by a rural GP that, since a rural centre for preschool education and care had opened, she had noticed a marked drop in mental health problems in young women. Such a claim, if true, must have major positive effects not just on the women themselves but on children and families and on the wider community.

The form of the preschool provision was important in terms of the community impacts. Some saw (voluntary or private) partner provision as evidence of abdication by the local authority of its responsibilities for preschool education in rural areas, and as further evidence of urban bias. Most respondents indeed favoured local authority provision. On the other hand, some (especially in the Western Isles) recognized the increased potential in voluntary provision for parents to be involved in the management, so developing their own skills (individual and community capacity-building) as well as improving local accountability and participation. Such a voluntary group may also act as a social centre for rural parents, integrating newcomers into the community as well as helping to overcome the social isolation of mothers at home. These parents wanted to retain local playgroups, often because of their community roots, their past contribution, and the opportunities afforded for parents to be involved. Some wanted to use a combination of both types of provision.

One thing that emerged clearly in this research was that an important dimension of quality for everyone is that they have in some way played an active role in defining their local provision, whether through a consultative process, through the exercise of personal choice in how it is used, or through active personal involvement. As noted above, the definition of quality is necessarily a political process and this may have a particular significance for rural areas.

First, the very diversity of rural areas makes the need to consult those who live in them and to understand their idiosyncrasies even more urgent, and these may change quickly because of the small numbers. Second, the interdependence of quality for children, families and communities may be particularly important in rural areas where options for alternatives will be limited and where compromise between the different claims of financial, social and educational aims is inevitable. This necessitates a continuing renegotiation of needs, definitions of quality, and of appropriate responses. Third, in rural areas, much more than in urban areas, the actions and choices of one group, even of individuals, may have profound effects on others.

Indeed, it was apparent in the study areas that attempts to provide choice for one set of parents had already diminished choice for others. This was evident in the necessity for the authority in the Sutherland and Western Isles case study areas to take into account the desire of some parents for Gaelic-medium provision for their children. The provision of choice for this group eroded the resources available for other groups and also reduced the pool of children available to keep existing local preschool groups viable. The same problem arose in the Killin area, where the provision of a centralized nursery for people who required extended care facilities had diminished the pool of children available for some of the local village playgroups, and has brought some of them close to extinction, thus inadvertently reducing choice for those parents who would wish their child to use a more local facility. The same threat lay over the effect that the proposed new all-day nursery in North Uist would have on the local *Croileagan*. Similarly, the loss of 3- and 4-year-olds to preschool provision in primary schools has threatened the viability of existing voluntary providers.

Of course, preschool groups will not necessarily be a focus of consensus. Consultation processes are as liable to lead to conflict as to consensus, but – well handled – they can be a very positive means of moving forward for the community as well as the individual stakeholders. In short, at its best, preschool education can be a focal point for community development and hence for social inclusion in a collectivist sense, as well as contributing to the social inclusion of the individual children themselves. In two of our study areas this was already acknowledged.

Discussion and Conclusion

This chapter began by summarizing a number of the ways in which social exclusion and inclusion have been conceived in the literature. In terms of agency and fundamental causes, three broad schools of thought were discerned: explanations which place individuals' behaviour and moral values at the centre; those which highlight the role of institutions and systems (such as the welfare state, late capitalism or globalization); and those which emphasize issues of discrimination and a lack of enforced rights. In the case of preschool education in rural areas of Scotland, we found no evidence that exclusion derives from individuals' deviant behaviour and moral failings.

On the contrary, our evidence highlighted the role of institutions and systems in social inclusion and exclusion, particularly administrative exclusion by the state, in so far as access to this basic educational service is frustrated or diluted by distance, transport costs, the high costs of providing for small, dispersed populations, and concerns about quality of provision. Moreover, the continuing renegotiation of needs, of definitions of quality, and of appropriate responses was rarely a priority for local authority providers and funders. But social exclusion goes well beyond these administrative aspects and must also be seen in the broader social context of late capitalism and the risk society, within which the provision of basic education (particularly in the preschool years) is seen as fundamental to promoting greater equality of future life-chances and enabling active citizenship. Inequalities of access to, and quality of, preschool education may therefore generate unequal capacities in relation to all four of Reimer's systems of inclusion. An additional and unexpected aspect of this was the incompatibility experienced by many families between the attendance of their children at preschool groups and the mother's labour market participation, as a result of high transport costs and the uncoordinated hours of preschool groups and primary schools. Ironically, the likelihood of child poverty and detachment from labour markets may thus be increased by the manner in which a social inclusion measure is implemented in rural areas.

Multidimensional conceptualizations of social exclusion and inclusion, such as Reimer's, also appear better able to capture the interconnectedness of the many different dimensions of service provision, transport, childcare, labour market participation, and community engagement which characterize the experience of preschool education in rural Scotland. Such a multidimensional framework allows us to consider the complex interactions between bureaucratic, associative, communal and market relations within particular social contexts which give rise to exclusion.

Our analysis also provides some evidence in line with the third school of thought, that is, those who view exclusion in terms of discrimination and a lack of enforced rights. The much lower levels of provision of preschool places relative to numbers of children in remote areas, the greater difficulties of transport and cost, and especially the suspicion that children in rural areas were receiving a second-class service, with fewer teachers, were all seen as evidence of urban bias by some respondents. Policies are often thought to discriminate against rural populations, if only through ignorance and oversight, and several European states have introduced procedures of 'rural-proofing' in explicit recognition of this. Certainly, if there is a lower quality, or diminished choice, in public service provision in rural areas, then this might be seen as a lack of enforced rights. This is not at all incompatible with a systemic explanation, of course. Reimer (2004: 79) notes that a 'critical feature of [administrative or bureaucratic] relations is the explicit or implicit articulation of rights and entitlements', and a discourse of entitlements was a notable aspect of our respondents' representation of these issues.

Finally, this chapter has sought to explore the implications of preschool educational provision not only for individuals but also for rural communities. Our evidence illustrates some of the ways in which inclusion may not merely be individualized but also has consequences for communities. Thus, a preschool group could encourage volunteering, it could nurture and develop management skills, it could bring different generations of adults together with children, it could help to integrate newcomers, it could provide training and employment opportunities and it could provide networks of friendship and common interests within the local community and beyond. Our research has also shown how individual decisions, taken together, may diminish choice for others within the locality. Finally, our empirical data and analysis lead us to endorse the adoption of an inclusionary paradigm whereby the whole community is involved in definitions of quality in preschool education, so going beyond the consumer–producer relationship, which is essentially private and individualistic, to reflect the essentially political and social nature of these decisions.

Notes

1. Andrew Copus, Scott Petrie, Janet Shucksmith, Mark Shucksmith, Maggie Still and Joyce Watt (2000), *Preschool Educational Provision in Rural Areas*, A Report to the Scottish Executive Education Department, Arkleton Centre for Rural Development Research, University of Aberdeen, Occasional Paper no. 1. The research was funded by the Scottish Executive Education Department and was undertaken between 1998 and 2000.

2. Byrne (1999) himself argues that there is a tension in the UNDP reports between liberal and collectivist conceptions.

References

Barry, B. (2002), Social exclusion, social isolation and the distribution of income. In J. Hills, J. Le Grand and D. Piachaud (eds), *Understanding Social Exclusion*, Oxford: Oxford University Press.

Berghman, J. (1995), Social exclusion in Europe: policy context and analytical framework. In G. Room (ed.), *Beyond the Threshold*, Bristol: Policy Press.

Burchardt, T., Hills, J. and Le Grand, J. (2002), Introduction. In J. Hills, J. Le Grand and D. Piachaud (eds), *Understanding Social Exclusion*, Oxford: Oxford University Press.

Byrne, D. (1999), *Social Exclusion*, Buckingham: Open University Press.

Commins, P. (1993), *Combating Exclusion in Ireland 1990–94: A Midway Report to the European Commission*, Brussels: European Commission.

Copus, A., Petrie, S., Shucksmith, J., Shucksmith, M., Still, M. and Watt, J. (2000), *Preschool Educational Provision in Rural Areas*, A Report to the Scottish Executive Education Department, Occasional Paper no. 1, Arkleton Centre for Rural Development Research, University of Aberdeen.

Duffy, K. (1997), *Review of the International Dimension of the Thematic Priority on Social Inclusion and Exclusion*, Report to the ESRC, Swindon: ESRC.

Farrington, J., Gray, D., Martin, S. and Roberts, D. (1998), *Car Dependence in Rural Scotland*, Central Research Unit, Edinburgh: Scottish Office.

Hayward, C., Simpson, L. and Wood, L. (2004), Still left out in the cold: problematising participatory research and development, *Sociologia Ruralis*, 44, 1: 95–108.

Howe, C., Foot, H., Cheyne, B., Terras, M. and Rattray, C. (1998), *Parents and Preschool Provision: Preferences, Involvement and General Satisfaction*, Glasgow: University of Strathclyde, Department of Psychology.

Jordan, B. (1996), *A Theory of Poverty and Social Exclusion*, Cambridge: Polity Press.

Lenoir, R. (1974), *Les Exclus*, Paris: Seuil.

Marshall, T. H. (1952), *Citizenship and Social Class*, Cambridge: Cambridge University Press.

Moss, P. and Pence, A. (1994), *Valuing Quality in Early Childhood Services: New Approaches to Defining Quality*, London: Paul Chapman.

Nussbaum, M. and Sen, A. (1993), *The Quality of Life*, Oxford: Clarendon Press.

Parkinson, M. (1998), *Combating Social Exclusion: Lessons from Area-based Programmes in Europe*, Bristol: Policy Press.

Paugam, S. (1995), The spirit of precariousness: a multidimensional approach to the process of social disqualification in France. In G. Room (ed.), *Beyond the Threshold*, Bristol: Policy Press.

Peace, R. (2001), Social exclusion: a concept in need of definition? *Social Policy Journal of New Zealand*, 16: 17–35.

Philip, L. and Shucksmith, M. (2003), Conceptualizing social exclusion in rural Britain, *European Planning Studies*, 11, 4: 461–80.

Polanyi, K. (1944), *The Great Transformation*, New York: Reinhardt.

Reimer, W. (2004), Social exclusion in a comparative context, *Sociologia Ruralis*, 44, 1: 76–94.

Scottish Office (1998a), *Services for Children 1996: Statistical Bulletin SWK/SC/1998/6 May*, Edinburgh: Government Statistical Service.

Scottish Office (1998b), Brian Wilson announces funding arrangements for preschool education, *News Release*, Scottish Office, 30 March.

Scottish Office (1999), £112 m. investment in preschool provides places for three year olds for the first time, *News Release*, Scottish Office, 2 February.

Shucksmith, M. (2000), Endogenous development, social capital and social inclusion: perspectives from LEADER in the UK, *Sociologia Ruralis*, 40, 2: 208–18.

Shucksmith, M., Chapman, P. and Clark, G. (1996), *Rural Scotland Today: The Best of Both Worlds?* Aldershot: Avebury.

Sparkes, J. and Glennerster, H. (2002), Preventing social exclusion: education's contribution. In J. Hills, J. Le Grand and D. Piachaud (eds), *Understanding Social Exclusion*, Oxford: Oxford University Press.

Stephen, C., Low, L., Brown, S., Bell, D., Cope, P., Morris, B. and Waterhouse, S. (1998), *Preschool Education Voucher Initiative: National Evaluation of the Pilot Year*, University of Stirling, Department of Education.

Teague, P. and Wilson, D. (1995), *Social Exclusion: Social Inclusion*, Belfast: Democratic Dialogue.

Waldfogel, J. (1998), Early childhood intervention and outcomes. In *Persistent Poverty and Lifetime Inequality: The Evidence*, CASE report 5 and HM Treasury Occasional Paper 10, London: LSE/HM Treasury.

7

Jobs in the Bush: Global Industries and Inclusive Rural Development

Robyn Eversole and John Martin

Introduction

When discussing rural change processes, *rural development, regional development* and *economic development* are familiar terms – along with more recent variants such as *human development* and *sustainable development*. All have the common denominator 'development', implying positive change. But who defines what change is 'positive'? *Development* is a value-laden term, and what comprises *development* varies according to context. Traditionally, proponents of regional, rural and economic development have looked to economic and material indicators to gauge the well-being of rural residents, and to determine whether or not things are changing for the better. In the 1990s, however, the United Nations promoted a broader concept of *human development,* via its *Human Development Reports,* drawing policy attention to the importance of non-material indicators such as life expectancies, literacy levels, and so forth. By the late 1990s, considerable policy attention was also focused on *sustainable development:* arguing that for things to change 'for the better' over the long term, it was important to consider both the state of society ('social sustainability') and the state of the environment ('environmental sustainability'), in addition to economic indicators.

Thus, when discussing rural development, it is valid to ask: What sort of development are we talking about here? *Economic* development? *Human* development? Different visions of development emphasize different points about what constitutes positive change. These different visions also vary considerably in the extent to which equity is part of the equation. Current international research on poverty argues that it is not enough for development to produce *more* (more money, more jobs, more schools) without taking distribution into account.[1] When seeking to create positive change, it matters who gets what: Who benefits from development – and who ends up at a disadvantage. For rural areas, often placed at a disadvantage by the concentration of resources and decision-making in urban centres, the equity consideration is particularly relevant. Development decision-making is thus interesting terrain in which to consider questions of rural governance and the agency of local rural communities. To what extent can members of these local communities benefit from development, and how much can local communities maintain a say over the kind of development that takes place?

This paper reflects on the experiences of the rural Western District of Victoria, Australia: a well-established rural agricultural and pastoral region, in a country where population and decision-making are strongly concentrated in urban centres. This paper demonstrates how, in the Western District, *rural development* and *regional development* have often meant the establishment of new regional industries coming in from elsewhere. Most recently, these have been tree farms (beginning in the 1990s, through the present) and mineral sands mining and processing (starting in 2004, having been under discussion and planning for several years). These new industries are part of international commodity chains and driven by international capital; however, at the local and regional level they have been actively promoted as examples of rural and regional development success.[2] This follows a typical pattern in 'local economic development' strategies internationally, in which attracting a new industry translates as successful regional development (see e.g. Beer *et al.* 2003). This paper looks more closely at this approach to development, arguing that it is problematic from an equity perspective, and underlines the need for stronger local, rural-based governance of rural development planning.

Development in the Western District

This paper is based on ethnographic fieldwork by two researchers, resident in the rural service town of Hamilton, the unofficial capital of Victoria's Western District. Specifically, the paper considers how local people in Hamilton define 'development' – often, with reference to indicators such as jobs, income into the region, industry diversification, and an expanded population base – then considers the implications of pursuing these goals via outside industries closely linked to international markets, and which operate largely outside local control. Drawing on recent experiences from Hamilton and its surrounding region, we argue that partnerships with outside industries to pursue development objectives need to be carefully planned and managed to ensure these partnerships meet local goals, and particularly, equity considerations. Equity considerations (e.g. that the 'whole community' will benefit) are often implied and assumed, but not specifically articulated or prioritized, in local people's understanding of development.

Rural development in Australia has traditionally taken as its starting-point the inequality between rural and metropolitan areas. Metropolitan areas in Australia concentrate approximately 90 per cent of the country's population, one of the highest proportions among OECD countries. The rural–urban divide in Australia has often been characterized as one between the urban centres and the peripheral farming areas, a stereotype which clearly overlooks the diversity of rural Australia and its importance to the national economy (Sher and Sher 1994). Popular as well as scholarly writings on the 'decline' of rural Australia have abounded in the past 20 years, signalling considerable loss of population and services in rural areas. Such losses have been common in the wake of industry restructuring and government cutbacks tuned to a neo-liberal philosophy of international free trade and competitiveness. Yet recent research demonstrates that the situation of rural Australian towns is more diverse than writings on rural decline would lead one to believe (Burnley and Murphy 2004). Rural areas vary greatly in their natural and built amenities, and in their proximity to urban centres and other desirable locations (e.g. the coast), leading to very different trajectories for different areas (Budge 2003).

In the context of this diversity, it is not surprising to find that some rural regions do not fit the stereotype of a declining rural Australia. The Western District of Victoria is one region that continues to do well, both economically and socially. The region comprises 100,000 people and 2.28 million hectares of rich grazing and agricultural land, with natural beauty along several hundred kilometres of coastline including the stunning geological formation, the Twelve Apostles. The region is also home to the Grampians National Park (the largest in Victoria), and the recently listed Budj Bim National Heritage Landscape, with archaeological evidence of an Aboriginal aquaculture industry dating back thousands of years. The region also includes extensive grape-growing and wine-making in the Henty Region, which lies adjacent to the world-famous Coonawarra wine region across the border in the state of South Australia.

Despite its abundant endowments, the Western District shares the plight of other Australian rural regions in that their local institutions, including local government schools and health services, are largely dependent on policies and policy-makers from far away. The people of the Western District often claim their region is overlooked by Federal and State policy-makers in the equitable distribution of intergovernmental revenue, especially around funding for roads, schools and health care. In the end, much of what impacts on the region is determined by policy-making from urban centres. At the same time, other levels of government claim they are empowering rural regions to determine the nature of their own economic and social development via 'Area Consultative Committees', 'Community Capacity Building Initiatives', and so on.

In Hamilton, local government, the press and the majority of the local population have embraced new industries such as plantation forestry and mineral sands, seeing these as comprising *development*. Development in Hamilton is most commonly defined as a more diverse and stable local economy, a more prosperous local economy (shop fronts occupied, real estate prices up, employment opportunities), and a greater number and diversity of local residents. Local people's agency in defining the rural and regional development agenda is mostly confined to supporting these outside initiatives (actively or passively) and attempting to benefit from them: for instance, by signing on to the queue for a job with the mineral sands industry, or attempting to put one's businesses in a position to tender for lucrative contracts. Yet it is uncertain to what extent such 'development' serves as a vehicle to address inequity and create opportunities for those who need them in the local area, because equity seldom emerges as a specific, articulated criterion in the way that development is understood. Rather, local people tend to adopt a generic, and often acritical, view of new industry development as 'good for the region' and 'good for the community'.

Given the current and past attempts of Australian central governments (both at state and national levels) to 'empower' local and regional communities and build capacity for local decision-making,[3] this paper asks: What influence do these communities really have upon rural development trajectories and their impacts on local people, in the face of competing demands from central governments and industries oriented to the world stage? In the following sections, we will review how Australia's central governments, while ostensibly encouraging local agency, in practice maintain control of regional and rural development processes through taxation policy (using tax breaks as an investment incentive for plantation forestry) and land use planning policy (via the approvals process for the development of the mineral sands mining and processing industry). These examples will serve to highlight the tension between the theory of local empowerment and the practice of central government control, and their implications for the deeper question of who benefits from rural and regional development initiatives.

Taxation Policy and the Plantation Forestry Industry

In the mid-1990s, the Australian Federal Government made direct investment in plantation forestry 100 per cent tax-deductible. This policy was designed to encourage investment in tree plantations as part of a long-term strategy to reduce logging in old-growth forests. It was intended to ensure a continuing supply of wood products without the need for old-growth logging and also, in the second instance, to encourage re-afforestation as part of Australia's contribution to the reduction of greenhouse gases. The policy has been very successful in encouraging the growth of the plantation forestry industry in Victoria; from 1996 to 2001, the amount of land under trees in South West Victoria increased significantly, from 50,000 to 85,000 hectares (Institute of Land and Food Resources 2002: 248). The Federal policy has been much less successful, however, in its primary goal of reducing logging in old-growth forests, which is largely a State government responsibility. Moreover, the predictions are that when the plantation forests come to harvest, there may be a glut in wood supply, leading to shocks through the regional economy (Clark 2002).

The publicly listed companies involved in the plantation industry are typically large, with their head office in an Australian capital city. These companies are not closely tied to the rural communities where their tree plantations are located, and they judge the success of their investment decisions primarily on economic criteria. Plantation forestry companies have simply responded entrepreneurially to an opportunity to realize good economic returns, taking advantage of the Federal Government's 100 per cent tax deductibility for investment in this industry. The government policy, for its part, has been designed to address important environmental issues. Yet both the Federal Government's taxation policy and the plantation forest companies' entrepreneurial economic behaviour have had local impacts that reach far beyond local control.

The 100 per cent tax deduction saw investors rush into the plantation forestry as they sought to gain financial advantage. The flow-on effect in the south-western region of Victoria has been significant. The demand for land for plantations has driven up the price of pastoral land to premium levels. Many farmers took the windfall and sold the family farm for a significant capital gain, many moving out of agriculture into early retirement. The plantation forestry industry's demand for land has provided a graceful exit for many farmers seeking to retire, or for those who had failed to keep pace with change in volatile commodity industries such as wool. On the other hand, it also led to population loss in many rural communities, and associated social impacts (Tonts *et al.* 2001; Schirmer and Tonts 2003). Meanwhile, for other farming properties, the forestry companies' land-leasing schemes have provided an additional, diversified source of income, as these farmers lease out portions of their properties for woodlots.

In 2001 the Australian Taxation Office (ATO) reviewed the 100 per cent tax deductibility for investment in plantation forestry. This hiatus sent shock waves through the Western District, creating uncertainty in landowners about how this change would impact on the value of their land and the likely future of the plantation industry – particularly given that many locals are also investors in prospectus plantation forestry companies. The ATO subsequently reinstated full tax deductibility the following year, and this has once again placed a premium on land in the region. The total area of plantation tree ownership in Victoria (of which the majority is in western Victoria) is now 366,611 hectares.

It is estimated that up to 10 per cent of agricultural land in the Western District – some of the richest agricultural land in the country – has been planted out to trees, with plantations expanding at an average annual growth rate of around 10,000 hectares (Commonwealth Department of Agriculture, Fisheries and Forestry 2004). This takes prime agricultural land out of annual production, locking it up in 10–15 year production cycles. With such long cycles, the vagaries of world timber prices have potentially more impact than the price fluctuations of agricultural commodities, where farmers have flexibility in their crop choice from season to season. Given these long cycles, it is conceivable that much of this timber may not be harvested at all, as world policy on carbon credits gains prominence with global warming, and as the Federal Government reviews its taxation policy towards investment in plantation forestry.

The rapid growth of the plantation forestry industry in the Western District has been driven from far away, but it has had significant local impacts. Artificial incentives have skewed local land-use regimes towards forestry, driving up the price of land to the point where agricultural and pastoral investment becomes costly, or even economically unsound. Yet the eventual pay-off of the forestry option for the region – in terms of a strong forestry industry with opportunities for wood processing and value-adding – is by no means certain. Meanwhile, the exchange of farming for trees over large portions of the region has meant a reduction in local labour needs, as the maintenance of tree plantations requires much less labour than agriculture. One local measure of good *development* is that it provides jobs; another is that it brings population; a third, that it enhances economic stability. Yet the plantation forestry industry has contributed to depopulating the countryside.

It provided, in the first instance, low-quality, short-term jobs (in tree planting); in the second instance, fewer employment opportunities than agriculture; and in the future, uncertain potential and even potential destabilization of the regional economy.

Planning Policy and the Mineral Sands Mining Industry

In June 2004 Iluka Resources Ltd's notice to the Australian Stock Exchange stated that its Board had approved an initial investment of A$270 million to construct and commission a mineral sands mine and concentrating facilities at Douglas, near the rural town of Balmoral, Victoria, as well as a mineral separation plant near Hamilton (Iluka Resources 2004). This was described by the local press as 'the biggest project in Hamilton's history'. The local State Parliamentary Representative cited the project's expected positive benefits to the local area, especially in terms of additional local employment. Proposals to mine mineral sands in the Douglas area (part of the Murray Basin deposits) had been under discussion for several years, as had the location of mineral sands processing facilities in the region. The mining exploration company Basin Minerals was a key player in early discussions. In May/June 2002, Basin Minerals was taken over by the Western Australia-based international mining company Iluka Resources Limited, the world's largest producer of zircon and second-largest producer of titanium minerals.

The process which has led to the Iluka board approval of an $A270 million investment in this region is instructive for understanding the nature of both local and external involvement in this major development initiative. First Murray Basin, and later Iluka, have been required by the Australian government to go through certain planning and consultative procedures as part of the new industry development process. The Environmental Effects Statement (EES) that Basin Minerals was required to prepare as a condition of government planning approval to mine at Douglas, involved consultation with a wide range of regulatory bodies, organizations, and members of the public. These included relevant local, State and Commonwealth departments and agencies – local Shires, Catchment Management Authorities, the Department of Natural Resources and the Environment, Department of Infrastructure, Environmental Protection Authority and various others – as well as infrastructure service providers, community groups (including Landcare groups), and individuals (Martinick McNulty 2001: 38, 75). Various studies were necessary (e.g. modelling the effects of tailings on groundwater; conducting a survey of native vegetation, archaeological survey, etc.). The public had the opportunity to comment on the EES report (available at local libraries and post offices) during a six-week review period; and an independent government panel of three reviewed submissions and made recommendations to the State Minister for Regional Development (Martinick McNulty 2001: 14–15, 102, 106, 137). The Environmental Effects Statement for the Douglas mine was then approved.

Unlike the mine, the proposal to establish a mineral separation plant on the outskirts of the town of Hamilton did not require the preparation of an Environmental Effects Statement; it only required that planning approval be granted by the local council. This appeared to be no obstacle: Basin Minerals' original announcement of the choice of Hamilton for the facility was greeted enthusiastically by most locals, including local government. Clearly phrased by the local press in terms of Regional Development, the project was described as the outcome of many months of effort by the town's then economic development manager. Described originally as a '$73 million sands processing plant' (later, a $90 million plant and, eventually, twice that size), it was tagged as a project which would easily be 'the biggest in Hamilton's history', could provide 'up to 500 permanent jobs', booms in housing and schools, and a reverse in the Shire's population decline of the previous two decades. In short, the project seemed a regional and rural development dream-come-true. Meanwhile, the company's environmental director assured that there would be 'no pollution and noise problems', recognizing that these could be issues for local people. Some (particularly neighbours of the proposed plant) expressed concerns about potential disbenefits of the plant such as discharges to air, noise, odour, discharge/leakage to groundwater, fallout affecting pasture animals, disturbance of lifestyle (auditory/visual irritation), and property values. These concerns were articulated early on, and they did not disappear.

The company's decision to locate the separation plant in Hamilton was made on the basis of geographic location, as well as by what could be termed existing local development advantages: the existence of good schools, local services, an attractive central business district, good highways, an existing railway line, natural gas line, and blue gum plantations which could be used as landscaping around the plant. Thus, other, previous actions and decisions had paved the way for this industry development opportunity. Shire employees actively highlighted these advantages to the company, and a grassroots group of local retail business people were vocal in their support of the company and its proposal. Other local residents, however, expressed their concerns about the lack of information available on the plant's potential impacts. They pressed for meetings with the Shire, the company, and the water authority to discuss various issues.

The mining company submitted the required planning permit application to the local council in December 2002; it was then put out for public comment. The planning permit application claimed the plant would create 350 direct and indirect jobs, using an employment multiplier of 4.1 based on 84 full-time employees; that these workers would be employed 'from the local area where possible . . . [as] most required skills are available locally'; and that the plant overall would earn an estimated $150 million a year in export revenue (Iluka 2002: 2, 19). In the end over 800 submissions were received to the permit application. All but about 30 were in favour of the plant, and the council approved the permit application unanimously.

An opposing local group then proceeded to take their case against the plant to the Victorian Civil and Administrative Tribunal (VCAT). It seemed that development was set to be negotiated in the courts. However, the State Planning Minister quickly 'called out' the case from the Tribunal to make a personal decision about the project's outcome 'because of its significance to Victoria'. The Minister for Regional Development observed, in the meantime, that the mining company was concerned about losing overseas investors if the planning approval was subject to delays in the Tribunal. Thus, the established citizens' appeals process was overturned, due to what was explained as the 'regional development significance' of the project.

In early September 2003, after considering the information presented, the State Government Planning Minister personally approved the planning permit for the location of the mineral separation plant in Hamilton. The local newspaper headline on the day of the Minister's planning approval read 'Green Light!' in large letters, conveying a strongly positive local response. In the article, the Mayor stated that he was 'absolutely thrilled' that the separation plant would be located in Hamilton; a local businessman was 'ecstatic'. The next issue, however, underlined another side to the local debate. The headline here was 'Denied Justice'. It referred to a local residents' group whose representatives felt 'disappointed and betrayed' that the planning minister had not allowed their case against the plant to be heard by the VCAT.

There has clearly been no unified 'community view' of this development initiative. The negotiations around the proposed mineral sands developments have been widely publicized in the local press, and people living and working in the area have had the opportunity to form opinions about the new industry. Most local people are expecting the new industry to bring some combination of 'development' advantages: jobs, population growth, increased demand for housing, schools, and local businesses' services, and increased confidence and general prosperity to the region. There has also been an expectation that the new industry will be a stabilizing force on the local economy, with diversification making it less vulnerable to fluctuations in other key local industries such as wool and trees. At the same time, there has also been recognition that the new industry may bring some problems such as increased traffic, damage to the road infrastructure, continuing high property prices (for those seeking to purchase a home), inconvenience for those living near the plant, and environmental damage (tree removal, soil damage). Moreover, the issue of water, specifically water allocations, has emerged as a serious issue in public debate regarding the mine, particularly in the region north of Hamilton.

As the construction phases for the mine, mineral separation plant, and related works (water pipeline, road upgrading, etc.) started in mid-2004, public opinion towards the new industry was still generally positive, but there were also some concerns. One was the water issue – although there must be at least 11 per cent capacity of water in the system before 'big users' like Iluka are allowed to take the allocation they have purchased from the water authority, water is still likely to remain a serious point of concern in a drought-stricken region where the local reservoir was at only 10 per cent capacity at mid-year (up from 3 per cent earlier in the year). Another concern was the reality of local jobs actually going to local people, given Iluka's overriding business imperative. While the company has worked closely with the government-funded Industry Capability Network to brief local suppliers about tendering for Iluka contracts, by mid-year 2004 two major contracts had already gone to out-of-state companies via competitive tendering, raising local complaints.[4] Such tensions draw attention to the fact that, although the mineral sands company has taken care to develop a good local image and to position itself as a partner in the region's development, its ultimate allegiances – to the economic interests of its shareholders – lie elsewhere.

Conclusion

The residents of the Western District of Victoria are generally very pleased to accept the economic benefits that will come from these two large new industries, regardless of the exposure these will bring to the vagaries of the world market. Local people are, in fact, quite aware of the potential impact of global economic forces on local livelihoods, having been highly dependent on export wool production when the 'reserve price scheme' for wool collapsed in the early 1990s. Global exposure is not a new issue for export-dependent rural regions, but it takes on a particular poignancy when newly arrived global industries are framed in terms of 'rural development'. The discourse of rural development speaks of the empowerment of rural regions and their residents – all residents, including the less-advantaged. It generally assumes local, rural participation in the governance of development, and equity in reaping development's benefits. Yet in practice, what influence do rural areas and their individual citizens really have on defining the terms of development, in the face of competing demands oriented to the world economic stage? Reflecting on the cases presented here, we would argue that they have minimal – and decreasing – control. Central governments and corporate board rooms far away, via their plans, policies, and processes, direct the long-term future of these communities.

Hamilton is a rural area in a relatively privileged position. But a reflection on economic restructuring and change in the Western District of Victoria has much to teach us about deeper issues in the governance of rural and regional development. Clearly, local people here are embracing the opportunity offered by new industries. Yet local people and local governments seem to be paying little critical attention to where the ultimate distribution of development costs and benefits will fall – who will be the 'losers' and 'winners' in the exciting new development scenarios that have come to town. Yet at least, local people are aware of some of the potential issues. At central government levels, on the other hand, policy-making and planning processes demonstrate little awareness of the potentially negative local impacts of new industry developments, and little time for local perspectives. Decisions are made, policies are put into place, plans are fast-tracked, and local communities in their turn do what they can with the circumstances they have been given. Australia's central governments, while ostensibly encouraging local agency, in practice maintain close control of regional and rural development processes.

The problem with this situation is that much of significance is overlooked when viewed from the centre. It is easy to assume, in a linear fashion, that more industry and more money in a region translate to a better lifestyle for rural communities. Yet as we have seen, other issues come into play: jobs may not be forthcoming, local resources may become scarcer as a result of the new industry's presence, and local expectations may not be met. New industry development is seldom if ever an unqualified success story for everyone concerned. There is much government can do, however, to promote more equitable, inclusive industry development. Specifically, governments can work to ensure that the costs associated with these new developments are shared equitably by the developers and the community, and that local people will also reap the benefits while these industries are doing well.

To ensure that local people – including less-advantaged people – benefit equitably from new industry development, investments in the future are key. Such investments include quality infrastructure; comprehensive, diverse and accessible education and training; additional new industry development; support for culture and the arts; and other investments that make the local area a better place to live in. Central governments can neither guess nor ordain the specific nature of local needs, but there are specific strategies that central governments can employ to authentically empower local communities in rural development decision-making. These include establishing local structures for community governance; for example, as with the current arrangement in the State Government hospitals, where local citizens apply and are appointed to local hospital boards. Another important strategy would be a requirement for full and open reporting of industry performance to the wider community, so that local people have an accurate and timely understanding of how their area's few large economic engines are performing. Too often, local communities are the last to know the fate of local industries that they rely so heavily upon.

As Sher and Sher (1994) so poignantly identified a decade ago, Australia does not have a coherent rural development policy. It is thus unsurprising to find the kinds of policy contradictions which we have highlighted in this chapter. Central government policy vis-à-vis rural communities is fragmented, ostensibly encouraging local control of development decision-making while at the same time using blunt policy instruments to steer rural development trajectories from the centre – with little room for attention to local needs or impacts. The nature of our federation, its competitive intergovernmental relations, and different demands of State and Commonwealth departments, mean that incoherence and inconsistency can easily persist. Clearly, rural communities will remain the poor cousins of urban Australia so long as public policy decisions continue to be driven from our urban centres. Given this continuing central-versus-devolved policy-making dilemma, we ask: What would it take to shift key relevant public policy decision-making away from urban centres to rural communities?

Recognition by central governments (both State and Commonwealth) that rural communities are capable of making local decisions in a global context is an essential first step. Given the current competitive state of Australian intergovernmental relations (where the Liberal–National Party Coalition are in power federally and opposition Labour governments are in power in all States) obtaining such recognition seems unlikely. Both of these levels of government currently compete to deliver services at the local community level, often unwittingly usurping local institutions (Martin 2005). Conversely, we also see, through much anecdotal evidence, rural communities making global decisions without the direction or support of central governments. There are communities that would benefit from the guidance and example of others, including central governments, to show them what other communities are doing and suggest viable strategies.

Global industries now recognize that there are real business returns riding on the nature of their relationship with people in the rural communities in which they seek to operate and do business. The International Council on Mining and Metals (2006), for example, has recently released its Community Development Toolkit, produced in collaboration with the World Bank's Oil, Gas and Mining Policy Division. While the focus is on work in developing nations, the Toolkit's approach is also relevant to developed nations where rural communities are in varying degrees of stress and would benefit from a more considered approach to development in their region by global mining companies. This point applies equally to agribusiness and advanced manufacturing industries that establish in rural communities to take advantage of the resources in these places.

Central to our view of rural development is the role of local communities themselves. They are the key source of change responding to global industries in their region. They have both the distinct advantage of local knowledge about their region and they have the networks which make a difference to the ability of global industries to succeed. Bryden and Hart (2001) came to this conclusion in their study of the dynamics of rural economies. It was the 'intangibles' of affiliation and association through community networks that made a difference in the economic performance of these regions. It is to these intangibles that governments can give much more attention – not by directly intervening in local communities, but by resourcing local and regional institutions in a long-term sustainable way. A focus on local knowledge and local decision-making – including the opportunity for locals to discuss and negotiate their different development agendas in responsive institutions – can empower rural communities to work with global industries in an inclusive and mutually productive manner.

Notes

1. See, for instance, Naschold (2002); also UNESCO (2000: 2): 'Poverty, a long-standing scourge on mankind, has been reduced significantly over the last century in a limited number of countries. But expectations that this progress would reach the world as a whole have not been fulfilled by development trends over the last decades. The process of globalization has brought about large increases in global wealth and income. Such gains have, however, been distributed very unequally and inequitably, both within and among countries, accentuating further already existing disparities and divides.'
2. In Australia, 'regional development' is most commonly used to refer to the development of rural (non-metropolitan) regions.
3. See e.g. Bryson and Mowbray (1981), Herbert-Cheshire (2000), and the recent efforts of the Department for Victorian Communities in the study area (http://www.dvc.vic.gov.au).
4. As described in the *Hamilton Spectator* (6 April 2004): 1.

References

Beer, A., Maude, A. and Pritchard, B. (2003), *Developing Australia's Regions, Theory and Practice*, Sydney: UNSW Press.

Bryden, J. and Hart, K. (2001), *Dynamics of Rural Areas (DORA): The International Comparison*, Aberdeen: Arkleton Centre for Rural Development Research, monograph.

Bryson, L. and Mowbray, M. (1981), Community: the spray-on solution, *Australian Journal of Social Issues*, 16, 4 (November): 255–67.

Budge, T. (2003), Country towns: more than just statistics, *Sustaining Regions*, 3, 1: 25–37.

Burnley, I. and Murphy, P. (2004), *Sea Change: Movement from Metropolitan to Arcadian Australia*, Kensington: UNSW Press.

Clark, J. (2002), Forest policy for commodity wood production: an examination drawing on the Australian experience. Paper presented to the Australia New Zealand Society for Ecological Economics conference 'Strategies into Action: Regional and Industry Policy Applications of Ecologically Sustainable Development', 2–4 December, University of Technology, Sydney.

Commonwealth Department of Agriculture, Fisheries and Forestry (2004), *National Plantation Industry Inventory Australia: 2004 Update*, Canberra: AFFA.

Herbert-Cheshire, L. (2000), Contemporary strategies for rural community development in Australia: a governmentality perspective, *Journal of Rural Studies*, 16: 203–15.

Iluka Resources Limited (2002), Planning Permit Application, Mineral Separation Plant, Hamilton, Western Victoria. West Perth: Martinick Bosch Sell Pty Ltd.

Iluka Resources (2004), Iluka Resources Commits A$270 Million to Develop the Murray Basin. Notice to the Australian Stock Exchange, Perth: Iluka Resources Ltd.

Institute of Land and Food Resources (2002), *Socioeconomic Impact of Changing Land Use in South West Victoria*, Melbourne: Institute of Land and Forest Resources.

International Council on Mining and Metals (2006), *Community Development Toolkit*, London: ICMM.

Martin, J. (2005), 'If you can't kill the guru . . .' Sustaining Communities in the Face of Bureaucratic Dominance. Western Decision Sciences Institute 34th Annual Meeting, Vancouver, Canada, April.

Martinick McNulty (2001), *Douglas Heavy Minerals Project Stage-1 Environmental Effects Statement*, Horsham, Victoria: Basin Mineral Holdings NL.

Naschold, F. (2002), *Why Inequality Matters for Poverty*, Overseas Development Institute briefing paper, London: Overseas Development Institute. Available at: http://www.odi.org.uk/pppg/publications/briefings/inequality_briefings/02.html (accessed September 2002).

Schirmer, J. and Tonts, M. (2003), Plantations and sustainable rural communities, *Australian Forestry*, 66, 1: 67–74.

Sher, J. and Sher, K. R (1994), Beyond the conventional wisdom: rural development as if Australia's rural people and communities really mattered, *Journal of Research in Rural Education*, 10, 1: 2–43.

Tonts, M., Campbell, C. and Black, A. (2001), *Socio-Economic Impacts of Farm Forestry*, RIRDC Publication no. 01/45, Canberra: Rural Industries Research and Development Corporation.

UNESCO (2000), *UNESCO's Strategy on Development and Poverty Eradication*, Paris: UNESCO. Available at: http://www.unesco.org/most/160ex13eng.pdf (accessed September 2002).

8

Older People 'on the Edge' in the Countrysides of Europe

George Giacinto Giarchi

Introduction

European countrysides constitute four-fifths of the continent's landmass. More than half of Europe's population lives outside its cities and major towns (Dower 1995). Also, European countrysides have a higher proportion of older people, aged 55 plus, than do Europe's urban areas (Countryside Agency 2000a, 2004; Eurostat 2000; Office of National Statistics 2002). Socio-economic and welfare implications were first noted by the International Expert Group Meeting (and Haute Report) on 'Ageing in remote rural areas: a challenge to the social and medical services' in Eymoutiers, France, in 1983. Experts from 16 European countries called for major research by the year 2000, to avert substantial breakdowns in rural services for older people (Maclouf and Lion 1984).

Responses in Europe to the Haute Report were minimal. Some authors in the UK did focus on older people in Europe, but most overlooked older rural people, apart from a few researchers, such as Scharf (2001) and Wenger (2001). According to Wenger, the study of rural ageing should be a discrete field of transnational research. Although recent major studies, such as those edited by Lowe and Speakman (2006), have focused upon older people in an ageing countryside, they have been confined to Britain. Comparative European analysis dealing specifically with the continent's older, rural residents is clearly called for. But how can it be carried out contextually, given the transnational cultural differences between European national settings?

C. Wright Mills (1959) stated in his *Sociological Imagination* that personal problems are best assessed within a broader societal context. Therefore, this chapter sets out to provide a European conspectus of older people's living conditions by considering the impact of socio-economic global macro forces within a centre–periphery overview. It does so by taking account of the interplay, and sometimes contraplay, of urban–rural parameters as they affect older Europeans, for better or worse within shifting global–local socio-economic landscapes. But certain preliminary factors need first to be identified.

Global Compression and Consequent Urban–Rural Outcomes

Globalization is the transnational socio-economic interconnection of localities. Woods (2005: 33) observes that it is characterized by 'the increasing subjection of rural regions to networks and processes of power that are produced and reproduced and executed on a global scale'. The European rural world within which these processes reside has been subject to ongoing, increasing, cumulative globalization processes over the centuries, but is now subject to more rapid changes (Robertson 1992). Giddens (1993) refers to the temporal-historical path to modernity with the creation of a transnational system. Within it, movements of people, capital, industry and technology are described as socio-economic and cultural flows. These run in different directions in time and place, affecting some areas more than others (Appadurai 1996; Mittelman 1997). Certainly the global impact, as Giddens stresses (1993: 528), is uneven, favouring some and disadvantaging others. As this chapter will show, the outcome for people in rural areas is largely dependent upon the relative nature of the nexus between city/town and countryside (Williams 1973). Global movements mainly flow via the major cities where the decisions of planners and providers help shape the global–local economy, benefiting some countrysides and not others

The rural environment is changing rapidly under the impact of global forces, with implications for older residents. Concomitantly, within globalization processes, counter-urbanization and the impact of modern agricultural industry have affected the physical environment and socio-economic landscape of continents such as Europe (Ilbery 1998). People in the changing countryside see their natural environment exploited and altered by counter-urbanization and accompanying new infrastructure, involving encroaching industrial ventures, outspill urban housing schemes, decanted populations and new highways. The erosion and rural pollution which follow – plus the loss of 'tranquil areas' – affect many rural residents (Woods 2005: 125) and alter the familiar landscape which older residents have valued over the years. In addition, modern industrialized agriculture removes hedgerows, while chemical pesticides destroy local indigenous plants, together with rare animal species. Graham Harvey (1998) describes such damage as 'the killing of the countryside'.

A major blighted area exists in the countrysides of Central and Eastern Europe, where pollutants from industrialized Western and Northern European urban areas are carried by prevailing winds from west to east. Drifting arsenic and cadmium have affected one million rural acres over the past thirty years and damaged many older residents' health in rural areas stretching from the Elbe to the mountains of Southern Bulgaria. (Thompson 1991; Giarchi 1996).

Another transnational phenomenon affecting global space and place has been the movement of urban residents in and out of rural areas, which Woods describes as the 'globalization of mobilization', when 'the coherence that once characterized rural communities has been eroded' (Woods 2005: 37–8). As a result of rapid population movements in and out of rural areas, people are less tied to a locality and to neighbours within rural communities, with implications for older people to be discussed and exemplified in this chapter.

Types of Countryside

Quality of life is inextricably interlinked to environmental settings affecting vulnerable older people in particular (Kahana 1982; Rubinstein and Parmelle 1992). Hence, there is a need to identify the types of settlements and countrysides in which older people reside. The UK's Office for National Statistics (ONS 2002) and Department for Environment, Food and Rural Affairs (Defra 2004), as well as the Census 2001 suggest a way of classifying rural settlements by introducing 'rural Census Output Areas' (rural COAs).

The smallest rural COA is identified as consisting of approximately 125 households (Countryside Agency 2004). These are located within less sparse to sparse/remote rural areas, at distances ranging from 10 to 30 km from a delivery service centre or a person's workplace. Although the same statistical indicators have not been adopted in continental Europe, the COA continuum – ranging from 'urban, town and fringe settlements' to villages, dispersed hamlets and isolated dispersed dwellings – is nonetheless useful when considering Europe's rural diversities in relation to older people. It largely coincides with Russell's (1986: 3) continuum, consisting of the following four types of rural location: urban shadow, accessible, less accessible and remote countryside areas. These are adopted in this chapter when considering accessibility and sparsity – critical factors when considering the notion of distance decay (Alun and Phillips 1984; Giarchi 1990).

Rural Deprivation and Distance Decay

The greater the distance, the greater the costs and problems affecting delivery of resources and access, especially for frailer and poorer rural residents in rurally deprived localities (Scharf and Bartham 2006). Services and volunteers can break the distance decay factor, as will be demonstrated, but costs often hamper outreach projects.

With regard to what constitutes rural deprivation, there is less agreement than there is over urban deprivation (see Room 1995; Shucksmith 2000; Blackman *et al.* 2001). Nonetheless, Key rural studies in Britain have identified the following factors as indicative of rural deprivation. Most go back to Walker's (1978) indices of rural poverty.

1. *Lower average income* (Simmons 1997; Chapman *et al.* 1998; Countryside Agency 2005; Lowe 2004).
2. *Not enough shops, amenities and domestic services* (Champion and Watkins 1991; Barnett 1999; Lowe 2003).
3. *Poor housing conditions* (Phillips and Williams 1984; Shucksmith 1991; Gummer 1999; Giarchi 2002; Herklots 2004).
4. *Inadequate transport provision* (Joseph and Phillips 1984; Giarchi 1990; Bell and Cloke 1991; Help the Aged and RDC 1996; Wiggans and Hillman 1998).

5. *Scarcities in health, social care, and welfare services* (Joseph and Phillips 1984; Giarchi 1990; Fernández-Ballesteros and Caprara 2003; Asthana *et al.* 2003; BMA Board of Science 2005).
6. *Increased burden of domestic care for frailer older isolated people* (Wenger 1984; Scharf and Wenger 2000; Wenger 2001; Scharf 2001).
7. *Lack of clubs, education and information services* (Giarchi 1990; Simmons 1997; Age Concern 1998).

Although some of these deprivations also disadvantage older people in urban settings, there are distinctive, experiential, socio-economic, and socio-political differences between deprivation in urban and rural settings, which call for a corresponding differentiation between urban and countryside solutions (Asthana *et al.* 2002; Milligan 2001). It is not possible for this chapter to consider all the above forms of rural deprivation in Europe, particularly because of incompleteness of data available for continental Europe. Nevertheless, some of more obvious and pertinent problems, such as lack of shops and of domestic services, health services, social care centres and transport, can be taken into account, as and when relevant.

With the above factors in mind, this exploratory overview will consider the nature of relevant urban–rural links (nexus) and diverse, contrasting consequences for older European residents within four urban–rural parameters to be identified and discussed each in turn.

When two-way urban–rural, socio-economic flows benefit the countryside

As already stated, the welfare of Europe's older rural residents is greatly dependent upon interaction between their countrysides and local and regional urban centres. The EU's rural LEADER schemes and the UK's White Paper, *Our Countryside* (MAFF/DEFR 2000) have stressed the importance of market towns in both top–down and bottom–up interplay between regional urban centres, small towns, and various countrysides.

Firstly, small rural towns (described by Frankenberg 1966, as urban–rural settlements) are often intermediate agents or rural hubs between city and countryside that facilitate the delivery of personal services for dependent older persons. Many provide amenities that raise standards of living locally, by providing, for instance, employment opportunities for older active persons and helping to create 'living countrysides' (Countryside Agency 2003). For example, in 499 out of 1,274 English market towns, 17.6 per cent of recent 'start-ups' were organized in the countryside by people aged over 55. By contrast, only 12 per cent of urban start-ups were organized from within the same age group (Countryside Agency 2004).

Secondly, within the global development process of counter-urbanization (Lewis 1998), there has been a 'filter-down', post-productionist shift of small and medium-sized businesses, high technologies and agro-food processing companies to small towns from the cities (North 1998). In such post-industrial countrysides older workers generally have more employment opportunities – and dependent older people have more accessible services – than do their counterparts in more isolated, less accessible and remote areas. Such post-industrial rurality, and the flexible work opportunities that part-time older workers can take advantage of, have been exemplified in Italy (Bagnasco 1977; in Spain (Precedo Ledo and Grimes 1991); in Greece (Papadopoulus 1985), in Southern France (Guesnier 1994), in Portugal (Lewis and Williams 1986); and in England's East Anglia (North 1998).

Thirdly, there exists a set of relatively few but interesting urban-fringe rural areas, whose traditional socio-economic urban–rural ties go back many years, springing from earlier pre-industrial developments (Robertson 1992; Giddens 1993). For instance, older sculptors and experienced skilled bronze workers, in the rural town of Pietrasanta at the foot of the Carrara Mountains, have produced art work for city galleries, and led and trained younger stone sculptors to provide monuments for nearby Florentine city patrons over the centuries. They now cater for wider global urban patrons and markets (Giarchi 1993). Similarly, skilled traditional leather work has been carried out for many years in small workshops in urban shadow countrysides in Tuscany, that now serve both piazza stalls and fashionable *botteghe* in Pisa, Florence, Milan and the wider global market. Again, in urban fringe/shadow country-sides in southern Germany, renowned, experienced older woodcarvers and woodworkers ply their skills side by side with younger woodcarvers whom they mentor in responding to and providing for urban commercial markets. Over the centuries, and especially in volatile markets, they have learned to adapt to demand and so have often managed to stave off workshop and studio closures. The rich diversity of traditional arts and crafts that are produced by active older Europeans in rural areas merit as much attention as do other forms of production. (See Fisher 1997, for an interesting exploration of the link between craft production and rurality in West Wales.)

Rather more has been reported about rural–urban agricultural projects in relation to older European farming families and workers, whose efforts are linked with city markets and food chains. In particular, the two-way urban–countryside burgeoning interrelationship provided by urban–rural wine pro-duction continues to be significant (although the industry has been weakened by recent overproduction). It involves older and younger co-cultivators in myriad European vineyards. These are located right across the rural con-tinuum ranging from urban fringe and accessible countrysides to less accessible and remote countrysides. Their wine bottles bear the name of the urban wine sellers, but are better known by their countryside of origin, such as: Chianti, Burgundy, Rioja, Madeira, Pfalz, etc. The final vintage quality is dependent upon the combined efforts and skills of older and younger countryside cultivators and fermenters sometimes within cooperatives in countryside vineyards of France, Germany, Italy, Spain, Portugal, Austria, Switzerland, Bulgaria, Hungary, and now parts of Southern England. Similar intergenerational two-way urban–rural ventures exist in the olive industry, mainly in countrysides of Greece, Spain and Italy (see Hawes's account, 2001).

A two-way urban–rural nexus may also exist with regard to the generation of social capital that provides informal care for dependent older people. Le Mesurier (2003, 2004, 2006) and Shucksmith (2000) have documented the supportive role of older people in urban–rural regeneration ventures in less accessible areas of England. These are often intergenerational, as exemplified by a Help the Aged and RDC (1996) project that is typical of many community care strategies. This scheme provided older, frailer residents with visiting and befriending schemes, rural transport and lifts to hard-to-reach shops, in dispersed, less accessible dwellings in 24 rural localities within Northumberland, North Yorkshire and Cumbria. Similar support projects and networks have been documented by: Giarchi (1996) in 29 European countries; Le Mesurier (2006) and Lowe and Speakman (2006) for rural England; Wenger (1984, 1992) for Wales; St Leger and Gillespie (1991) for Northern Ireland; Scharf (2001) for Germany; and Paúl et al. (2003) for Portugal. Older rural residents' quality of life has been enhanced by the combined intergenerational efforts sustained by two-way urban–rural flows, between regional agency urban outreach centres, involving market towns, village local coordinators and volunteers.

In addition, quality of rural life is dependent upon security. In response to rural demand, a NACRO and the Countryside Agency project (2000) in England, directed by Lawley and Deane (2000), has introduced centre–periphery community safety schemes in an effort to minimize rural crime in areas where older residents have been victims of 'distraction burglary' (Help the Aged 2004). A partnership now exists, in some areas in England, between central urban crime squads and local parish councils. However, we know little as yet about comparable police protection arrangements in continental rural Europe.

Lastly, two-way urban–rural links can be strengthened by ICT to create more interactive two-way services within localities, strengthening informal ties between older people and their families and offering emedicine programmes to rural health care patients. Dower (1995: 6), for instance, refers to the creation of Euro-telecottages, making it possible for remoter areas to be in touch whatever and wherever the need. Unfortunately, however, although older rural users of services can in principle be in digital touch with service providers, the majority of them remain out of touch, especially in less accessible rural areas. There are, in any case, disparities between the availability of computer connections for rural and urban households. In England, for instance, broadband internet connection in villages amounts to 16 per cent (in remote areas it is only 4 per cent), whereas in urban areas it amounts to 95 per cent (Countryside Agency 2004). It is fortunate that, over the longer term, in spite of the slower uptake of today's older rural ICT users, increasing numbers of older people (the 'silver surfers') can be expected to be communicating with one another and their distant family members via email. Even so, Castells (1989a, 1998b) remains convinced that ICT will be the domain of the more educated.

When a long-standing two-way impasse hampers urban–rural socio-economic flows

Manifestly, the globalization process favours some and disadvantages others at local levels. Long-standing injustices and divisions not only persist, they are often increased (Bradshaw and Wallace 1996). Here, layers of encrusted peripheralisms may have been built up over time (see Tarrow 1977), resulting in 'closed economies', as have existed in the former communist 'eastern semi-peripheries of Europe' (Wellman 1999). Older people, especially the lonely, can so easily be trapped within closed cultures in isolated and remote communities. Within these, local people may seek independence, in what has sometimes been described as 'internal colonies' (Halliday 1959; Payton 1993). Historic ethnic divides and racist feuds may, from time to time, block urban–rural communication and possible collaboration and mutual help for older, frail and dependent people. They themselves may be carriers of discrimination within inward-looking racist communities.

We are acquainted with walled cities, less so with walled countrysides. Over time, some more isolated rural areas may well have been exploited by regional centres. For example, the suffix -*wall* in the placename of largely rural 'Cornwall', UK, is derived from the Anglo-Saxon term *wealh* ('foreign'). As part of the Celtic fringe, Cornish people, particularly country elders, hold on to what they see as their separate, beleaguered culture. Payton (1993: 17) quotes Linda Christmas's trenchant remark:

> Cornwall does not wish to be ignored and does not wish to be hyphenated to Devon, as though 'Cornwall and Devon' were like Gilbert and Sullivan, nothing without each other, devoid of a separate identity.

In some parts of Europe, cultural and/or political 'walls' have divided large numbers of countrysides and their older residents from regional centres. Some such 'walled' countrysides are to be found in vast rural tracts of Europe, such as those of Basilicata and Campania (Italy); Asturias, Beira, Castilla-La Mancha, Castilla Leon, Litoral and Extremadura and Galicia (Spain); Salonika (Greece), and Alentejo, Algarve, and Açores (Portugal); Tropoje, Puke, Mirdite and Kolonje (Albania), and in isolated villages in Central Anatolia (Turkey) (Fernández-Armesto 1994). In such semi-closed culturescapes the seniors or elders can conserve and pass on cultural and sectarian separatism, as in many Serbian, Macedonian, Croatian and Slovenian countrysides (*ibid.*). Semi-closed villages (both Protestant and Catholic) in Northern Ireland have perpetuated sectarian divides.

There are also marginalized travelling groups in rural parts of Europe, such as Romanian, Hungarian and British gypsies, whose older people are especially vulnerable. In addition, many of the 16 million Europeans who have a minority language (for instance Occitan, Galician, Sardinian, Gaelic, Breton, Friulian, West Frisian, Corsican and Welsh) often reside in less accessible countrysides (Fernández-Armesto 1994; Hoggart *et al.* 1995). In the vocabulary of the anti-discrimination literature, older people within such ethnic groups may be both 'othered' and 'othering' because of separatist 'cultural accounts' of their own identity (Cohen 1982). The extent to which this occurs has so far been under-researched.

When regional and local urban centres block or cut socio-economic flows to the countryside

McLaughlin (1986) refers to 'planned deterioration' in rural areas caused by government's urban-led priorities. Urban service providers face ever-increasing socio-economic and health care demands in Europe's countrysides that have implications for older Europeans seeking essential services. The underlying problem is that European urban centres prefer larger contracts at cheaper prices within a more competitive global economy. Global events beyond the control of planners thwart efforts to meet demand. For instance, they can be frustrated by global movements of younger European 'out-migrants' and of older 'in-migrants', within open EU frontiers. Each form of migration poses its own problems.

The movement of younger people from Europe's more remote rural areas to the cities worsens rural deprivation, particularly in the less accessible and remote countrysides. They often leave older residents behind in semi-desolate villages, particularly in Central and Eastern Europe. The exit of younger people is often accompanied by the migration of professionals who move out, once regional centralized authorities allow decay to set in. For instance, Warnes *et al.* (2004: 317) record how a mass exodus of younger people from the Adriatic Islands of Croatia has caused rural dereliction by leaving older local inhabitants behind. The researchers described how frail older residents were 'abandoned' and their traditional cycle of life disrupted. No longer were there baptisms, marriages or festivals – only funerals and burials.

In other areas, the opposite scenario occurs when older people are moving into the countryside, adding to demands for housing, health and social care, often in less accessible and remote areas. This situation can pose quite different problems for planners and providers, who are caught up in global, national and regional competitions for the same resources that are also demanded by urban electorates.

In other instances, a laissez-faire disregard for rural needs would seem to account for the lack of rural services. In England, for instance, post offices decrease as one moves from market towns into less accessible countrysides (Woods 2005; Countryside Agency 2004). With regard to rural transport, buses are either unreliable or few, or in some areas do not run at all. And yet reliance upon public transport increases with age. Although 85.5 per cent of persons in England aged over 50 in rural areas own a car, they are less likely to do so after 65 years of age (Lowe and Speakman 2006; Gilbert *et al.* 2006). The UK Rural Development Commission (1996: 47) has stressed that 'transport is the most important factor in determining degrees of isolation experienced by many rural residents'.

The costs of supplying health and social care services are certainly higher per capita in rural areas (Asthana *et al.* 2003; Scharf and Bartlam 2006; Bevan and Croucher 2006). Thus, with regard to health care provision in England and Wales, there has been a 6 per cent decrease in the number of surgeries over the last twenty years, affecting 23,000 villages. Rural dentistries are also in short supply (Clark and Woollett 1990; Cloke and Little 1997; Furuseth 1998; Countryside Agency 2005). By 2000, some 83 per cent of country parishes in England did not have a local resident GP (Countryside Agency 2001). Where the number of older rural people has increased, the numbers of health and social care rural centres have paradoxically decreased (Furuseth 1998; Milligan 2001). Data with regard to the extent of any corresponding decrease in continental Europe are unfortunately lacking. Walker and

Maltby (1997: 90–1) have stressed the high fragmentation of health and social care services available to older people, but say nothing about rural provision.

EU measures to improve health care can actually make them worse, in deprived rural areas. For example, the European Working Time Directive (in force from 1998) imposes a maximum 48-hour working week for doctors, which the BMA has identified as problematic in remote rural areas, where back-up and out-of-hours cover can take up a disproportionate amount of time (BMA Board of Science 2005: 27). An infrastructure for out-of-hours health care across the EU (currently being tackled in England) is essential for the sustainability of isolated and remote community medical services in rural localities.

Because of health problems caused by older people's poor housing conditions, regional planners often face increased demand for health and social care services. In spite of the search for Arcadia's idealized rural dwelling close to nature, many older people live in inadequate housing. In general, the more remote European houses are, and the more aged local residents happen to be, the more dilapidated their homes are likely to be (Giarchi 2002). Older people are not only living longer, they are also residing in older houses for longer. These dwellings are often in need of repair, especially in less accessible and remote countrysides where rundown conditions often go unnoticed (Giarchi 1996, 2002). Data indicate that significant numbers of older people in such areas are residing in leaking, damp and cramped houses (Giarchi 2002). Elder housing conditions are particularly poor in countrysides of Portugal, Spain, Italy and Greece (see Giarchi 1996, 2002). Yet chocolate-box or table-mat images of picturesque rural dwellings continue to be in vogue (Wenger 2001).

The majority of older Europeans' rural houses are owner-occupied – and it is owner-occupied countryside properties which are among the most run-down in continental Europe. Older people's houses tend to be in better condition when located closer to urban centres (Giarchi 2002). Also, there is a greater provision of special needs housing in urban areas; however, such houses, together with domestic repair services, tend to be more available in the north-west regions of Europe. Houses in disrepair may be located anywhere in Europe, but they are especially to be found in the more isolated, more remote eastern countrysides, primarily in Hungary, Bulgaria, Romania, Slovakia, Albania, and scarred war-torn zones of the former Yugoslavia (Giarchi 1996, 2002).

The demand for welfare services located in urban centres can also be aggravated by older workers' unemployment. In the face of global competition and depression in commodity prices the European agricultural labour force has recently decreased by over 2.2 million workers (Eurostat 2000). This has affected active older farm labourers, who are often the first to be laid off and whose average income is among the lowest in Europe. In more remote peripheries of eastern Poland, for instance, country household incomes (mainly pertaining to older rural residents) are 86 per cent less than the national average (Wilson 1998; Hoggart et al. 1995). It is estimated that some 750,000 small farms in Poland have closed down (Hoggart et al. 1995). The situation has been worse in Bulgaria, Romania and the Slovak Republic (Giarchi 1996). Věra Majerová (2006), commenting on conditions in Czech rural areas, has shown how difficult has been the transfer from state controls to a thoroughly different socio-economic system, especially for older owners of smaller farms.

In the face of blocked resources or cutbacks, the voices of countryside communities have less political influence than those of city electorates. Furthermore, 'Euro-ageism' can affect urban planners' judgement as to the formulation of health and social care policies and priorities (Vincent 1999; Walker and Naegele 1999). Indeed, older people's needs in general are not being adequately represented politically, nationally or regionally in most EU countries (Walker and Naegele 1999). Nonetheless, some representative organizations continue to voice countryside concerns in urban municipalities: for instance the 'National Federation for Clubs for Older People in Rural Parts of the Country' (FNCRA: 1.2 million members) in France; 'Dane Age' and 'Aeldre Mobiliseringen' (Mobilizing the Elderly) in Denmark; 'Age Concern', the 'National Association of Old Age Pension Associations', 'National Pensioners' Convention', 'Help the Aged', and the recently government-led 'Better Government for Older People' in the UK. Also, cooperatives can be successful in providing and organizing replacements for rural services that have been withdrawn by urban planners. In a recent case study in the Republic of Ireland, Casey *et al.* (2006) describe how the Bantry Rural Transport Group that included older people set up its own transport services in the West Cork rural area.

When rural areas resist socio-economic regional and local urban flows to the countryside

As already considered, one major urban outflow to the countryside has been that of retirees. Champion and Shepherd (2006) refer to this as the global 'cascading down' from urban to rural settlements. Apart from negative factors discussed above, in-migration in some instances can benefit the rural economy and may also provide a rich source of local social capital. Yet the flow can become an avalanche, disturbing the social equilibrium of villages and their cultural ethos and conserved traditions. Culture clashes result. In addition, in competing for scarce local commodities, the newcomers may also outbid older-established consumers.

Also, more affluent incoming retirees can contribute to an increase in local relative poverty in select areas of scenic beauty, as a result of visible gaps in income/capital resources between incomers and indigenous older residents. Simmons (1997) refers to 'well-to-do' folk in England with 'city ways' who are buying into countrysides in search of the rural idyll, as researched in East Anglia, the South-West and Cambridgeshire. The same has been noted recently in Hungary (Salinow 2006). Moreover, such largely urban retirees can add further to what Gilbert *et al.* (2006: 90) have declared to be 'a clear geographical variation in income status', with indigenous older people faring worst of all, especially in less accessible and remote rural areas. Incoming affluence can also add to the deprivation experienced by poor pensioners in countrysides, wherever costs of food and domestic goods soar and house prices escalate.

Furthermore, there are also disruptive planned urban-into-rural developments. According to Rena Sarumpaet (2006), 'globalization has overwhelmingly been an urbanizing phenomenon and is creating inequalities both within and between cities and their rural hinterlands'. David Harvey and John Wiseman (cited in Sarumpaet 2006: 1–17) support this view. Nairn (1956) once referred to 'place annulling forces of urban uniformity'. He predicted a wholesale loss of distinctiveness of place, as a result of the disruptive inroads of subtopia and the march of bricks and mortar into green pastures. In Northern Europe, urban retail parks and shopping malls have edged their way into green belts (Barker 1999). Some older people may have welcomed their advent, but other indigenous older residents resent and resist the plans of 'scene-changers' and entrepreneurs, drawn up in faraway urban landscapes. Sights, smells and sounds can alter local-scapes, or *heimat*, which Huber and O'Reilly (2004) (after Neumeyer 1992: 127) interpret as 'the immediate and subjective life-world' of the place that is 'home' for them. Older indigenous residents can be most bewildered by the intrusion of multinational corporate investments. They see their countryside becoming a 'company region', such as has long existed in Niedersachsen (VolksWagen), Bavaria (BMW), Northern Italy (Fiat), and North-West France (Renault) (see Hoggart *et al.* 1995: 171).

Local rural older people can also feel hemmed in by urban encroachment in those parts of Europe's remote countrysides that have progressively been commodified as global city playgrounds (Williams and Baláz 2000), or 'urban playspace' (Butler 1998). Mass tourism has spread well beyond established continental inland retreats, such as in remote countrysides of Bratislava-District, Stará Lunbovna and Dolny Kubín regions (Slovakia). Nature-based tourism has also become a major attraction in remote landscapes of Central and Eastern Europe (Williams and Baláz 2000). Townsend (1991: 91–2) has commented upon significant increases in 'day tourism' and short-term weekends in isolated countrysides. Although some older local people profit from the additional income that visitors bring to the local economy, many do not. In my 1992 interviews in Chianti, most local people complained of their villages being invaded by chanting bands of urban *stranieri* (Giarchi 1993). In my Ligurian study (1996), an older Italian sitting in the shade of his small shed ruefully referred to 'summer hordes invading our village like the Lombardi did long ago'. Bailey (1992: 242) similarly cites Urry's (1990) reference to people becoming 'objects of the tourist gaze', epitomized by ageist portrayals of 'wrinkled older rustic faces' as depicted in holiday postcards and travel brochures. Increasing 'consumption' of the countryside – initiated and financed by urban elites, public services and entrepreneurs – has appropriated some of the most scenic landscapes of Europe. Part of this process, for instance, has been the creation of at least 65 national country parks in twelve EU countries (Ministère de l'environnement 1994). Although some indigenous older people have accepted or welcomed conservation areas and parks, many others have not. (Some Cornish people, for instance, describe the summer incomers as 'emmets' – which is old Cornish for 'ants'.)

Summary and Conclusion

In providing a framework for an overview of the 'life-world' of older Europeans, this chapter has taken account of the nature and extent of interaction between urban centres and rural peripheries. On the basis of available research in Britain and continental Europe, the chapter has proposed and formulated an urban–rural framework consisting of four parameters within which to focus upon salient, possible socio-economic and socio-political outcomes that can affect older people in diverse rural countrysides.

The first parameter consists of two-way urban–rural socio-economic flows that benefit older people, especially in urban fringe/shadow countrysides and accessible settlements. Here, fitter older people often contribute to the well-being of local people. Services are usually more accessible, and there are more opportunities locally for willing volunteering, and more employment for the active older residents than there are in less accessible and remote country-sides. Also, dependent senior citizens are more likely to have better usage of support services than in scattered and less accessible countryside dwellings.

The second parameter concerns the impact upon older persons in country-sides, wherever urban and rural domains cut themselves off from one another. Urban–rural socio-economic flows are hampered when there exists a socio-political and long-standing cultural deadlock between regional urban centres and rural localities. Older residents in such an impasse can be trapped within 'internal colonies' that are virtually closed rural communities.

The third parameter identifies the situation when regional and local urban centres block or cut socio-economic flows to diverse countrysides. Transport costs, and the additional time it takes to provide goods, health and social care, affect service delivery to older people in the less accessible and remote countrysides, especially to those living in scattered, isolated dwellings.

The fourth parameter takes account of countryside resistance to urban–rural developments ushered in by globalization. Grassroots action has been mobilized to resist urban–rural developments or to protest about the lack of countryside services. This may occur when older residents in pursuit of the rural idyll view new infrastructures as a threat to their peaceful countryside. Incoming retirees can also disrupt the traditional village ethos.

Throughout this prospective overview, account has been taken of the significance of socio-political power and influence within the global interplay of urban centres and rural peripheries. In addition, reference has been made to the import of values taken by planners and providers, on the one hand, and of the stance of older people themselves over rural issues, on the other. Given the gaps revealed in the empirical data within rural studies regarding the welfare of older residents, especially in continental Europe, an expansion of comparative studies in this area is clearly called for.

Acknowledgements

The author is indebted to earlier funding provided in the 1970s, 1980s and 1999s by the Esme Fairbain Trust, ESRC, and the EC Social Fund for research he carried out in the rural areas of Argyll, Cornwall and Devon in the UK, Tuscany and Liguria in Italy; and County Cork in the Republic of Ireland.

I am grateful to Professor Catherine Jones Finer, the series editor, and to Dr Gai Harrison, Dr Penny Price and Dr Joyce Halliday (University of Plymouth) for their invaluable comments and ideas while writing this chapter.

References

Age Concern (1998), *Developing Rural Services to Older People*, Resource Pack, London: Age Concern.

Alun, F. J. and Phillips, D. R. (1984), *Accessibility and Utilization: Geographical Perspectives on Health Care Delivery*, New York: Harper and Row.

Appadurai, A. (1996), *Modernity at Large*, Minneapolis: University of Minnesota Press.

Asthana, S., Halliday, J., Bingham, P. and Gibson, A. (2002), *Rural Deprivation and Service Need: A Review of the Literature and an Assessment of Indicators for Rural Service Planning*, Plymouth: South West Public Health Observatory, University of Plymouth.

Asthana, S., Gibson, A., Moon, G. and Bingham, P. (2003), Allocating resources for health and social care: the significance of rurality, *Health and Social Care in the Community*, 11, 6: 486–90.

Bagnasco, A. (1977), *The Italie*, Bologna: Il Mulino.

Bailey, J. (ed.) (1992), *Social Europe*, London: Longman.

Barker, P. (1999), Edge city. In A. Barnett and R. Scruton (eds), *Town and Country*, London: Random House, pp. 206–16.

Barnett, A. (1999), Securing the future. In A. Barnett and R. Scruton (eds), *Town and Country*, London: Vintage.

Barnett, A. (1999), Securing the future. In A. Barnett and R. Scruton (eds), *Town and Country*, London: Vintage, pp. 339–42.

Bell, P. and Cloke, P. (1991), Public transport in the countryside: the effects of bus deregulation in rural Wales. In T. Champion and C. Watkins. *People in the Countryside*, London: Chapman, pp. 125–43.

Bevan, M. and Croucher, K. (2006), Delivering services for older people in rural areas. In P. Lowe and L. Speakman (eds), *The Ageing Countryside*, London: Age Concern, pp. 147–63.

Blackman, T., Brodhurst, S. and Convery, J. (2001), *Social Care and Social Exclusion*, Basingstoke: Palgrave.

BMA Board of Science (2005), *Health Care in a Rural Setting*, London: British Medical Association.

Bradshaw, W. and Wallace, M. (1996), *Global Inequalities*, California: Pine Forge.

Butler, R. (1998), Rural recreation and tourism. In B. Ilbery (ed.), *The Geography of Rural Change*, Harlow: Longman, pp. 211–32.

Casey, E., Enright, P. and O'Shaughnessy, M. (2006), Exploring the role of social enterprises in meeting the needs of rural citizens: a case study of rural transport in Ireland. Paper presented at The Rural Citizen Conference: Governance, Culture and Wellbeing in the 21st Century, Plymouth University, 5–7 April.

Castells, M. (1998a), *The Rise of the Network Society*, Oxford: Blackwell.

Castells, M. (1998b), *The Power of Identity*, Oxford: Blackwell.

Champion, T. and Watkins, C. (eds) (1991), *People in the Countryside*, London: Chapman.

Champion, T. and Shepherd, J. (2006), Demographic change in rural England. In P. Lowe and L. Speakman (eds), *The Ageing Countryside*, London: Age Concern, pp. 29–50.

Chapman, P., Phimister, E., Shucksmith, N., Upward, R. and Vera-Toscano, E. (1998), *Poverty and Exclusion in Rural Britain: The Dynamics of Low Income and Employment*, York: YPS.

Christmas, L. (1991), *Chopping Down the Cherry Trees: A Portrait of Britain in the Eighties*, London: Penguin, p. 262.

Clark, G. and Woollett, S. (1990), *English Village Services in the Eighties*, Rural Research Series no. 7, London: Rural Development Commission.

Cohen, A. P. (ed.) (1982), *Belonging*, Manchester: Manchester University Press.

Cloke, P. J. and Little, J. (1997), *Contested Countryside Cultures*, London: Routledge.

Countryside Agency (2000a), *The State of the Countryside*, Cheltenham: Countryside Agency.

Countryside Agency (2000b), *Not Seen Not Heard? Social Exclusion in Rural Areas*, London: Countryside Agency.

Countryside Agency (2001), *Rural Services in 2000*, London: Countryside Agency.

Countryside Agency (2003), *Quality of Life in Tomorrow's Countryside*, Cheltenham: Countryside Agency Publications.

Countryside Agency (2004), *The State of the Countryside*, Cheltenham: Countryside Agency.

Countryside Agency (2005), *The State of the Countryside*, Cheltenham: Countryside Agency.

Defra (2004), *Rural Strategy 2004*, London: Department for the Environment, Food and Rural Affairs.

Dower, M. (1995), Rural well-being in Europe. Unpublished paper presented at University of Plymouth Geography Department Symposium, Plymouth, 28 April.

Eurostat (2000), *Europe in Figures*, Luxembourg: Office for Official Publications of the European Communities.

Fernández-Armesto, F. (ed.) (1994), *Guide to the Peoples of Europe*, London: Times Books.

Fernández-Ballasteros, R. and Caprara, M. (eds) (2003), Psychology of Aging in Europe, *European Psychologist*, 8, 3 (September).

Fisher, C. (1997), I bought my fist saw with my maternity benefit. In P. Cloke and J. Little (eds), *Contested Countryside Cultures*, London: Routledge, pp. 232–51.

Frankenberg, R. (1966), *Communities in Britain*, Harmondsworth: Penguin.

Furuseth, O. (1998), Service provision and social deprivation. In B. Ilbery (ed.), *The Geography of Rural Change*, Harlow: Longman, pp. 133–56.

Giarchi, G. G. (1990), Distance decay and information deprivation: health implications for people in rural isolation. In P. Abbott and G. Payne (eds), *New Directions in the Sociology of Health*, London: Falmer Press, pp. 57–69.

Giarchi, G. G. (1993), *Community Actions for the Elderly*, funded by Commission of the European Communities, Social Fund: Brussels.

Giarchi, G. G. (1996), *Caring for Older Europeans*, Aldershot: Arena Books.

Giarchi, G. G. (2002), A conspectus of types, options and conditions of elder accommodation in the European continent, *Innovation: The European Journal of Social Science Research*, 15, 2: 99–120.

Giddens, A. (1993), *Sociology*, 2nd edn, Cambridge: Polity Press, Blackwell.

Gilbert, A., Philip, L. and Shucksmith, M. (2006), Rich and poor in the countryside. In P. Lowe and L. Speakman (eds), *The Ageing Countryside*, London: Age Concern, pp. 69–93.

Guesnier, B. (1994), Regional variations in new firm formation in France, *Regional Studies*, 28: 347–58.

Gummer, J. (1999), The four million houses. In A. Barnett and R. Scruton (eds), *Town and Country*, London: Vintage, pp. 177–89.

Halliday, F. E. (1959), *A History of Cornwall*, Letchworth: Duckworth.

Harvey, D. (1998), *The Killing of the Countryside*, London: Vintage.

Hawes, A. (2001), *Extra Virgin Amongst the Olive Groves of Liguria*, London: Penguin.

Herklots, H. (2004), Rural infrastructure. Paper presented at Ageing and the Countryside Conference, Age Concern and Defra and the Countryside Agency, Victoria Park Plaza: London.

Help the Aged and Rural Development Commission (1996), *Growing Old in the Countryside*, London: RDC.

Help the Aged (2004), *Beat the Bogus Caller*, London: Help the Aged.

Hoggart, K., Buller, H. and Black, R. (1995), *Rural Europe: Identity and Change*, London: Arnold.

Huber, A. and O'Reilly, K. (2004), The construction of *Heimat* under conditions of individualised modernity: Swiss and elder migrants in Spain, *Ageing and Society*, 24, 3: 307–51.

Ilbery, B. (ed.) (1998), Dimensions of rural change. In B. Ilbery (ed.), *The Geography of Rural Change*, Harlow: Longman, pp. 13–30.

Joseph, A. E. and Phillips, D. R. (1984), *Accessibility and Utilization*, New York: Harper and Row.

Kahana, E. A. (1982), A congruence model of person–environment interaction. In M. P. Lawton, P. G. Windley and T. O. Byerts (eds), *Aging and the Environment: Theoretical Approaches*, New York: Springer, pp. 87–121.

Lawley, A. and Deane, M. (2000), *Making Rural Communities Safer: Consultation on Community Safety*, London and Cheltenham: Nacro/Countryside Agency.

Le Mesurier, N. (2003), *The Hidden Store*, London: Age Concern.

Le Mesurier, N. (2004), Older people's involvement in rural communities. Ageing and the Countryside Conference, Age Concern, Defra and Help the Aged, Victoria Plaza, London.

Le Mesurier, N. (2006), The contributions of older people to rural community and citizenship. In P. Lowe and L. Speakman (eds), *The Ageing Countryside*, London: Age Concern, pp. 133–46.

Lewis, G. (1998), Rural migration and demographic change. In B. Ilbery (ed.), *The Geography of Rural Change*, Harlow: Longman, pp. 131–60.

Lewis, J. R. and Williams, A. M. (1986), Factories, farms and families: the impact of industrial growth in rural Central Portugal, *Sociologia Ruralis*, 26, 3/4: 320–44.

Lowe, G. (2003), Regions for all ages. Age Concern and English Regions Network Conference, Birmingham.

Lowe, G. (2004), Population ageing and rural policy. Paper presented at 'Ageing and the Countryside Conference', Age Concern, Defra and Help the Aged, Victoria Plaza: London.

Lowe, P. and Speakman, L. (eds) (2006), *The Ageing Countryside*, London: Age Concern.

McLaughlin, B. (1986), The rural deprivation debate: retrospect and prospect. In P. Lowe and S. Wright (eds), *Deprivation and Welfare in Rural Areas*, Norwich: Geobooks, pp. 43–54.

Maclouf, P. and Lion, A. (1984), *Report of the International Group Meeting on Aging in Remote Rural Areas: A Challenge to Social and Medical Services*, Vienna: Eurosocial reports, no. 24.

MAFF/DEFR (2000), *Our Countryside: The Future. A Fair Deal for Rural England*, London: Stationery Office.

Majerová, V, (2006), From citizenship to rural civil society: Czech rural areas after the transformation of agriculture. Paper presented at The Rural Citizen Conference: Governance, Culture and Wellbeing in the 21st Century, Plymouth University, 5–7 April.

Milligan, C. (2001), *Geographies of Care*, Aldershot: Avebury.

Ministère de l'environnement (1994), *L'Environnement en France*, Paris: Dunod.

Mittelman, J. (ed.) (1997), *Globalization: Critical Reflection*, London: Lynne Rienner.

Nairn, I. (1956), Counter attack, *Architectural Review*, December: 20–30.

Neumeyer, M. (1992), *Heimat zu Geschichte und Begriff eines Phänomens Selbstverlag des Geographischen*, Instituts der Universität Kiel: Kiel, Germany. Cited in Huber and O'Reilly (2004).

North, D. (1998), Rural industrialization. In B. Ilbery (ed.), *The Geography of Rural Change*, Harlow: Longman, pp. 161–88.

Office of National Statistics (2002), *Census 2001: First Results on Population for England and Wales*, London: Stationery Office.

Papadopoulus, S. (1985), La découverte muséologique du paysan en Grèce. In M. P. Canapa and associates, *Paysans et Nations d'Europe Centrale et Balkanique*, Paris: Maisoneuve et Larose, pp. 87–93.

Paúl, C., Fonseca, A. M., Martin, I. and Amado, J. (2003), Psychological profile of rural and urban elders in Portugal, *European Psychology*, 8, 3: 160–7.

Payton, P. (ed.) (1993), *Cornwall Since the War*, Redruth: Institute of Cornish Studies.

Phillips, D. and Williams, A. (1984), *Rural Britain: A Social Geography*, Oxford: Blackwell.

Precedo Ledo, A. and Grimes, S. (1991), Urban transitions and local developments in a peripheral region: the case of Galicia. In M. J. Banton, L. S. Bownes and R. Sinclair (eds), *Urbanization and Urban Development*, Dublin: University College Dublin, pp. 97–107.

Robertson. R. (1992), *Globalization, Social Theory and Social Culture*, London: Sage.

Room, G. (1995), *Beyond the Threshold: The Measurement and Analysis of Social Exclusion*, Bristol: Policy Press.

Rubinstein, R. and Parmelle, P. (1992), Attachment to place and representation of life course by the elderly. In I. Altman and S. Low (eds), *Human Behaviour and Environment*, vol. 12: *Place Attachment*, New York: Plenum, pp. 139–63.

Rural Development Commission (1996), *Disadvantage in Rural Areas*, Salisbury: RDC.

Russell, A. (1986), *The Country Parish*, London: SPCK.

Salinow, J. (2006), The Hungarian countryside. Unpublished seminar proceedings, The Rural Citizen: Governance, culture and wellbeing in the 21st Century, University of Plymouth, 5–7 April.

Sarumpaet, R. (2006), *Globally Speaking – The Politics of Globalisation*. Program 5: *Global Cities*. Available at: http://www.abc.net.au/global/radio/radio05.htm

Scharf, T. (2001), Ageing and international relationships in rural Germany, *Ageing and Society*, special issue: 547–66.

Scharf, T. and Bartlam, B. (2006), *Rural Disadvantage: Quality of Life and Disadvantage Amongst Older People – A Pilot Study*, London: Commission for Rural Communities.

Scharf, T. and Wenger, G. C. (2000), Cross-national and empirical research in gerontology: the OPERA experience, *Education and Ageing*, 15, 3.

Shucksmith, M. (1991), Still no homes for locals? Affordable housing and planning controls in rural areas. In T. Champion and C. Watkins (eds), *People in the Countryside*, London: Chapman, pp. 53–66.

Shucksmith, M. (2000), *Exclusive Countryside? Social Exclusion and Regeneration in Rural Areas*, York: Joseph Rowntree Foundation.

Simmons, M. (1997), *Landscapes of Poverty*, London: Lemos and Crane.

St Leger, F. and Gillespie, N. (1991), *Informal Welfare in Belfast Caring Communities?* Aldershot: Avebury.

Tarrow, S. (1977), *Between Centre and Periphery: Grassroots Politicians in Italy and France*, New Haven, CT: Yale University Press.

Thompson, J. (1991), East Europe: dark dawn, *National Geographic*, 179, 6: 37–68.

Townsend, A. (1991), New forms of employment in rural areas. In T. Champion and C. Watkins (eds), *People in the Countryside*, London: Chapman, pp. 84–95.

Turnock, D. (ed.) (1998), *Privatization in Rural Eastern Europe*, Cheltenham: Edward Elgar.

Urry, J. (1990), *The Tourist Gaze: Leisure and Travel in Contemporary Societies*, London: Sage.

Vincent, J. A. (1999), *Politics, Power and Old Age*, Buckingham: Open University Press.

Walker, A. (1978), *Rural Poverty: Poverty, Deprivation and Planning in Rural Areas*, London: Child Poverty Action Group.

Walker, A. and Maltby, T. (1997), *Ageing Europe*, Buckingham: Open University Press.

Walker, A. and Naegele, G. (1999), *The Politics of Old Age in Europe*, Basingstoke: Open University Press.

Warnes, A. M., Friedrich, K., Kellaher, L. and Torres, S. (2004), The diversity and welfare of older migrants in Europe, *Ageing and Society*, 24, 3 (May): 307–26.

Wellman, B. (ed.) (1999), *Networks in the Global Village*, Boulder, CO: Westview Press.

Wenger, G. C. (1984), *The Support Network: Coping with Old Age*, London: George Allen and Unwin.

Wenger, G. C. (1992), *Help in Old Age: Facing up to a Change: A Longitudinal Network Study*, Occasional Paper 5, Liverpool: Institute of Human Ageing.

Wenger, G. C. (2001), Introduction: intergenerational relationships in rural areas, *Ageing and Society*, special issue: 537–45.

Wiggans, D. and Hillman, M. (1998), Railways, settlements and access. In A. Barnett and R. Scruton (eds), *Town and Country*, London: Vintage, pp. 21–44.

Williams, A. and Baláz, V. (2000), *Tourism in Transition: Economic Change in Central Europe*, London: I B Tauris.

Williams, R. (1973), *The Country and the City*, London: Chatto and Windus.

Wilson, O. (1998), East Germany. In D. Turnock (ed.), *Privatization in Rural Eastern Europe*, Cheltenham: Edward Elgar, pp. 120–44.

Woods, M. (2005), *Rural Geography*, London: Sage.

Wright Mills, C. (1959), *The Sociological Imagination*, London: Penguin.

9
Spinning the Rural Agenda: The Countryside Alliance, Fox Hunting and Social Policy

Alison Anderson

Introduction

Protest groups that mobilize concerns about the countryside and the environment often embrace a much broader agenda encompassing social, economic and political issues. The strategic integration of this wider agenda is beneficial as there is less likelihood of the groups becoming labelled as a single-issue pressure group. Traditionally, social policy is seen as bound up with questions of human welfare and has tended to focus on urban spaces. However, campaigns over 'rural' issues have fundamental implications for sustainability, in terms of both the economy and the environment. Changes in rural traditions, services and leisure pursuits have direct effects upon livelihoods within rural communities, although the extent of this impact is hotly debated. Recent years have witnessed both the increasing emergence of direct action protests and a rapid growth in the PR industry. Such developments have important implications for social policy since the battle over 'countryside' issues reflects wider concerns to do with inequality, citizenship and power. To what extent do such protests constitute the democratic voice of rural publics? What role does cultural capital play in influencing the outcome of protest activities? How influential are the protests in shaping rural policy? Through examining a case study of the UK campaign against the ban on fox hunting this chapter seeks to highlight how the analysis of popular protests over rural restructuring is of central relevance for contemporary social policy.

Until the 2005 ban, fox hunting, as a traditional sport, had been practised in the UK for some 300 years. However, by the 1990s mounting political pressure from backbench Labour MPs mobilized by powerful anti-hunting pressure groups, such as the League Against Cruel Sports (LACS), the Royal Society for the Prevention of Cruelty to Animals (RSPCA) and the International Fund for Animal Welfare (IFAW), posed an increasing threat to this controversial pastime. This chapter focuses in particular on the public relations campaign that was mounted by the Countryside Alliance (CA) to oppose the 'Hunting with Dogs' Bill. The CA is a lobby group established 'to campaign for the countryside, country sports and the rural way of life' (CA website). Like the fuel protests of 2000, which drew on overlapping activist networks, the CA campaign raised issues of broader social policy relevance concerning the power of vocal minority groups to claim the countryside agenda (Barry and Doherty 2001).

Both sides of the hunting debate have skilfully used the news media to wage a symbolic war concerning issues of morality, identity and the ownership of the countryside. The degree of access to the news media that the pro- and anti-hunting lobbies have enjoyed has varied over time, with both sides frequently complaining about bias and misrepresentation (*Daily Telegraph* leader, 26 September 2002; Leonard *et al.* 2002; Real Countryside Alliance (spoof website); *UK Press Gazette* 2005; Windeatt 1982). While news media reporting has not always neatly followed simple political divides, UK national press coverage has clearly been influenced by political partisanship, with the right-leaning *Daily Telegraph* and *Daily Mail* providing the most sympathetic coverage of the pro-hunting alliance, and the left-leaning *Guardian* and *Daily Mirror* offering most sympathetic coverage of the anti-hunting cause (Stokes 1996; Thomas 1983).[1] However, to date there has been little in-depth, systematic examination of the role of the news media in studies of the UK fox hunting debate. Researchers have tended to restrict their focus to the 'quality' press and have generally shown little engagement with mainstream media studies research, nor an appreciation of the complexities of news production and media influence in terms of framing and agenda-building (e.g. Evans 2000; Norton 2000; Wallwork and Dixon 2004). This study therefore aims to develop new insights about the shifting media politics of the hunting debate and constructions of rurality. It is based upon an examination of CA press releases, together with a detailed qualitative textual analysis of the framing of the CA Liberty and Livelihood March in the British newspaper press during the period 17–23 September 2002.[2] This covered the period leading up to, and the day after, the reporting of the march in London on 22 September.

The case study illustrates how the hunting lobby succeeded in gaining extensive press coverage of its Liberty and Livelihood March. With the rise of new media, the absence of marked ideological divides between the main political parties, and a growing sense of disillusionment with party politics among voters, some commentators claim that the relationship between protest movements and the press has been transformed in recent years. Indeed Milne (2005) argues that these factors have led to a shift from the press manufacturing consent to a new emphasis upon what she calls 'manufacturing dissent'. Thus she observes:

> The lack of fit between party platforms and protesters' concerns suggests a dissonance between politics and public opinion. The axis with media organizations creates powerful if short-lived coalitions capable of competing with governments to frame the political agenda. The trend towards instant, PR driven protest risks giving newspapers disproportionate power. It pushes politicians into the role of rapid reactors to majority pressure, rather than arbiters of different interests. (2005: 12)

However, this chapter questions the claim that the press are becoming actors or agents of social movements for the first time. Through a focus upon the case study of the CA campaign, it argues that such claims are ahistorical and tend to isolate the press from the broader policy-making arena. Before examining newspaper representations of the protest, it is first necessary to consider briefly the CA's historical origins so as to gain an appreciation of movement–media relations over time.

The Rebranding of the Hunting Lobby

The CA was established in 1997 in the widely predicted run-up to the New Labour government. It resulted from an amalgamation of the British Field Sports Society (BFSS), the Countryside Movement (CM) and the Countryside Business Group (CBG). The CA currently claims to have over 105,000 full ordinary members, together with approximately 250,000 associate members through affiliated clubs and societies (CA website). Previous experience had taught the leadership of the BFSS that broad public support for its cause could not be generated on the hunting issue alone. Public opinion polls had consistently demonstrated majority public support for a hunting ban and, according to former CA press officer Janet George, there was a concerted attempt by hunt supporters to 'wrap hunting up in the wider rural fabric. Because everyone loves the countryside and hates hunting' (Beckett 1998). As Daniel (1997) commented:

> The Alliance hopes to tap into the rich vein of frustration felt by 'rural folk' towards week-enders and starry-eyed city migrants, and their sense that the bright lights of the city have blinded politicians to issues such as rural poverty and lack of services . . . rural frustration is certainly a better button to press than asking people to defend a sport pursued by a minority.

As far back as 1995 the BFSS provided financial support to the newly created Countryside Movement (CM), which consisted largely of pro-hunting interests and campaigned 'for tolerance to be shown towards hunting and other minority sports' (Clover 1995). However, the CM was mired in controversy concerning its sources of funding (the Duke of Westminster reportedly provided £1 million in funding to rescue the organization after it had overspent), and, despite these sources, failed to reach the levels of income anticipated at the launch (Younge 2000). The BFSS saw an opportunity to capitalize on the mistakes made by the CM, and announced a merger with it and another pro-hunting organization, the Countryside Business Group. It was felt the newly created CA could muster support from a broad range of countryside interests, to form a powerful coalition which any government could not afford to ignore. From the start it sought to build relations with the government rather than launch a strategy of outright hostility, despite relying on anti-Labour feeling among traditionally Conservative rural voters for its core support (Ward 2002). It appointed the Labour peer Baroness Mallalieu as president, and eventually a Labour-supporting chairman and chief executive.

In the run-up to the ban on hunting with hounds, which came into effect on 18 February 2005, the CA was able to capitalize on a variety of rural crises over issues such as foot and mouth disease, dwindling rural services, the rising cost of fuel, concerns about government proposals to increase access to the countryside, as well as a more general dissatisfaction with Labour government policy (Lusoli and Ward 2003, 2005; Milbourne 2003). It positioned itself as a body that exists to protect 'the rural way of life' – a way of life that is frequently romanticized and portrayed as under threat from an increasingly distanced urban, political elite. This tapped into, and resonated with, powerful symbolic metaphors of the land associated with national identity and the rural idyll – going to the very heart of what it means to be 'British' (see Wallwork and Dixon 2004). With the absence of an effective rural lobby group, what followed was

> a skilful exercise in re-branding which coincided with a dramatic slump in the fortunes of rural Britain . . . The Alliance, with its recent make-over, was perfectly poised to step into the void and bring together the disparate discontent in the countryside. (Younge 2000)

This strategy involved a number of different tactics to try to spin the 'countryside agenda' in its favour, one of which involved concerted attempts to influence the outcome of news media opinion polls on fox hunting through using the CA email distribution list to encourage supporters to make multiple calls (see Mathiason 2004). For example, in 1999 the *Daily Mirror* claimed the CA rigged their poll (Jones *et al.* 1999). In 2000 the CA appointed David Burnside to launch a major PR campaign. Burnside was previously head of public relations at British Airways and engineered the 'dirty tricks' campaign against Virgin (Dillon and Goodchild 2000). By this point the CA had 80 full-time staff and 10 regional press and public relations officers (Younge 2000) and considerable financial backing.[3]

One of the difficulties that the organization faced was how to broaden support for a minority interest through mobilizing concerns about a host of other rural issues. The idea that one can have a 'countryside' alliance is itself questionable, given the sheer diversity of rural issues and the increasing blurring of the urban and the rural, and it was not long before major rifts began to appear, with splinter groups developing, such as the Real Countryside Alliance and the Countryside Action Network. In 2002 the CA conducted a survey among its members on 'What is rural?' In the selection of definitions provided on the CA website there is an emphasis on the 'rural' as 'a state of mind' rather than a location. If the definition of rural is framed in terms of a state of mind, then attitudes and opinions that are not consistent with the CA are implicitly framed as anti-rural. In this way, 'any attack on hunting threatens other components of rurality' (Milbourne 2003: 290).

Despite public hostility from the government, it was essential for the CA to continue to court various countryside interests if its strategy of widening its support base was to succeed. However, between 10 January and 4 November 1998, Evans (2000) discovered that 43 out of 74 news releases available on its website related specifically to hunting. Also, out of the 124 press releases in 1999 listed by the CA on its website, over half (69) were primarily about hunting. Many of the remainder related to other 'country sports' or organizational developments, and a small proportion, just 16 per cent (20), primarily related to other countryside issues. In the year 2000 internal CA documents suggested that just 3 per cent of its budget was spent on the development of policy areas such as post offices and transport, whereas £1.2 million was allocated to campaigns to defend hunting, shooting and fishing, with a further £1.5 million allocated to political lobbying and public relations to fight attempts to ban hunting (Woolf 2001). Nevertheless, the leadership of the CA continued to claim to speak on behalf of rural Britain, and undoubtedly succeeded in attracting large numbers of people to its march who were not principally concerned with a ban on hunting.

The Liberty and Livelihood March

Besides utilizing the network of hundreds of hunts and coursing clubs, the CA made more effective use of ICT to mobilize its supporters than it did in the earlier Countryside March of 1998. Through a regular 'grass-e-route' electronic newsletter, supporters were kept up to date and urged to participate in a variety of activities from voting in phone-in polls on hunting to attending regional as well as national demonstrations. In August 2002 the CA announced plans to use an Internet webcast to promote the march (CA 2002a). Also, it created a separate march website which contained march-related information, and it was easy for sympathetic newspapers to post the website address for readers to visit. For example, anonymously authored articles in the *Daily Telegraph* regularly reproduced information taken from the website and CA press releases with details such as: 'Marchers who haven't registered, including those from overseas, should do so now (0900 102 0900; www.march-info.org) so that organizers can collate numbers expected and confirm arrangements with the Metropolitan Police' (17 September 2002). According to Lusoli and Ward (2003, 2005), the march website attracted 120,000 visits in total, and the average number of monthly visitors to the main CA site grew from 40,000 to 160,000 in September 2002.

The timing of the march, just one year after the number of reported cases of foot and mouth had reached a peak, was fortuitous for the CA. As Lusoli and Ward observe:

> Arguably, much of the success of the CA has been its ability to act as a focal point for a range of sometimes-contradictory rural issues . . . though the pro-hunting cause is by far away the most prominent issue, the CA have tapped into and encouraged the perception of a growing urban–rural divide in the UK. The CA has consistently argued that rural issues and countryside pursuits have been misunderstood and discriminated against by an essentially urban political class. (2003: 3)

The march was also scheduled to take place a matter of weeks after a series of public hearings, organized by the government, as part of its consultation process before introducing legislation on hunting.

The Liberty and Livelihood March attracted widespread coverage in the UK press. The CA claimed that over 400,000 people took part, although this figure was challenged by an independent count conducted by MORI (LACS 2002). Unusually, there was a considerable amount of coverage of the march in the national press in the two weeks leading up to it. However, most coverage was generated on the day of the march, with particularly extensive coverage the following day, much of it focusing on the CA appeal to English libertarian values. On Monday 23 September, the day after the march, all of the UK national daily newspapers carried the story on the front page, apart from the *Daily Star* – although it devoted its editorial, 'The Daily Star Says Hunt Down Real Issues', to arguing that there were too many other important issues for parliament to spend more of its time debating fox hunting. The coverage in the red-top and mid-market press centred on members of the royal family and their support for the march. For example, the *Daily Star* focused on Prince William – 'Wills On Razzle With Marchers', while the *Daily Express*, the *Daily Mirror* and the *Sun* focused on Prince Charles's intervention into the debate. The *People* urged Prime Minister Tony Blair to see through the ban on hunting in its leader the day before commenting: 'This newspaper has always despised fox hunting.' At the same time it called for the prime minister to listen to the 'genuine concerns' of the marchers about rural policy.

The *Daily Express*, though not leading on the story, printed a special souvenir edition with three pages devoted to the march and an editorial headed 'Charles Must Desist From Expressing Political Views'. The *Sunday Express* meanwhile took a clear line against hunting, arguing in its own leader column: 'Where we part company with the marchers is on the issue that is to many of them fundamental: hunting. Despite their claims that only hunters understand the hunt, we can see no justification for a practice that is both cruel and unnecessary.' To provide an appearance of impartiality, this was accompanied by a leading article on the same page written by John Jackson, former chairman of the CA. Jackson implied that rural people unanimously opposed the ban on hunting: 'Rural people find it hard to understand how anyone could even question the role of hunting in rural life, let alone ban it.' Further on in the same edition a piece on 'Fifteen Foxy Facts' was authored by Professor Stephen Harris, providing details of the anti-hunting National Fox Welfare Society. At the same time a piece taken straight from a CA press release provided readers with 'March dos and don'ts', including advice on what to bring, how to behave and recommending restaurants and pubs along the route.

The march was given particular prominence in the *Daily Mail*'s 'Souvenir issue of the great march', which provided 15 pages of reports, comment and pictures, including an 8-page picture pull-out. The front page featured the headline: 'So Where Were You, Prime Minister? (Weekending in the Country Actually . . .)'. Each page devoted to the march bore the slogan 'Save Our Countryside' and the front page featured a photograph of a boy on his father's shoulders proudly displaying the *Daily Mail* 'Save Our Countryside' poster featuring the picturesque, affluent Cotswold village of Snowshill (see Morris 2002). It described the protesters as 'defenders of Britain's rural way of life'. The newspaper distributed plastic-backed versions of the poster on the route for marchers to display. On page 5 it carried a prominent article reporting Prince Charles's comments concerning what he saw as the victimization of a minority group by the government. In its editorial it contrasted Prince Charles's 'instinctive, profound and active interest in the countryside and the people who live and work in it' with Prime Minster Tony Blair, who is said to show 'no concern for the marginalization of rural Britain, nor any sympathy for those whose rural traditions, values and livelihoods are under threat'.

Many newspapers went to great lengths to provide the appearance of impartiality on the hunting debate. The *Daily Mail* distanced itself from supporting the pro-hunting case: 'As we have stressed repeatedly, this paper holds no brief for fox-hunting. But fox-hunting itself is not the issue. What matters is, once again, Labour's aloof metropolitan elite insists on imposing its values on others.' The piece finished by claiming: 'Ultimately what is at stake is Britain's priceless and enviable tradition of live-and-let-live, which has made us a beacon of tolerance and liberty down the centuries.' The *Daily Mail* used this opportunity to attack Labour Party policies through an appeal to history and tradition. Its coverage of the march emphasized support for its demands from royalty, celebrities and Mr Iain Duncan Smith, the then Conservative Party Leader. In an article on 27 September 2002 it described anti-hunting proposals as stemming from 'ignorant, urban class-hatred' and was highly critical of what it perceived as the BBC's relatively low-key coverage of the march.

The *Western Morning News* was also highly supportive of the March. On 23 September the whole of the front page was taken up with a photograph showing crowds of protesters with their placards, most prominent of which was a *Shooting Times* poster, 'Ban(g) Out of Order'. It claimed that 407,791 'country folk filed up to the Big Smoke'. In addition to the six pages on the 'Great Countryside Protest', the newspaper carried a 32-page march souvenir pull-out, containing a two-page article written by the south-west spokesman for the CA and two one-page articles by representatives of Endangered Exmoor Campaign Group, which describes itself as 'an organization formed by local people to fight for a traditional way of life under threat on Exmoor . . . and to highlight the devastating consequences a ban on hunting with hounds would have on this unique rural community' (Endangered Exmoor website). The coverage emphasized the respectability and sincerity of the marchers: 'this was not an unruly mob but the backbone of England on the move. Parish councillors, Women's Institute ladies, priests, village squires, woodland workers, agricultural labourers, yeomen, farmers.' While the newspaper steered clear of commenting on the hunting issue in its regular editorial column (that looked at the European Union and the beef ban), it carried a whole-page editorial on the march in its pull-out supplement. Here it stated:

> We have no desire to take sides in what is unquestionably a sensitive debate, evoking powerful and sincere emotions amongst pros and antis alike . . . If there be a case for distinguishing between one form of vermin control and another, then it must be made clearly, succinctly, and without

a trace of personal emotion. Thus far, we have not heard the case so stated. Until it be so, the pro-hunting fraternity can, with reason, claim that an urban government is, simply, throwing its weight about.

In this way the *Western Morning News* gives the appearance of impartiality and yet implicitly associates the anti-hunting case with emotion while clearly associating the pro-hunting case with rational thought. It presented 'the countryside' as having one voice, with the march bringing together people from all ages and walks of life in their common grievance in phrases such as 'Travellers unite in their desire to protect all aspects of country life.'

Among the national daily newspapers, the left-learning *Daily Mirror* came out most strongly against moves to stop the government from banning fox-hunting, declaring in its editorial: 'Many serious grievances were aired on yesterday's huge march but it was hijacked by the pro-hunters, including Prince Charles . . . The people with a genuine complaint are those who can't understand why it hasn't been banned before.' However, the *Sunday Mirror* was less forthright in its editorial on the day of the march, observing: 'The countryside is on the march today. Good luck to them. The countryside has been a forgotten land under new Labour.'

Even the largest-circulating newspaper, the *Sun*, devoted five pages to the march and took up the whole of the front page with a photograph of the protest alongside the headline: '400,000 March For Countryside: The Wonder Of Wellies'. Its coverage focused on how the 'green welly brigade' were marching to 'protect country life', the backing from celebrities such as Elle MacPherson and topless country girls. Its editorial focused on the march but, in sharp contrast to the *Daily Mirror*, it clearly perceived this to be an issue low down on its readers' agenda of concerns: 'And why does Blair feel the need to ban hunting? It is not an issue our 10 million readers list among their top five worries. Labour is fighting a class war in the country and we do not like this spectacle.'

Coverage of the march in the *Guardian* and the *Independent* was low-key. Both newspapers also gave front-page prominence to a news story about the German Green Party. Interestingly, both newspapers featured a Reuters photograph of a ferret on its owner's shoulder on their front page rather than a crowd scene. The *Independent* reported that while the CA estimated that the number of marchers was over 400,000, the metropolitan police estimated it to be 300,000. Its editorial included a brief comment attacking Prince Charles's intervention in the debate. The march did not even get a mention in the *Guardian*'s editorial, which instead focused on the German Greens, the Liberal Democrat party conference and climate change. The *Observer* led on the march, arguing: 'If hunts want to continue, then let them win licences from their local authorities, who should be obliged to hold referendums on the question.' Alongside this was a letter from Sir Patrick Moore, a supporter of LACS, which reiterated their position that 'hunting with dogs is cruel and unnecessary and has no place in modern Britain'.

The news frames adopted by the *Guardian* sharply contrasted with those of the *Daily Telegraph*, which provided extensive coverage of the demonstration. The latter has a long history of staunchly supporting fox hunting. Indeed, the then editor, Charles Moore, is said to have told its owner, Conrad

Black: 'The *Daily Telegraph* stands for foxhunting plus a few other things' (see McCann 2001). The march took up the whole of the front page on 23 September, and there were over eight pages of news and features. The front-page article attacked the perceived bias of the BBC's coverage of the march and, like the *Western Morning News*, claimed that there was considerable diversity among the supporters: 'As hard as a BBC presenter might try, you could not generalise about these people. No cosy British social snobbery or inverted snobbery helps you out, for the crowds were so socially and geographically diverse', a point that was reiterated in much of the reporting. For example: 'The biggest ever protest in Britain breaks barricades of age and class.' This strongly contrasts with the *Guardian*'s coverage, which suggested that 'if the political, social and racial diversity of the marchers was limited, the causes that they lead were eccentrically diverse'; the *Independent on Sunday*: 'This is not a unified movement'; the *Observer*: 'Damaging rifts within the rural lobby are threatening to overshadow today's countryside march'; and *The Times*: 'there are already signs that the fragile coalition of the alliance could be starting to splinter.' A MORI poll found the majority of marchers were right-wing and middle-class; 82 per cent of the protesters said they were most inclined to support the Conservative Party and 52 per cent were from classes A and B (professional/managerial) while 27 per cent were from the C1 group (clerical) (MORI 2002). This was broadly similar to the findings of a MORI poll conducted at the time of the 1998 march when 79 per cent of marchers said they would be most inclined to vote Conservative and 47 per cent were in the class AB group, with 35 per cent in the class C1 group (MORI 1998).

The *Daily Telegraph* emphasized national identity and tradition through comments such as: 'Despite the crisis in crime, the countryside and education brought about by cool Britannia, England can still regain its age-old position as the country of deeply-held beliefs and order', and 'One's idea of one's own culture is formed by many things . . . You won't spend much time talking about Britishness but you will recognise its symptoms, and you will mind if they are attacked'. Similarly, in the lead-up to the march, the *Daily Mail* compared the crowds likely to attend to those on Armistice Day in 1918 and VE Day in 1945. On the day of the march the *Sunday Telegraph* led with: 'Prince Charles tells Blair: "Farmers are being treated worse than blacks or gays."' It also included a piece written by Iain Duncan Smith, the then leader of the Conservative Party, arguing for the need to preserve freedom and tolerance. Although many items focused on the hunting issue, some mentioned broader issues affecting the countryside. For example, one feature article emphasized the human interest angle through an interview with an old farming family, united through generations in their place in the local rural community. The piece, written in a literary style, begins with an image of the sun shining through a stained glass window reflecting on to gravestones and ends with the prospect of the light being extinguished if nothing is done to protect livelihood and heritage: 'It is important to know your heritage, your roots . . . gazing down at his cracked and calloused knuckles. Hands like these say it all . . . I reckon we Rashs are *genetically programmed* to farm here: we are a bit like hefted sheep. Born knowing we belong.'

The *Daily Telegraph*'s coverage similarly emphasized the way in which it saw support for hunting and farming as a natural and integral aspect of rural communities and instinctively supported by rural people. The then editor, Charles Moore, claimed:

> In that still large part of British culture which has any link with rural life, hunting is firmly ingrained, and so is farming. If you are part of that culture, you may not yourself know very much about either, and you may dislike some of the practices of both, but your prejudice – your cultural DNA – is invincibly on their side.

Coverage in *The Times* and the *Sunday Times* focused more on how the march had been 'hijacked by the hunting lobby'. *The Times* reported that 'the vast majority of protesters said that they were moved to march on London by the proposal to ban foxhunting', and the *Sunday Times* claimed: 'The march would be more accurately described as for "Foxhunting and Fossilisation". What most of the marchers want is that the countryside should remain exactly as it is and that, through higher taxes or higher food prices, the urban masses should pay for them to go on looking after it'. The *Times* leader argued that the government should develop a new rural strategy.

The *Financial Times* focused upon economic factors affecting the countryside and emphasized the involvement of 'ordinary farming folk' and business people on the March: 'yesterday was not just a demonstration of the gentry: just as many people were going into McDonalds as into the Travellers' for lunch. An overwhelming majority of marchers were ordinary farming folk. Their banners reflected the range of issues in the minds of this diverse crowd. "Born to hunt – ready to fight", screamed one; "The rural economy is our business" read another.'

Battle metaphors were prominent in both the news coverage and CA press releases over the period. For example, the CA warned: 'Government declares war on the countryside.' Articles in the *Daily Telegraph* referred to the marchers as an 'army' or 'an army of 400,000 grass warriors' contrasted with 'Labour's class warriors'. Similarly, the *Daily Star* referred to the marchers as 'a country army', the *Observer* reported 'Countryside sounds call to arms' and the *Mail on Sunday* observed: 'Marchers fight for countryside'.

On the day of the march the press was far more likely to refer to the Urban Alliance, a militant anarchist group opposing fox hunting, than it was to refer to LACS. On that day the Urban Alliance was mentioned by the *News of the World*, the *Mail on Sunday* and the *Sunday Times*; the *Daily Express* had previously mentioned the group on the day prior to the march, and the *Guardian* on the day after the march. Several of these articles quoted comments made on the group's website such as: 'If you really want to stop the [Countryside] Alliance, don't go to London to boo them, get out into the countryside and hit them where it really hurts – in their own backyard.' Indeed, the only UK national newspaper to provide a direct quote from LACS on the day of the march was the *Independent on Sunday* – in response to comments made by a militant wing of the CA that they would target the prime minister's wife, Cherie Blair. And there were only two mentions (in passing) of the National

Fox Welfare Society; one in the *Sunday Telegraph* and one in the *Sunday Express*. Only one newspaper, the *Mail on Sunday*, referred to the National Anti-Hunt Campaign. The day after the march the *Guardian* provided a direct quote from a spokesperson for IFAW and another from the RSPCA. However, LACS gained more coverage on 24 September when its joint MORI opinion poll survey (with IFAW) on the Countryside March was released (IFAW 2002). This was reported by *The Times*, the *Financial Times* and the *Independent*. The *Daily Express* referred to the MORI poll but did not say who it was carried out on behalf of and in the same edition an anonymously authored article released the results of the newspaper's own questionable 'internet poll' which suggested that 46 per cent of readers supported Prince Charles's intervention on behalf of the pro-hunting lobby. However, the prime purpose of the MORI poll was to influence government rather than public opinion, with its emphasis on demonstrating that there were no votes to lose from this section of the electorate (pers. comm., LACS, December 2005).

The views of the then chairman of the CA, John Jackson, were directly referred to by the *Independent on Sunday* on the day of the march and he authored his own article in the *Sunday Express*. The following day his views were directly quoted by all national daily newspapers apart from the *Daily Mail*, which instead chose to print the views of Labour peer Baroness Mallalieu, president of the CA. She was also directly quoted on 23 September by the *Guardian*, the *Independent*, the *Daily Telegraph*, *The Times* and the *Daily Mirror*. Richard Burge, the CA's former chief executive, was directly quoted by the *Daily Telegraph*, the *Daily Express*, the *Guardian*, the *Daily Mirror* and the *Sun*. The views of Douglas Bachelor, chief executive of LACS, were completely absent on both days. The single most widely referred to individual in the coverage was Prince Charles, and following him it was Alun Michael, Rural Affairs Minister.[4]

However, it is important to bear in mind the complexity of uncovering source-media dependence, given the frequent non-attribution of news sources in news stories and the historical shifts in relations over time (Anderson 1997; Manning 2001). Pressure groups are sometimes used as unpaid researchers by the news media, their investigative research being presented as the journalist's own discovery, with no reference being made to the source. Moreover, a news source may hold back from proactively targeting the news media at a particular juncture in its campaign where public opinion is on its side and it is directing most of its attention to directly lobbying government. Also, restricting focus to the newspaper press means that it is not possible to consider patterns of coverage in the broader media environment; the requirement for 'balance' may lead radio and television to seek out a wider range of perspectives since they have strictly defined codes of conduct.

Discussion and Conclusions

Like the Countryside March before it, the mish-mash of interests represented in the 'Liberty and Livelihood' March created an impressive turn-out. However, in trying to attract as many groups as possible to join the march, the CA was unable to capitalize on this success in the long term. A YouGov poll of public opinion following the march found that 18 per cent of respondents thought it had made them 'less sympathetic' to the countryside's concerns and 57 per cent said that it had made no difference; only a quarter of those surveyed claimed it had made them 'more sympathetic' to the march. Although some newspapers attacked Prince Charles for intervening in the debate, a majority of respondents (64 per cent) claimed they thought he was right to write to the prime minister to express his views on the problems in the countryside. The public appear to have been divided on the organizers' motives, with 37 per cent viewing the march as mainly about fox hunting and 31 per cent as representing a genuine concern to 'preserve the countryside's way of life' (King 2002). Moreover, an ICM poll found that only 29 per cent of respondents thought that the CA and pro-hunting demonstrations were 'definitely justified' (ICM 2004).

One of the main reasons for the difficulties experienced by the CA in capitalizing on the march is that the countryside consists of a wide variety of (often conflicting) interests which cannot possibly be catered for effectively within a single pressure group. A MORI poll conducted on behalf of IFAW among those attending the Liberty and Livelihood March showed that only 27 per cent of respondents thought 'fox hunting/hunting with dogs' should be the main priority for the CA, with another 11 per cent of respondents indicating that 'country sports/pursuits generally' should be its main priority. A majority of respondents thought other issues should be the main focus, and, unsurprisingly, there was a wide variety cited, from 'farming generally', to 'rural businesses/small businesses', 'government interference/not under-standing' and 'affordable housing' (MORI 2002). While a majority may well have been sympathetic to the CA's campaign to save hunting, the polling suggests the main concerns of most marchers were other issues and the continued focus of the CA on hunting ensured the impact of the march was short-lived. As Milne observes:

> The Telegraph and the Mail did not manufacture indignation over foxhunting, but they helped the Countryside Alliance evoke a gulf between rural and urban life when the countryside's most acute prob-lems, such as lack of affordable housing, apply equally to cities. (2005: 59)

In an attempt to address this problem, apparent in the aftermath of its previous march, the CA announced on the day of the Liberty and Livelihood March that it would invite 'all rural organizations to a major rural conference . . . with a view to setting up a new Rural Council to represent the whole of the countryside' (CA 2002b). The CA managed to attract 35 rural organi-zations to attend the conference, which included many other field sports groups, but influential rural organizations, such as the Council for the Protection of Rural England and the National Trust, were absent. Within six months the idea of establishing the Rural Council was shelved (see First for Farming 2003).

In December, less than three months after the Liberty and Livelihood March, the government introduced another Hunting Bill, this time a compromise proposal which would outlaw hare coursing and deer hunting, but permit limited fox hunting if it could be demonstrated to meet tests of cruelty and utility. Most Labour MPs regarded the proposal as a fudge, which they would be prepared to rebel against if necessary (Webster 2002). The CA dismissed 'entirely' the proposed ban on stag hunting and hare coursing (CA 2002c). Within a matter of days more than 100 MPs, including former ministers and their parliamentary aides, had signed an Early Day Motion calling for a complete ban on hunting.

Having organized three large-scale peaceful protests, the CA was finding it increasingly difficult to control its more aggressive pro-hunting members. Several thousand of its supporters attempted to 'lay siege' to Parliament during the second reading of the Hunting Bill (Jones and Sparrow 2002). *The Times* reported that the CA had 'lost control' of its militants, arguing it had been 'out-manoeuvred' by more militant splinter groups such as the Countryside Action Network.

Through the Liberty and Livelihood March the CA gained enhanced visibility, but this should not be confused with securing lasting political influence. As Milne (2005) acknowledges, the House of Lords delayed a hunting ban but it did not prevent it. It is questionable whether the publicity thus generated forced the Labour government to pay attention to rural issues, as Milne contends. Moreover, the argument that, instead of simply reporting it, the press is starting to *manufacture* dissent through actively playing a campaigning role is historically short-sighted and exaggerates the power of the media by failing to consider the broader policy-making arena. A snapshot analysis of press coverage of a protest organization at a particular point in time is inevitably limited, and glosses over the ebbs and flows in media–movement relations. There is a long history of press backing in the hunting debate. On 4 January 1910 the front page of the *Daily Mirror* pictured the blooding of the Marquis of Worcester, the 10-year-old son of the Duke of Beaufort, showing him holding up a dead hare for the hounds, to the delight of onlookers (see Salt 1915). Also, the *Daily Mirror* ran a number of hard-hitting campaigns against fox hunting during the 1980s. For example, in 1981 it published major hunting items on consecutive days, starting with a centre-fold of pictures depicting hounds killing a fox in a village street, followed the next day by an editorial condemning the practice (26 and 27 November).[5] There are also many earlier instances of politicians and protest groups using the 'countryside agenda' or the environment in an attempt to broaden public support (see Anderson 1997; Bettelheim 1995).

The protest march did not occur abruptly; rather, it was a last-ditch attempt to try to sway public opinion against a ban on hunting emanating from a long campaign. The evidence presented here suggests that the protesters were largely middle-class, Conservative voters, and opinion polls indicated little support for attempts to oppose the proposed hunting ban (e.g. MORI 2003). This suggests that the marchers were hardly representative of 'public opinion', casting doubt on Milne's claim that this sort of protest illustrates a 'synthesis between protest movements, press campaigns and public opinion' (2005: 11). What distinguishes such recent protest groups (including the fuel campaigners that gained prominence in the UK press) from earlier cases is that they are all reactionary forces, with very close connections with the Conservative Party. The *Daily Telegraph* reported that over half of the Shadow Cabinet and more than 100 Conservative MPs registered to join the march (Jones 2002), and, as mentioned earlier, the then leader, Iain Duncan Smith, authored his own article in support of the protest in the *Sunday Telegraph*. Indeed Toynbee recently observed: 'The "countryside" as a surrogate for the Conservatives is increasing its breadth and range of issues with which to attack Labour' (Toynbee 2004). During the course of controversy over hunting the focus in the newspaper press shifted away from a public debate with two principal campaigning organizations to a situation where it became the CA campaigning against the government. With a weak party in opposition the press turned to organizations such as the CA to fill the void.

This study suggests that the success of the Liberty and Livelihood March was likely to be short-lived. Afterwards the issue faded quickly from the public agenda and the idea of establishing a Rural Council was rapidly shelved. Within the three years following the march hunting was banned completely and, despite subsequent coverage of attempts by the hunting community to get around the law, there have been no further 'countryside' marches or high-profile campaigning on rural issues. This provides further evidence of the centrality of hunting to the CA campaign. The findings suggest that, through rebranding itself, the hunting lobby managed to gain extensive press coverage but this did not mean that it was successful in its aim of overturning the proposed ban on hunting. Future studies would benefit from considering the less visible processes of news production within historical context, and in relation to the broader policy-making arena, to adequately assess whether there has been a significant shift in the relationship between protest movements and the press in recent years.

A central tenet of the later stages of the CA campaign was the emphasis on 'Livelihood' and 'Liberty'. Here it is important to ask: whose livelihood and whose liberty? Issues of social exclusion and rural deprivation did not feature as a central concern of this campaign. Examining the representation of popular protests in the news media raises key questions about how 'public opinion' on social policy issues is being constructed. There is little evidence to suggest that the CA campaign against the ban on fox hunting represented the democratic voice of rural publics regarding the crisis in the countryside. The challenge for social policy is to rethink traditional notions of welfare and to critically examine how policy agendas are shaped by protest activity and news media attention.

Notes

1. A MORI poll conducted in 1997 found that the greatest level of support for the Foster Bill to outlaw fox hunting was to be found among readers of the *People* and the *Daily Mirror*, while the highest level of opposition was among readers of the *Sunday Telegraph* and the *Daily Telegraph*. Yet even in the case of the latter two newspapers, a majority of readers (57 per cent in each case) supported the ban.
2. The sample included all the principal UK national daily and Sunday newspapers. It also included one regional newspaper, the *Western Morning News*. This paper serves parts of the south-west of England, where the hunting lobby has the greatest

presence, and is owned by Northcliffe Newspapers, part of the Daily Mail and General Trust Group. Each item within the sample was analysed using qualitative methods to ascertain its leading news frame, and particular attention was paid to the use of metaphors.

3. Although it emerged that some of its funding came from unlikely sources such as Persimmon Homes, McAlpine and Sunley, that build on greenbelt land. According to a leaked report published by the *Observer* on 26 September 1999, donors included Prince Charles, the Duke of Westminster, the Duke of Northumberland and Christopher Bland (formerly Chair of the BBC).

4. Prince Charles previously intervened in debates on GM foods and crops in 1999, and later on nanotechnologies in 2003 (see Anderson *et al.* 2005).

5. The *Daily Mirror* was also very vocal during the Greenpeace campaign against the deep-sea disposal of the Brent Spar oil platform in 1995. The newspaper cast itself as not only having reported the case against the dumping of the installation at sea but as bringing about Shell's U-turn. It frequently referred to 'people power' and 'victory for the people' and congratulated itself in a piece entitled: 'How We Did It: Brent Spa [*sic*] scandal was first revealed by Daily Mirror which highlighted potential disaster' (21 June 1995).

References

Anderson, A. (1997), *Media, Culture and the Environment*, London: University College London Press.

Anderson, A., Petersen, A., Wilkinson, C. and Allan, S. (2005), The framing of nano-technologies in the British newspaper press, *Science Communication*, 27, 2: 200–20.

Barry, J. and Doherty, B. (2001), The Greens and social policy: movements, politics and practice? *Social Policy & Administration*, 35, 5: 587–607.

Beckett, A. (1998), Blood on the saddle, *Guardian*, 13 August.

Bettelheim, B. (1995), A war we can win, *The Field*, November: 9.

Clover, C. (1995), Howlers as children fail the countryside test, *Daily Telegraph*, 17 November.

CA (2002), What is Rural? Available at: http://www.countryside-alliance.org/policy/whatis/index.html (accessed 16 October 2005).

CA (2002a), Alliance to use Internet web-cast to promote Liberty and Livelihood March, press release, 16 August. Available at: http://www.countryside-alliance.org/news/02/020816cjc.htm (accessed 16 October 2005).

CA (2002b), Alliance proposes new rural body, press release, 22 September. Available at: http://www.countryside-alliance.org/news/02/020923march.htm (accessed 16 October 2005).

CA (2002c), Countryside Alliance responds to proposed hunting bill, press release, 3 December. Available at: http://www.countryside-alliance.org/news/02/021203res.htm (accessed 16 October 2005).

CA (website), available at: http://www.countryside-alliance.org (accessed 16 October 2005).

Daniel, C. (1997), Hunters lay a false scent – campaign on rural poverty issues, *New Statesman*, 24 October.

Dillon, J. and Goodchild, S. (2000), 'Dirty tricks' PR expert hired to take on anti-hunt campaigners, *Independent*, 28 May.

Endangered Exmoor (website), available at: http://www.exmoor.org.uk/ (accessed 29 November 2005).

Evans, R. (2000), Contesting spaces and places: conflicting geographic imaginaries in the Countryside March, London, March 1, 1998. In H. Hillebrand, R. Goetgeluk and H. Hetsen (eds), *Plurality and Rurality: The Role of the Countryside in Urbanised Regions*, The Hague: Agricultural Economics Research Institute (LEI).

First for Farming (2003), Rural council plan shelved, 28 February. Available at: http://www.first4farming.com/F4F/news/index.jhtml?article_id=fwi9347 (accessed 29 November 2005).

ICM (2004), 'State of the Nation' poll. Available at: http://www.jrrt.org.uk/FINDINGS.pdf (accessed 29 November 2005).

IFAW (2002), Countryside Alliance march to save hunting backfires, 23 September. Available at: http://www.ifaw.org/ifaw/general/default.aspx?oid=83959 (accessed 29 November 2005).

Jones, G. (2002), Duncan Smith to lead the Tory battalions, *Daily Telegraph*, 19 September.

Jones, G., Alford, D. and Dennis, S. (1999), Tally blow! *Daily Mirror*, 3 November.

Jones, G. and Sparrow, A. (2002), Angry hunt supporters lay siege to Commons, *Daily Telegraph*, 17 December.

King, A. (2002), Foxhunting divides nation into tribes, *Daily Telegraph*, 28 September.

LACS (2002), Campaigners call for scepticism on march figures, press release, 22 September.

Leonard, T., Born, M. and Clover, C. (2002), Country marchers accuse BBC of pro–Government bias, *Daily Telegraph*, 24 September.

Lusoli, W. and Ward, S. (2003), Hunting protesters: mobilization, participation and protest online in the Countryside Alliance. Paper presented at the ECPR Joint Sessions, University of Edinburgh, 23 March to 2 April.

Lusoli, W. and Ward, S. (2005), Hunting protesters: mobilization, participation, and protest online in the Countryside Alliance. In S. Oates, D. Owen and R. K. Gibson (eds), *Civil Society, Democracy and the Internet: A Comparative Perspective*, London: Routledge, pp. 59–79.

McCann, P. (2001), Clash of the torygraphs, *The Times*, 20 July.

Manning, P. (2001), *News and News Sources: A Critical Introduction*, London: Sage.

Mathiason, N. (2004), A £1bn industry is accused of distorting results to produce what clients want to hear, *Observer*, 6 June.

Milbourne, P. (2003), The complexities of hunting in rural England and Wales, *Sociologia Ruralis*, 43, 3: 289–308.

Milne, K. (2005), *Manufacturing Dissent: Single-issue Protest, the Public and the Press*, London: Demos.

MORI (2003), Most say hunting should not be legal, November. Available at: http://www.more.com/polls/2003/cpha.shtml (accessed 29 November 2005).

MORI (2002), *The Countryside March survey*, 23 September. Available at: http://193.114.101.164/polls/2002/ifaw3.shtml (accessed 29 November 2005).

MORI (1998), *The Countryside March – Who Was Really There?* 24 February. Available at: http://193.114.101.164/polls/1998/hunting3.shtml (accessed 29 November 2005).

Morris, S. (2002), Do they mean us? *Guardian*, 19 September.

Norton, A. (2000), The relationship between hunting and country life, *Countryside Recreation*, 8, 1: 8–12. Available at: http://www.countrysiderecreation.org.uk/journal/spring2000/4-hunting.pdf (accessed 18 October 2005).

Real Countryside Alliance (spoof website), available at: http://www.realca.co.uk/media_bias.htm (accessed 29 November 2005).

Salt, H. (1915), The blooding of children. Available at: http://www.henrysalt.co.uk/index_old.html (accessed 29 November 2005).

Stokes, E. (1996), *Hunting and Hunt Saboteurs: A Censure Study*, London: University of East London.

Thomas, R. (1983), *The Politics of Hunting*, Aldershot: Gower.

Toynbee, P. (2004), Countryside Alliance, *Guardian*, 13 August.

UK Press Gazette (2005), Wildlife changes ad policy after calendar row, 27 January.

Wallwork, J. and Dixon, J. A. (2004), Foxes, green fields and Britishness: on the rhetorical construction of place and national identity, *British Journal of Social Psychology*, 43: 21–39.

Ward, N. (2002), Representing rurality? New Labour and the electoral geography of Britain, *Area*, 34, 2: 171–81.

Webster, P. (2002), Labour MPs reject hunt fudge, *The Times*, 4 December.

Windeatt, P. (1982), *The Hunt and the Anti-Hunt*, London: Pluto Press.

Woolf, M. (2001), Rural lobby 'spent £3m defending blood sport', *Independent*, 13 August.

Younge, G. (2000), Back in the hunt, *Guardian*, 4 October.

Index

Abild, Carsten   22
acute respiratory infections (ARI)
    in developing countries   72, 73
    Progresa Programme   74, 77, 82,
        86–9, 90–4
Adivasi Kshema Samithi   66
adivasis (Kerala indigenous people)
    impact of changing politics   xii,
        63–6, 67, 68
    impact of neo-liberalism   61–3, 66,
        67, 68
    inclusion in decentralized
        planning   54, 57, 58–60, 68
'agricultural welfare state'   3
agriculture/farming
    changing public attitudes   4
    decline economic significance   4, 18
    decrease in labour force   22, 131–2
    discrimination in   11
    domination of rural politics   2–4
    effects of neo-liberalism   5, 60–1,
        62–3, 68
    effects of plantation forestry   115
    'killing of the countryside'   124
    rural-urban projects   127
    and rural way of life   6, 148, 149
Albania
    rural housing conditions   131
    small farm closures   131
    'walled countrysides'   129
America *see* North America; US
American Country Life Association
    6
arts and crafts   127
asylum reception centres   12–13
Australia   ix, xi, xii
    bank closures   7
    compulsory competitive
        tendering   46
    lack of rural development policy   xiv,
        120
    neo-liberal reforms   5, 8
    post office closure protests   7
    rural public services   6
    rural rights campaigns   8
    rural-urban divide   112
    see also Western District of Victoria
Australia Post   7
Australian Taxation Office (ATO)   115
Azeez, A.   61

Bachelor, Douglas   150
bank closures   7
Bantry Rural Transport Group   132
Barry, B.   101
Basin Minerals   116, 117
BBC   146, 148
Black, Conrad   147–8
Blair, Cherie   149
Blair, Tony   145, 146, 147, 148
BMA Board of Science   xi
Boyne, G. A.   46
Britain *see* UK/Britain
British Columbia, rural school closures   9
British Field Sports Society (BFSS)   142
Browne, W. P.   4
Bryden, J.   121
Bulgaria
    countryside vineyards   127
    pollution   124
    rural housing conditions   131
    small farm closures   131
Burchardt, T.   98
Burnside, David   143
Byrne, D.   98, 99

California   47
Campaign for Rural Europe   21

Campaign to Protect Rural England
(CPRE)   12
Canada
post office closure protests   7, 8
rural school closures   9
threat to rural postal services   47–8
Canadian Royal Post   47
capitalism   4, 98, 107
Caravan Sites (Amendment) Act
(1993)   12
Casey, E.   132
Castells, M.   2, 128
Central Europe
blighted countrysides   124
rural exodus of younger people   130
rural tourism   133
centralization   xi, 18, 28
Champion, T.   x, 132
Charles, Prince   145, 146, 147, 148,
150, 151
child health   72–3
Progresa Programme   xiii, 72–96
Christmas, Linda   129
civil society
and destatization   53
effects of politicization, Kerala   57–8
'embedded autonomy'   55–6
importance of participation   18
role of rural movements   28, 29, 31
'state-in-society' approach   55
Clean Water Act (US)   36
Clinton Administration   36
Common Agricultural Policy   3
Communist Party of India (Marxist)
(CPI/M)   53, 56, 57, 59
Communist Party-led (Left) coalition,
Kerala   53–4, 55, 56–7, 59,
64–5, 68–9
communities see rural communities
Congress Party-led (Conservative)
coalition, Kerala   53, 54, 55, 56,
57, 59, 63, 67
Conservatives, UK   97, 142, 146, 148,
153
Council for the Protection of Rural
England   151
Council of Rural Districts (LDF)   23
counter-urbanization   x, 4, 124, 126
Countryside Action Network   143, 152
Countryside Agency   xi

Countryside Alliance   7–8
historical origins   142–4
Liberty and Livelihood march   141,
144–50, 152, 153
reasons for short-lived success
151–3
Countryside Business Group
(CBG)   142
Countryside Movement (CM)   142
crime and security   128
Criminal Justice and Public Order Act
(1994)   12
Croatia, rural exodus of younger
people   130
Czech Republic, small farm
difficulties   131–2

Daily Express   145, 149, 150
Daily Mail   141, 143, 145–6, 148, 150
Daily Mirror   141, 143, 145, 147, 150,
152
Daily Star   145, 149
Daily Telegraph   141, 144, 147–8, 149,
150, 153
Daniel, C.   142
Danish Village Association (LAL)   22
Deane, M.   128
decentralization   xii
concept of   53
rotation with centralization   xi
and spatial inequality, US   xii, 34–6,
48
decentralized planning, Kerala   53–4,
55–8
adivasi inclusion   54, 57, 58–60, 68
changing politics and adivasi
development   xii, 63–6, 67, 68
Denmark
agricultural decline   18
rural elder organizations   132
rural movement   22–3, 27
destatization   xii, 53, 54
developing countries
common childhood diseases   72
risk factors for infectious diseases   73
development
concept and indicators   111
of rural space   1, 5–6, 14
diarrhoea
in developing countries   72, 73

Progresa Programme   74, 77, 79–81,
    83–6, 90
discriminant analysis   43–4
discrimination
    difference and   10–13
    and rural elders   129
    against rural populations   8, 108
distance decay   125
domestic air pollution, and child
    respiratory infections   77
Dower, M.   128
Duncan Smith, Iain   146, 148, 153

Eastern Europe
    agricultural decline   18
    blighted countrysides   124
    rural exodus of younger people   130
    rural housing conditions   131
    rural movements   xii, 19, 23–4,
        25–6
    rural tourism   133
education
    Progresa benefits   73, 90
    see also preschool education; schools
'embedded autonomy'   55–6
employment
    and access to preschool
        education   103, 107
    adivasis   60, 62, 66
    decrease in agricultural   22, 131–2
    local variations in training   36
    rural elders   126–7
ENCEL survey   76
Endangered Exmoor Campaign
    Group   146
England   xi
    decline in rural health services   130
    post office closures   130
    rural broadband access   128
    rural elder employment   127
    rural elder support schemes   127–8
    urban retirees   132
    urban-rural crime prevention
        partnerships   128
environment
    effects of mineral sands mining   116,
        117
    impact of agriculture   4, 124
    and plantation forestry   114
    sustainability   140

Estonia
    agricultural decline   18
    importance of the village   26
    rural movement   23, 25, 26, 30
Euro-ageism   132
Europe   ix
    pressure for agricultural reform
        5
    rural elders   xiv, 123–39
    rural movements   18–33
    rural public services   6
    social inclusion agenda   98
European Rural Alliance   19, 28
European Union (EU)   21, 23, 31
    agricultural focus   19
    impact of rural movements   27, 28,
        30
    internal market forces   18
    migration   130
    national country parks   133
    neglect of elders' needs   132
    promotion of social inclusion   98
    rural LEADER schemes   126
European Working Time
    Directive   131
Evans, P.   55–6
Evans, R.   143

farming see agriculture/farming
Farrington, J.   102
Financial Times   149, 150
Finland
    agricultural decline   18
    rural movement   20–1, 25, 26, 27,
        28, 29–30
    rural school closures   9
Finnish National Organization for
    Village Action   20
Foundation for the Bush   8
fox-hunting debate, UK   xiv, 140–56
France   123
    origins of 'social exclusion' term
        98
    post office closure protests   7
    rural elder employment   127
    rural elder organizations   132
    rural school closures   9
    urban encroachment   133
free trade agreements   47–8
Fysh, Betsy   8

General Agreement on Trade in
 Services (GATS) 36, 48
George, Janet 142
Germany
 rural elder employment 127
 rural elder support schemes 128
 post office closure protests 7
 rural school closures 9
Giddens, A. 124
Gilbert, A. 132
Glass, R. x
globalization
 and 'closed economies' 128–9
 competing globalizations xi
 effect on health and welfare
  services x
 of markets 18
 of mobilization 124–5
 negative consequences, Kerala 61
 resurgence of the city 35
 and 'rural development' 119
 and social exclusion 98
 uneven urban-rural outcomes xiv,
  124–5
 and urbanization 132–3, 134
Greece
 rural elder employment 127
 rural elder housing conditions 131
 'walled countrysides' 129
Guardian, The 141, 147, 148, 149, 150
Gurukkal, R. 57

Halfacree, K. x, 12
Hamilton, Victoria 112, 113, 119
 mineral sands mining industry
  116–19
Harris, Stephen 145
Hart, K. 121
Harvey, Graham 124
Haute Report 123
Hautemaki, Lauri 20
Hayward, C. 99
health services
 decline in rural provision,
  Europe 130–1
 effects of neo-liberalism, Kerala
  62
 effects of globalization x
 local variations, US 36
 rural policy agendum, UK xi

Hefetz, A. 43
Hela Norden Ska Leva (HNSL) 19
Help the Aged and RDC community
 care project 128
housing
 adivasis 59–60
 older Europeans 131
Howe, C. 105
Hubbard, P. 12–13
Huber, A. 133
human development 111
Hungary
 countryside vineyards 127
 rural school closures 9
 rural housing conditions 131
 urban retirees 132
Hunting Bills 140, 151–2

Iceland ix
ICT
 Countryside Alliance use 144
 rural access 36, 128
Iluka Resources Ltd 116–17, 118–19
Independent 147, 150
Independent on Sunday 148, 149, 150
India xi see also Kerala, India
Indian Constitution 54, 55, 66–7
in-migrants (urban villagers) x, xi
 anti-discriminatory 11
 challenge to agricultural elites 4
 and Danish rural movement 22
 retirees 130, 132, 134
 rural service expectations 6
Integrated Tribal Development
 Programme 58
Inter-America Development Bank 74
'internal colonies' 129, 134
International City/County Management
 Association surveys (ICMA) 37,
  38, 43, 46
International Council on Mining and
 Metals Community Development
 Toolkit 121
International Expert Group Meeting on
 rural ageing 123
International Fund for Animal Welfare
 (IFAW) 140, 150, 151
Ireland
 bank closure protests 7
 post office closure protests 7

rural school closures 9
see also Northern Ireland; Republic of
    Ireland
Italy
    rural elder employment 127
    rural elder housing conditions 131
    rural tourism 133
    urban encroachment 133
    'walled countrysides' 129

Jackson, John 145, 150
Jansen, A. 35
Japan ix
    postal service privatization 7
    pressure for agricultural reform 5
Jordan, B. 99

Katz, Michael 36
Kerala, India xii, 53–71
    changing politics and *adivasi*
        development xii, 54, 63–6, 68
    compatibility of new politics with
        Indian Constitution 66–7
    decentralized planning xii, 53–4,
        55–60, 68
    neo-liberalism xii, 54, 60–3, 67, 68
Kerala *Panchayat Raj* Act (1994) 55
Kodukant 23

Labour/New Labour, UK 97, 140,
    142, 143, 146, 147, 152, 153
Lapland, village associations 20–1
Latin America 94
Lawley, A. 128
Le Mesurier, N. 127–8
League Against Cruel Sports
    (LACS) 140, 147, 149, 150
Lisbon summit 98
local authorities (Scotland), and rural
    pre-school provision xii, 97,
    100–1, 102
Lowe, P. x, 123, 128
Lusoli, W. 144

MacPherson, Elle 147
Mail on Sunday 149, 140
Majerová, V. 131–2
Mallalieu, Baroness 142, 150
Maltby, T. 131
market towns 126

market-based approaches
    challenge for rural governments,
        US xii, 34–52
    see also decentralization; neo-
        liberalism; privatization
Marshallian citizenship 99
McLaughlin, B. x, 129
Mexico xi
    child health and Progresa xiii,
        72–96
    North American Free Trade
        Agreement 47
Michael, Alun 150
Migdal, J. S. 55
Milne, K. 51, 141, 152
mineral sands mining industry 112,
    113
    planning policy and 116–19
minority groups 10–13, 129
Moore, Charles 147–8, 149
Moore, Patrick 147
Mormont, M. x, 1, 5, 10, 12, 13, 14
Moss, P. 104
MTBE (gasoline additive) 47
multi-purpose preschool education
    centres 103

NACRO and Countryside Agency
    community safety project 128
Nairn, A. 133
National Anti-Hunt Campaign 150
National Fox Welfare Society 145,
    149–50
national identity 143, 148
National Institute of Public Health
    (INSP) survey 76–7, 79, 82
National Trust 151
'National Village Action
    Programme' 21
neo-liberalism
    effect on rural politics 5
    effect on rural service provision 6–7,
        8
    in Kerala xii, 54, 60–3, 67, 68
    and rural 'decline' 112–13
    and social exclusion 98
new age travellers (NATs) 11–12
New Zealand xi, xii
    neo-liberal reforms 5
    post office closure protests 7

rural public services 6
rural school closures 9–10
New Zealand Post 7
news media
    press coverage of Liberty and
        Livelihood March 141, 145–50
    relationship with protest
        movements xiv, 141–2, 150,
        152, 153
News of the World 149
Nordic countries *see* Scandinavia
Nordic Network 19
North America xii
    rural public services 6
    see also Canada; US
North American Free Trade Agreement
    (NAFTA) 47
Northern Ireland
    rural elder support schemes 128
    'walled countrysides' 129
nutrition
    and child health 73, 75
    Progresa supplements 73, 74, 75,
        83, 85–6, 89, 94

O'Reilly, K. 133
Observer 147, 148, 149
older people, rural Europe xiv, 123–39
oorukkoottams 64–5
Oportunidades 73, 94
out-migrants 18, 130

panchayats 55, 56, 58, 59, 60, 63, 64,
    65–6
participation, and social inclusion 99
participatory democracy
    growing interest 18
    role of rural movements 28–9
Pence, A. 104
People 145
People's Planning Campaign (PPC),
    Kerala 54, 55, 56, 57–8, 59, 60,
    63, 68
People's Science Movement (KSSP)
    59
planning
    and the mineral sands mining
        industry 116–19
    and rural values xi
    see also decentralized planning

plantation forestry (tree farms) 112,
    113
    taxation policy and 114–16
Poland, small farm closures 131
'politics of the rural' xi–xii, 2, 5–14
pollution 124
Poothady *panchayat*, Wayanad
    district 54–5, 59, 64, 66
Popular Movement Council (PMC) 22
Portugal
    rural elder employment 127
    rural elder housing conditions 131
    rural elder support schemes 128
    'walled countrysides' 129
postal services
    effect of free trade agreements,
        Canada 47–8
    neglect by Countryside Alliance 144
    post office closures 7, 8, 130
poverty
    and attractiveness for market
        providers 42
    and child health 73
    and equitable development 111
    in-comers and indigenous
        populations 132
    severity, and impact of Progresa 76,
        79, 89–90, 94
PREPARE Programme 19
preschool education, rural
    Scotland xiii, 97–8, 100–7
    accessing 'entitlements' 101–3
    and conceptualizations of social
        exclusion 103, 107–8
    individualized and collective
        aspects 104–7, 108
privatization 34, 53
    challenges for rural governments,
        US xii, 36, 38, 39–48, 48–9
    effect on rural service provision
        6, 7
    effect on rural politics 5
    impact on *adivasis* 62, 66
    local government use by metro status,
        US 37–9
    structural/attitudinal constraints
        on 39–43
Progresa, Mexico xiii, 72–96
    research analysis methods 77–9
    research background 72–6

research enquiry 76–7
research results 79–90
protest movements *see* social/protest
    movements
Public Choice theory 35
public distribution system (PDS),
    Kerala 60, 61–2
public services
    blocked by urban centres 129–32
    rural challenges of market-led delivery,
        US 34–49
    rural services and rural rights 6–8
Putnam, R. 57

racism 11, 129
Reagan, Ronald 36
Real Countryside Alliance 143
Reeder, R. 35
Regional Women's Alliance 8
Reimer, W. 98, 108
Reinventing Government (Osborne and
    Gaebler) 44
Republic of Ireland, rural transport
    cooperative 132
respiratory infections *see* acute
    respiratory infections
Romania
    small farm closures 131
    rural housing conditions 131
Royal Society for the Prevention of
    Cruelty to Animals (RSPCA) 140,
    150
rural ageing studies 123
rural Census Output Areas
    (COAs) 125
Rural Coalition 11
rural communities
    centrality of rural schools 8–10
    health risks 72
    and rural development, Western
        District xiii–xiv, 111–21
    value of preschools 105–6, 108
rural decline
    Australia 112–13
    Europe 18–19, 22
rural deprivation 125–6
    neglected by Countryside
        Alliance 153
    and urban-rural socio-economic
        flows 126–33

rural development, Western
    District xiii–xiv, 111–22
Rural Dignity 8
rural forums 23, 25–6
rural identity 2, 14
    and public services 7–8
    role of rural movements 28
    and 'stability' 11
rural movements, Europe xii, 18–33
    factors promoting growth 18–19
    characteristics 24–8
    development 19–24
    future directions 30–1
    impact 28–30
Rural Parliaments 22, 23, 24, 25, 30
'Rural Policy Programme', Finland 21,
    27
rural politics
    domination by agriculture 2–4
    domination by land use 1
    transition to 'politics of the rural'
        xi–xii, 4–6, 13–14
rural poverty 125–6
    and capitalist agriculture 3–4
'rural proofing' 14, 108
rural space
    contested function 1
    development debates 1, 5, 14
rurality
    contested meanings ix–x, 2, 5, 13,
        14
    contrasting values x–xi
    Countryside Alliance definitions 143
    degrees of ix
    population-based descriptors ix
Russell, A. x, 125

Sarumpaet, R. 132–3
Scandinavia/Nordic countries
    rural decline 18
    rural movements xii, 20–3, 25
    weakening of local democracy 28–9
Scharf, T. 123, 128
Scheduled Castes 59, 67
Scheduled Tribes 54, 59, 67
schools
    effects of neo-liberalism, Kerala 62
    rural closures 9–10
Scotland xi, xiii
    'golliwog' controversy 11

preschool education in rural   xiii,
    97–8, 100–8
Sheingate, A. D.   3
Shepherd, J.   132
Sher, J.   120
Sher, R. K.   120
Shucksmith, M.   x, 102, 127–8
Sibley, D.   13
Simmons, M.   132
Slovak Rural Parliament   23, 24
Slovakia
    importance of the village   26
    mass rural tourism   133
    rural housing conditions   131
    rural movement   23–4, 25, 26, 27,
        30
    small farms closures   131
Smith, Susan   11
social capital
    importance as force for action   18
    individual/collective conceptions   99
    location in civil society   57
    role of rural movements   29–30
    urban-rural nexus   127–8
social exclusion/inclusion   xiii, 97
    adivasis, Kerala   xii, 54, 61, 68
    contested conceptualizations
        98–100
    neglected by Countryside
        Alliance   153
    and preschool education,
        Scotland   97–8, 101–7, 107–8
social/protest movements   xi
    campaigns for rural services   7–8, 10
    'new social movement'   xii, 5, 10, 14
    opposition to travellers' camps and
        asylum centres   12–13
    reactionary nature   152–3
    rejection in Kerala   55
    relationship with news media   xiv,
        141–2, 150, 152, 153
    widening agenda   140
    see also Countryside Alliance
social policy
    anti-discriminatory   11
    agricultural policy domination   3–4
    and the meaning of rurality   6
    and 'politics of the rural'   xii, 1–2,
        6–13, 14
    promotion of inclusion   101

relevance of popular rural
    protests   140, 153
Spain
    rural elder employment   127
    rural elder housing conditions   131
    'walled countrysides'   129
Speakman, L.   x, 123, 128
'state in society'   xii, 55
state-society relations   55–6
Subrahmanian, K. K.   61
Sun   145, 147, 150
Sunday Express   145, 150
Sunday Mirror   147
Sunday Telegraph   148, 150, 153
Sunday Times   149
sustainability   111, 140
Sweden   24
    rural school closures   9
    rural movement   21–2, 25, 26, 29,
        30

taxation policy
    and plantation forest industry,
        Western District   114–16
    and local government competition,
        US   35
Teague, P.   99
Tharakan, P. K. M.   57
Tiebout, Charles   35
Times   148, 149, 150, 152
Tönnies, F.   ix
tourism   133
Townsend, A.   133
Toynbee, P.   153
Trade Related Intellectual Property
    Rights (TRIPS)   62
Trans-European Rural Network
    (TERN)   19
transport
    and access to preschool education,
        Scotland   102–3
    deregulation   6
    importance to rural elders, UK   130
    neglect by Countryside Alliance   144
travellers/gypsies   129
    and Countryside Alliance
        March   147
tribal sub-plan (TSP), Kerala   58, 59,
        63–4, 66
Turkey, 'walled countrysides'   129

UK/Britain   ix, xii
   ageing countryside studies   123
   agrarian-dominated rural councils   3
   asylum reception centres   12–13
   compulsory competitive
      tendering   46
   fox-hunting debate   xiv, 140–56
   new age travellers   11–12
   post office closure protests   7
   postal service privatization   7
   Our Countryside White Paper   126
   parental labour market
      participation   103
   rural elder organizations   132
   rural health and welfare agendum   xi
   rural movements   25–6
   rural school closures   9
   social inclusion agendum   98
UK Census 2001   125
UK Department for Environment, Food
   and Rural Affairs (Defra)   125
UK Office for National Statistics   125
UK Rural Development
   Commission   130
UN Development Programme
   (UNDP)   99
UN *Human Development Reports*   111
'underclass'   98–9, 99–100
United Parcel Service   47–8
Urban Alliance   149
urban encroachment   132–3
urban politics   2
urban-fringe rural areas   127
urban-rural socio-economic
   flows   124–5
   benefiting countrysides   xiv, 126–8,
      134
   blocked by regional/urban
      centres   xiv, 129–32, 134
   hindered by two-way impasse   xiv,
      128–9, 134
   resisted by rural areas   xiv, 132–3,
      134
urbanization   18, 31, 132–3
Urry, J.   133
US   ix, xi, 24
   'agricultural welfare state'   3
   discriminatory practices   11
   limited rural programmes   4
   market-based governance   xii, 34–52

North American Free Trade
   Agreement   47
   pressure for agricultural reform   5
   rural school closures   9, 10
   'underclass'   98–9
US Census of Government
   Finance   37–8
US Census of Population and
   Housing   42
US Rural Coalition   11

'Village Action 1976'   20
'Village Action Association of
   Finland'   20, 29–30, 31
village action movements   20, 23, 25,
   29–30
village associations   20–1, 21–2, 26–7,
   28
village committees   20
Village in Denmark Association
   (LID)   22
village movements   26
village planning   21

Wales   xi
   campaigns against school
      closures   10
   decline in rural health services   130
   rural elders' support schemes   128
Walker, A.   125, 130–1
'walled countrysides'   129
Ward, S.   144
Warner, M. E.   43
Warnes, A. M.   130
welfare services
   effects of globalization   x
   effects of neo-liberalism, Kerala
      61–2
   local variations, US   36
   rural policy, UK   xi
Wenger, G. C.   x, 123, 128
Western District of Victoria, Australia
   development in   112–14
   mineral sands mining industry   112,
      113, 116–19
   need for stronger local
      governance   xiii–xiv, 119–21
   plantation forestry industry   112,
      113, 114–16
Western Morning News   146–7, 148

William, Prince   145
Williamson, O. E.   46
Wilson, D.   99
wine production   127
women
    development projects, Kerala   60
    impact of PDS dismantling,
        Kerala   62
    rural movements, Australia   8
Woods, M.   ix, x, 124

Workforce Investment Act (1998,
    US)   46–7
World Bank   57
    Oil, Gas and Mining Policy
        Division   121
World Trade Organization   62
Wright Mills, C.   123

Yugoslavia, former, rural housing
    conditions   131